Debating Durkheim

'An excellent collection of essays, which will make a useful addition to the English-language literature on Durkheim.'

William Outhwaite, *School of European Studies, University of Sussex.*

In *Debating Durkheim*, leading international scholars are brought together to discuss controversial issues in the work of this increasingly important founding father of sociology. The subjects covered relate to Durkheim's Jewish background and its influence on his life and thought; a positive reinterpretation of Durkheim's study of primitive thought in terms of social classification; an attempt to shed new light on his book on methodology, *The Rules*, which has been much criticized; a philosophical and sympathetic analysis of the notion of the social; a discussion of Durkheim's sociology of morals based on a study of social facts; a careful consideration of the problems of Durkheim's references to state, nation and patriotism; and finally, an application of *The Rules* to data relating to first names and raising the issue of social imitation. The appendix is an extension of the first chapter and covers new translations and hitherto unpublished material by Durkheim on the issues of Jewishness and anti-semitism. As these essays will show, Durkheim raises basic issues which must be examined if contemporary society is to be understood.

William Pickering has devoted much of his academic life to the study of Durkheim. He is currently honorary organizing secretary at the British Centre for Durkheimian Studies, Oxford. **Herminio Martins** is a Fellow of St Antony's College, Oxford.

Contributors: N. J. Allen, Philippe Besnard, Mike Gane, Margaret Gilbert, Josep R. Llobera, W. S. F. Pickering, W. Watts Miller.

Debating Durkheim

Edited by W. S. F. Pickering
and H. Martins

Published in conjunction with
the British Centre for Durkheimian Studies

London and New York

First published 1994
by Routledge
11 New Fetter Lane, London EC4P 4EE

Simultaneously published in the USA and Canada
by Routledge
29 West 35th Street, New York, NY 10001

Typeset in Baskerville by Florencetype Ltd, Kewstoke, Avon
Printed and bound in Great Britain by
Mackays of Chatham PLC, Chatham, Kent

British Library Cataloguing in Publication Data
A catalogue record for this book is available from the British Library.

Library of Congress Cataloging in Publication Data
Debating Durkheim / edited by W.S.F Pickering with Herminio
Martins.
        p.   cm.
    "Published in conjunction with the British Centre for Durkheimian
Studies."
    Includes bibliographical references and index.
    ISBN 0–415–07720–6: $59.95
    1. Durkheim, Emile, 1858–1917.   2. Sociology—France—History.
3. Sociology—Philosophy.   I. Pickering, W.S.F.   II. Martins,
Herminio.   III. British Centre for Durkheimian Studies.
HM101.C458   1994
301′.01–dc20   93–46095
                                                                      CIP

ISBN 0–415–07720–6

Contents

Figures

Biographical notes on the contributors

N. J. Allen won a scholarship in classics to New College, Oxford in 1957. He studied medicine there and later in London. He returned to Oxford to study social anthropology, basing his D. Phil. on fieldwork in Nepal. He lectured at Durham from 1972 to 1976. Since then he has been a lecturer in the Social Anthropology of South Asia at Oxford (Wolfson College). His main interests are: the Himalayas, Hinduism, kinship theory and Indo-European comparativism.

Philippe Besnard was born in 1942. He is director of research at the Centre National de la Recherche Scientifique in Paris and teaches at the Institut d'Études Politiques. He is joint-editor of the *Revue française de sociologie*. He was for many years an active member of the Groupe d'études durkheimiennes, an international network he created. Among the several books he has published are *The Sociological Domain. The Durkheimians and the Founding of French Sociology* (1983), *L'Anomie* (1987), *Un prénom pour toujours. La cote des prénoms* (1986).

Mike Gane is Senior Lecturer in the Department of Social Sciences at Loughborough University. He was educated at Leicester University and the London School of Economics. He has written *On Durkheim's Rules of Sociological Method* (1988) and edited *The Radical Sociology of Durkheim and Mauss* (1992). He has also recently edited a book of interviews with Jean Baudrillard and written a book on theory, theorists and gender, both published by Routledge in 1993.

Margaret Gilbert is currently Professor of Philosophy at the University of Connecticut, Storrs. She studied in Cambridge and

Oxford, and has taught at a number of universities in Britain and the United States, including Princeton and UCLA. For many years she has specialized in the philosophy of social science.

Josep R. Llobera is Senior Lecturer in sociology and social anthropology at Goldsmiths' College, University of London. He has published extensively on the history of the social sciences and on nationalism. His latest book is *The Development of Nationalism in Western Europe*, to appear in 1994.

Herminio Martins is a fellow of St Antony's College, Oxford. He has published papers in sociological theory, the sociology of knowledge, and on Portugal and Brazil. He has recently edited *Knowledge and Passion: Essays in Honour of John Rex* (1993), contributing a chapter on the philosophy of technology.

William S. F. Pickering formerly lectured in sociology in the University of Newcastle upon Tyne. He has now retired. Much of his academic life has been devoted to the study of Durkheim. He has edited and assisted in translations of Durkheim's works, *Durkheim and Religion* (1975), *Durkheim On Morals and Education* (1979). In 1984 he published *Durkheim's Sociology of Religion: Themes and Theories*. He is currently involved in setting up the British Centre for Durkheimian Studies at the Institute of Social and Cultural Anthropology in the University of Oxford.

H. L. Sutcliffe was Earl Gray Memorial Fellow and subsequently lecturer in French language in the University of Newcastle upon Tyne until 1976. Since 1981, he has worked full-time as a freelance translator and précis writer, largely within the United Nations system. He has published many translations of items by or about Durkheim.

Willie Watts Miller lectures in sociology and philosophy at the University of Bristol, writes on ethics, and is completing two books on Durkheim. One is a critical commentary on his study of moral life. The other develops and applies his approach to contemporary issues.

References and notation

The Harvard system of referencing has been employed throughout this book. The details of each reference in the text can be found in the appropriate section at the end of the book. The name of the author of the citation, the date of the publication and, where applicable, the page number or numbers are given in the text itself.

Just as Mozart's works are now universally referred to by their Köchel numbers, and other composers' works by their opus numbers, so it is hoped that the use of the dating enumeration created by Steven Lukes (see Lukes 1992: 561ff.) for Durkheim's writings will receive general agreement. The call for uniformity in using such a dating enumeration arises from the fact that scholars referring to Durkheim's works often give different dates derived from different reprints. This causes confusion and doubt on the reader's part. Here, in employing the system of Lukes, the date of a later edition, which has different page numbers, is associated with the original date of publication. For example, (1893b/1902b: 21) refers to page 21 of the 1902 edition of the *Division of Labour* (1893b). The details of a given work by Durkheim are to be found under the original date of publication or the date when the contents of what Durkheim had written became public knowledge. These details also include those of translations.

Translations of Durkheim's works are preceded by the prefix 't.' to make them quickly identifiable as such. Some works of Durkheim have been translated more than once and it is therefore necessary to differentiate these translations by reference to a date.

Some authors of the chapters ahead have included the page

numbers for both the French and the corresponding English translation. Others have been content with just the pages of the translation. In this respect there has been no attempt to bring about uniformity.

Acknowledgements

The editors and publisher express their gratitude to the editor of *Genèses*, Paris, for permission to translate into English 'Rapport sur la situation des Russes en France' by Emile Durkheim (see Appendix 2). Similar gratitude is also extended to the authorities of the Yivo Institute for Jewish Research, New York, for the translation of Durkheim's 'Note sur les mesures ayant pour objet d'obliger les Russes réfugiés en Angleterre s'engager dans l'armée anglaise ou rejoindre l'armée russe', to be found in the David Mowshowitch Collection (see Appendix 3).

The editors warmly thank H. L. Sutcliffe for his translation of all the items by Durkheim in the Appendix and also for translating Chapter 7.

Dedicated to Steven Lukes
to whom we owe so much

Introduction

Much of what great writers have written has given rise to contention. To be sure, what they wrote and thought has been highly praised and has been seminal for those who followed them. By this means much of their thought has been developed or adapted. This also implies that debate and argument have arisen around their work. One is tempted to say that the more heightened and prolonged the debate, the more influential has been the thought. Put negatively and more strongly, an absence of debate suggests that there has been nothing worthy of argument. And in turn that has meant that, on the one hand, what a person wrote was of no consequence or was incorrect and can, therefore, be disregarded; or, on the other, that it immediately found its way into received thought, where the origin of the contribution was quickly forgotten.

One of the hallmarks of a classic is that all of it or parts of it have to be taken seriously. The process of acceptance may happen immediately or occur slowly, as the importance of the ideas is realized by the intellectual community. Although a classic cannot be disregarded – a fact implied in the notion of a classic – not everyone accepts it in its entirety. The greatness is seen on all sides due to the new ground it breaks but with it come questioning and challenge. New ideas are seldom immediately taken for granted. Debate is the life-blood of the continuing quest. Where there is no debate, there is no life or living tradition.

The debate at the core of this book is a sociological tradition which, far from being dead, shows vigorous signs of growth. It centres on the French sociologist Emile Durkheim (1858–1917). From the time that he started writing in the late 1880s, it was obvious that he was destined to be a controversial figure who rejected much that was currently held to be sociology. The subject was not deemed academic enough to be taught in French or any other universities. It was confined to a reading public and was dominated by the thought of Saint-Simon and Auguste Comte. Due almost entirely to Durkheim's efforts, his ability and determination, as well as backing by the government of the day, sociology became a recognized subject in various university faculties in France and then spread to other countries. But the offensive which he commanded drew blood and he faced opposition, not least from philosophers, in whose discipline sociology had one of its many roots. Other academics joined in the fray, notably those in disciplines loosely grouped under what we would call today the human and social sciences. Durkheim drew blood not just over his claim that sociology was a science but because his creative influence spread well beyond the narrow confines of sociology itself. He succeeded in making his 'science' of social reality extend beyond the disciplines of sociology and anthropology as we know them – and he did not distinguish the two subjects. It was his aim to apply sociology to history, politics, economics, linguistics, philosophy, psychology, and so on. This intention was realized, in part, by drawing around him a group of young scholars who were specialists in various fields and who were enthusiastic to apply his approach. Under his direction the *équipe* based on a division of labour produced what was to become the very influential journal, the *Année sociologique* (see *RFS*, XX). Durkheim's leadership, together with the loyalty and endeavours of his disciples, was the starting point of an important academic tradition. The spread of Durkheim's ideas over a number of disciplines is paralleled by the achievements of Freud and Marx, and, as has been noted often enough, all three were of Jewish origin. Moreover, they have been the originators of some of the fiercest intellectual debates of modern times.

The influence of Durkheim reached its zenith in France immediately before the First World War. Thereafter it tended to decline. After the Second World War there were signs of revival as sociology began to be taught more extensively, particularly in the United States, although Durkheim was well recognized there in the late 1930s, largely through the work of Talcott Parsons. Durkheim is now universally recognized as one of the founders of sociology, along with Weber and Marx. Translations of his books were made or promoted by American scholars, and then by British academics, largely under the initiative of the professor of social anthropology in Oxford, E. E. Evans-Pritchard. Indeed, in Britain, most of the efforts to propagate the works of Durkheim and the school he founded were made by social anthropologists as much as, or even more than, by sociologists.

In more recent times, a significant advance in Durkheimian scholarship came with the publication in 1973 of Steven Lukes's *Emile Durkheim: His Life and Work; A Critical and Historical Study.* It was not without significance that Evans-Pritchard was the supervisor of the thesis which was virtually reduplicated for the book. It greatly extended the debate on Durkheim, which started, as we have said, in the early days of Durkheim's professional career and has continued with varying intensity ever since.

Lukes's extensive research and comprehensive coverage of Durkheim's work opened a new chapter in studies on the master. The book achieved this in two ways. First, it challenged some of the established interpretations of Durkheim. Second, it set his work in a larger framework which covered his entire *œuvre.* It brought to light heretofore little-known or totally unknown pieces written by Durkheim. Further, it stimulated others to look again at the contribution which the master made to sociology and to late nineteenth- and early twentieth-century thought. Not only have a series of books and numerous articles been published over the last twenty years, but the Groupe d'études durkheimiennes was opened in Paris in 1978. Unfortunately it was closed ten years later, but the bulletin it started, which covered research on Durkheim and his school, is now being published in Urbana, Illinois. In October 1991, the British Centre for Durkheimian Studies came into existence in Oxford.

Lukes himself was by no means an uncritical exponent of the master he so assiduously studied. Although he expounded many of his ideas, Lukes's conclusions were far from definitive. He left many of the questions open, since it was impossible for him to develop in detail all the issues he had raised. It was left to others to deal extensively with such subjects as method, religion, suicide, the division of labour and so on.

The introduction to this book would extend to an inordinate length if the many controversies arising out of Durkheim's work were described, even briefly. Nevertheless, some kind of indication is required to show the general areas of controversy which have arisen over the years.

Inevitably, argument has prevailed about what Durkheim actually wrote. This is not really a matter of textual criticism in the classical sense of comparing variant texts which have been handed down over the ages and which differ at some points. In the case of Durkheim, the actual words that he wrote or used are not seriously in question. Rather, controversy has centred on the meaning or interpretation of what he wrote. And here a number of issues are at stake.

Doubt or misunderstanding arises because Durkheim does not always define key words or concepts, and that despite his commitment to some form of rationalism and the implied need for definition; for example, the words society, *représentations*, effervescence, are never defined or are only obliquely defined. He seems to assume that his readers know what he means by the word in question. Take another case. Only later on in his academic career did he define religion, which was such a key concept in his thinking. And when he did put forward a definition, it became a source of controversy (Pickering 1984: ch.9; see Lukes 1973: 1–36).

Again, although he claimed to be writing as a 'scientist', his language was not free from ambiguity. In relating two entities he sometimes implies that A causes B or A influences B, and on other occasions that B causes A, etc. A slightly different kind of ambiguity lies in the way in which he relates key social concepts when, for example, he relates society to the individual or religion to society. The priority or primacy of one of the terms of the relationship is not stated, at least not in a consistent way. Sometimes one or sometimes the other of a pair is given primacy. Is he arguing 'scientifically' (or 'rationally')? Or, on the other hand, in terms of unresolved dualisms, even dialectically?

In this connection it should not be overlooked that English-speaking scholars, who do not read the French texts, have had to rely on poor translations. Indeed, Durkheim has not been served well by English translators, save for certain exceptions.

Further, scholars of all nationalities have tended in the past, if not so much today, to rely on only one or two of Durkheim's major works. They have not troubled to examine his thought on a particular topic across the entire range of his writings.

Standard phrases, sentences, quotations, have all been worked over *ad nauseam* without trying to discover other examples or to see a word or words in different contexts. The result has been a conventional or limited interpretation. However, scholars are now taking pains to examine more carefully the corpus of Durkheim's works.

One of the key approaches to understanding a text is, as has just been hinted, to place it in its historical context. What is important is to examine the background against which Durkheim was writing, both in France at the time and in the academic world itself.

The matter of personal or hidden intention has also been raised. Can one discover what the author was intending to do, when he wrote, for example, *The Rules of Sociological Method* (1895a; see Chapter 3 in this volume). To what extent intention can actually be found, and its significance for analysing Durkheim's work, have been debated by R. A. Jones, who has employed some of the thinking of the Cambridge historian of ideas, Quentin Skinner.

The second type of debate turns on the contention that what Durkheim wrote does not have application to society today. To establish the 'science' of sociology, Durkheim drew on empirical data ranging from preliterate societies to early twentieth-century conditions in Europe. But do the conclusions of Durkheim have any meaning for contemporary European and Europeanized societies?

The way in which sociology has emerged has meant that for many of its advocates, its long-term aim is, like that of the natural sciences, to discover laws or correlations. It is assumed that such generalizations are without reference to time or to specific societies. Here, it is argued, Durkheim's achievements fell very short of his aims. But what he often projected were generalizations which were specific to certain societies and to certain periods of history. Even if they were generally held to be valid, it is questionable whether they are adequate for present-day society. One might cite the example of the relative absence of social conflict and class tension in his thought. Such an in-adequacy is evident in his thesis, *De la Division du travail social* (1893b). Another example is his treatment of religion. As he progressed in his professional career, he became increasingly convinced that religion was the key to the understanding of society (see Pickering 1984). This idea was enshrined in perhaps his greatest book, *Les Formes élémentaires de la vie religieuse* (1912a), in which he used extensively material from a preliterate society, the Arunta of Australia. But his theories, based on totemism, have little relevance for later major religions of the world. And when he started to analyse the contemporary European situation, he admitted that it was in the process of what we would call secularization, in which case, some would argue, religion ceases to be a key to understanding it. To attempt to be consistent, Durkheim pointed to what he held was the emerging religion of modern society, namely, the cult of the individual. But precisely here there are those who would see a number of theoretical and empirical weaknesses, not least whether the cult of the individual performs the same function in a society as does a primitive religion.

Up to this point, and by way of illustration, we have referred to only one or two substantive issues which have broken new ground and given rise to controversy. This is because some of the other issues are raised specifically in the chapters which follow. The list of such issues emerging from Durkheim's work is endless, and quite obviously only a handful are raised here. We name at random some of those which are not raised here: the distinction between egoism and individualism in modern society, the nature of anomie (also in modern society), the influence of social factors on the formation of abstract categories, such factors in understanding suicide, a religious base for morality, the need for a sociological analysis of educational processes, the idea of the human person as a socialized being, and so on. As might be realized, the list is very long. It is for this reason that Durkheim is the classical writer he is.

The papers forming the substance of this book were originally given in seminars at St Antony's College, Oxford, in the years 1990 to 1992, in a series entitled 'Durkheim and French Sociology'. In some cases the papers have been rewritten or expanded specifically for the book.

The fact that Durkheim was of Jewish origin, the son of a rabbi, has prompted some scholars to relate such a background to his sociological thought. Whether one can reach definite answers about this is questioned by W. S. F. Pickering in the opening chapter of the book. He focuses on Durkheim's attitude to Judaism itself and his coming to terms with his ethnic background. This was highlighted by the Dreyfus Affair and current anti-semitism. Primarily, Durkheim wanted to be seen as a loyal Frenchman and an unquestioned supporter of the Third Republic. His attitude to Judaism was ambivalent. The Appendix contains three items (with introductions) relating to anti-semitism, two of which have only recently come to light.

As we have noted, Durkheim made little distinction between anthropology and sociology, and one early monograph, written in conjunction with his nephew Marcel Mauss, in 1903, has caused a great deal of controversy among members of the two disciplines, both of which are interested in part in knowledge and its relation to social life. The monograph broke new ground in relating abstract concepts in terms of classification with what might be called social structure. Rodney Needham (1963) in his introduction to the English translation of the text, claimed to identify its many weaknesses. Nick Allen (Chapter 2) would contest such criticism. By bringing to bear the work of Dumézil and de Saussure he finds the general thesis of the monograph acceptable. He then directly challenges many of the criticisms of Needham as ill-founded.

Perhaps one of the most contested books of Durkheim is his *Rules of Sociological Method* (1895a). This charter for making 'sociology a science' has been criticized on at least two grounds – that Durkheim's notion of science was inadequate and that his treatment of social reality was unscientific and did not follow his own canons. A large number of sociologists have written off the book as being unhelpful for the development of sociology. Mike Gane (Chapter 3) attempts to restore it to its rightful place by challenging some of the criticisms. He holds that the *Rules* must be viewed not in a piecemeal fashion but holistically. What is needed for a sympathetic reading of Durkheim, argues Gane, is to see that Durkheim calls for an exposition of the various complex positions with regard to social reality to be established before judgment is given. Avoiding empiricism and mysticism, Durkheim felt that a complex rationalism was the answer, which included an optimistic faith in science. Further, sociology offers a logic of explanation which is also oriented towards practical intervention by which abnormal phenomena become revealed.

Central to Durkheim's methodology as laid down in the *Rules* is the concept of a social fact. Exactly what a social fact is has always been a source of puzzlement. And coupled with it, the notion of society as a *sui generis* synthesis of individuals has always given rise to questioning and rejection. Margaret Gilbert, a philosopher, maintains that many of the criticisms levelled against Durkheim's formulation of these two concepts are ill-founded (Chapter 4). She holds that collective beliefs exist on their own, independent of their manifestations in individuals, though no social group can be independent of the individuals who make it up. Thus, it can be said that social facts are group facts. It is the case that in everyday speech people ascribe beliefs to groups, an instance of what might be called 'pre-theoretical intuition'. Collective beliefs require for their existence a social group, and 'inhere' in such a group, which consists of plural subjects, forming a *sui generis* human association.

Durkheim held that the starting point of ethics had to be a science of moral facts. Both the possibility and desirability of such an exercise have been challenged. Willie Watts Miller (Chapter 5) takes up these ideas in terms of the importance, as Durkheim saw it, of identifying societies according to type and stages of development, that is, in an evolutionary framework. This allows for the notion of deviancy relative to a particular type or stage of development. At the centre of Durkheim's interest is the role of and importance given to the individual, the human personality and the idea of freedom. These ideas in turn lead to issues of conflict and cohesion. One of the accusations levelled against Durkheim was that his neutrality, arising from a scientific outlook, meant that he could not condemn human atrocities. Watts Miller takes a contrary view and holds that Durkheim's ethical stance does condemn man's inhumanity to man. He also analyses aspects of the French Revolution to show how radical change can be understood in Durkheim's terms.

A quick reading of Durkheim's better known-books, those published while he was still alive, might suggest that he was unconcerned with the issue of nationalism – a subject so important at the present time. As Josep Llobera argues, a closer examination of Durkheim's writings, including pamphlets written in the First World War, shows that he was deeply concerned with the subject (Chapter 6). Durkheim brought out both the positive and normative aspects of the nation and tried to relate them to ethnicity. He also differentiated nationalism from patriotism. In opening a controversial issue, Durkheim felt forced to differentiate morbid from non-morbid forms of the state and of nationalism. He held that in modern times force should not prevail in the formation or preservation of states.

In joining in the continuing debate about the nature of social facts and the impingement of the social on the individual, Philippe Besnard, in the final chapter, considers one of the most basic of all social facts, the naming of a child. He maintains that a study of Christian names or first names perfectly exemplifies Durkheim's approach to sociology. Naming is also related to ideas of fashion and diffusion as expounded in *The Rules of Sociological Method*. This in turn encourages Besnard to consider the well-known debate between Durkheim and Tarde on the issue of imitation, for which it is necessary to consider various meanings of the concept. Besnard, employing contemporary research on first names in France, considers that fashion in names is a cyclical development of preferences – a *sui generis* process – and not an expression of 'the spirit of the times'.

From what has been said already and from what is to follow, an outsider might wonder whether sociology is nothing more than debate, rather like philosophy. Certainly, debate has surrounded sociology ever since it emerged in the nineteeth century as a 'scientific' means of settling social and political debates. If nothing more, that debate has helped enormously to clarify differences. One crucial debate has centred on the realization that a crude empirical approach to the data of social life cannot produce simple scientific laws which were at one time thought to be immanent. The debates will continue as the issues become more refined. In this Durkheim has a key role to play, not so much by offering definitive answers, but by raising key questions which must be explored, if we are to understand the society in which we live.

Chapter 1

The enigma of
Durkheim's Jewishness

W. S. F. Pickering

INTRODUCTION

Several years ago Rodney Needham, reviewing a book on
Durkheim, wrote: 'The suggestion has even been made by a
Jewish scholar (a historian and social anthropologist) that there
is something about those characteristic virtues and viewpoints
[of Durkheim] which cannot well be understood by gentile
readers' (1978). This raises the age-old question of whether a
gentile can correctly interpret Judaistic thought or understand
Judaism at any historical period. And it applies equally to an
examination of Durkheim's thought itself. *A prima facie*, a wise
policy in dealing with hermeneutical issues, is to go, at least
initially, to those who have worked directly with them as part of
their inherited culture.

On the other hand, the logic of all this, and particularly *vis-à-
vis* Durkheim, is that only a Jew can understand him and his
sociology. Durkheim himself would have protested against such
an outlook, for it is a rejection of the objectivity of sociology and
its claim to some kind of universality. Further, for him science
and all worthwhile knowledge was not skewed by cultural
interpretations.

There is a parallel here in the story that a French academic is
said to have told Steven Lukes that his attempt to write an
intellectual biography of Durkheim was doomed to failure from
the start. Why? Because he was not a Frenchman! There was no
reference in the story to Lukes having a Jewish background.
The prophecy that he was incapable of writing the book has
been silenced by its very success (1973).

The question of who can or cannot correctly interpret a

religious or ethnic situation can never be solved *a priori*. In the end the hermeneutical solution has to be decided empirically or pragmatically. The question of who can speak on Durkheim's Jewishness remains unsolved and is open to all comers. Judgment has to rest on what is presented.

The subject of Durkheim's Jewishness, however, has never been dealt with systematically. As we have just seen, the call that it should be tackled has come from scholars such as Rodney Needham and others (ibid.). No convincing response, however, has emerged. Perhaps the stubborn silence persists because the subject is a very tricky one and one on which a conclusion is difficult to reach. That is really what I want to demonstrate. Some aspects of it have been considered, notably Durkheim's early years, his parental background, and his alleged rejection of the rabbinate (see, for example, Meštrović 1988: 27ff.).[1] The events have also been subject to some form of psychoanalytic interpretation (see Pickering 1984: 13–14). There is no intention here to rework this ground, for it has serious limitations, owing to the paucity of knowledge of Durkheim's personal life.[2] Instead, I intend to look at possible influences on his life and thought, primarily in terms of social and historical factors, rather than possible influences emanating from Biblical or Judaistic sources.

ASSIMILATION, INCORPORATION AND ACCOMMODATION

The Durkheimian scholar, Tiryakian, has referred to Durkheim as an assimilated Jew (1979: 111). What does such an assertion mean?

Assimilation has been an ever-recurrent problem for Jews of the Diaspora. Today it remains an issue of great importance and Jewish identity persists just because of a refusal on the part of Jews to accept total assimilation. The issue of identity has deep theological roots which certainly in Europe, if not in Asia, have been the foundation of the remarkable ability of Jews to stand firmly against social and religious absorption. The tap-root of this resistance is the very strongly held doctrine that Israel is a separated and holy (*qodesh*) people, specially chosen and sustained by God. Such separation has inevitably demanded the maintenance of well-marked boundaries. The Diaspora could never have remained in existence for about 2,000 years without upholding such boundaries and manning firm walls of demarcation. Persecution at the hands of the Romans, and then at various times by Christians and Muslims, has been weathered at great cost through a stubborn refusal on the part of large numbers of Jews to lose their identity. They have mounted this determined resistance, never having had, until very recent times, a country or base from which to draw strength, or in which to take refuge. That is a quite remarkable feat.

The maintenance of identity is not only a social or corporate problem in 'keeping the people together', it is also one for the individual. In the face of the desire of the individual Jew to succeed and live peaceably in a foreign society, even to remain alive and survive in times of persecution, there has always been the temptation to take the easy way out and to become assimilated. This can be achieved in various ways, which are not mutually exclusive. One can convert to the dominant religion, usually Christianity, and less frequently Islam. Although such a step might seem logical, apostasy was never an easy step to take. Again, one can repudiate the Judaism of one's birth by marrying a gentile. Or one can deliberately deny or hide one's Jewish background, and in so doing sever links with the Jewish community completely. A common method of disguise was, and still is, to change the surname, for example, from Gottmann to Goodman, from Weinstein to Kasparov. With the rise of industrial society in Western Europe from the early nineteenth century onwards, and with the accompanying growth of tolerance, which sprang earlier from some Enlightenment philosophers, there emerged a growing tendency towards assimilation. In the face of a slowly growing but seemingly assured religious pluralism in Europe, where Catholics and Protestants were forced to tolerate one another, Jews, supported by legal emancipation, felt they could be accepted and could be assimilated without having to deny or conceal their Jewishness. This offered them a non-compromising form of assimilation whereby they could still identify themselves as Jews and worship in the synagogue, but at the same time they could adopt to a very large measure, though never completely, the dominant culture of the society in which they lived. In this way they were accommodated within the society and were not forced to renounce openly their own religion and culture. In brief, there was the possibility of a peaceful compromise, undergirded by legal rights, which meant that they could live as Jews in an essentially gentile world. It is important to make this differentiation in considering the position of Jews in nineteenth-century Europe because of the opportunities which became available to them that had not occurred before. In this respect France was a pioneer in granting emancipation to Jews. Initiated by the Revolution of 1789, emancipation extended to other countries in Europe, not least through the conquests of Napoleon.

A recent writer on anti-semitism in France has held that assimilation occurs when Jews are taken as 'Frenchmen like any other' (Marrus 1971: 2). But 'like any other' in what sense? What of Alsatians? Basques? Or those of minority religions – what of Protestants? There were some ardent nationalists at the time of the Dreyfus Affair who said that Protestants 'were artificial Frenchmen, outside the reality of the nation' (Kedward 1965: 30). The notion of assimilation, which is essentially concerned with culture and acculturation, is complex and too much of a blanket term to cover the various responses of Jews to the new, freer, nineteenth-century situation which confronted them in many western countries, especially in France (for a rejection of the term in a strictly historical context, see Sorkin 1990). The word implies both a final position and a process towards a goal that is to be achieved (Gordon 1964: 631).[3] Marrus has written of Jews in France that 'their assimilation was never complete and was thus a continuing problem' (1971: 2).

The problem is this. Assimilation means to be both similar to and also identical to. The differences in the meanings must be stressed but at the same time each must be refined. Common usage demands that the word has to be retained. But within it should be included two concepts, namely, the notion of incorporation on the one hand, and of accommodation on the other. Incorporation is taken to mean identification or absorption. It implies what some people mean by assimilation, as with Marrus, when he says, 'by assimilation we are referring to the process by which individuals of Jewish background assumed an *identity* which is essentially French' (ibid.: 2; and see Meštrović 1988: 32). But incorporation is of two types. One involves radical changes in the life-style of the individual, generally by converting to Christianity, thereby severing all contact with the Jewish community, and demonstrating to all the unequivocal wish for identification. This might be called positive incorporation. Negative incorporation means hiding one's identity and trying to pass as a gentile. It usually involves cutting oneself off from one's fellow-Jews and, if necessary, withdrawing from the synagogue. *Les juifs honteux* were those who unashamedly became incorporated.

In contrast to incorporation, accommodation is a much less radical form of assimilation. Here the individual retains much of her or his Jewish culture, including synagogue worship perhaps, but at the same time becomes closely associated with the larger society by adopting as much of gentile culture as is possible without denying Jewish culture. One attempts to become, or is seen to become, as much a 'normal' citizen as is a Catholic in Britain, or a member of the Mormons in Germany, but one does not cut one's social tap-root or cultural orientation. As religious pluralism and agnosticism began to emerge in the nineteenth century, so it was possible to be a Frenchman but at the same time not a Catholic.

Where do the secular Jews of the past century, and especially those of today, fit into these terms? Some have adopted one path; some another. The secular Jew might veer towards negative incorporation, but is more likely to be one who is accommodated to the gentile society. Such Jews will probably never deny their Jewishness, but at the same time they will have little or no connection with the synagogue, they are likely to be agnostic, and in public will be reluctant to acknowledge their Jewishness.

The adoption of the responses just outlined, or the possibility of a number of variations between them, has caused division among Jews themselves, as well as various reactions among gentiles. Total incorporation into gentile society has brought with it bitterness and distress to most Jews, who have remained faithful to their roots. On the other hand, converts themselves may be received in gentile groups with some suspicion. Among anti-semites in France in the late nineteenth century there were those who thought that the most dangerous Jews were those who accommodated themselves to the society of their day by playing down their Jewishness, but at the same time did not cut themselves off from their local communities (Derczansky 1990: 157–8). In this respect the notion of a 'dirty' Jew can have two connotations – it may refer to physical traits or habits thought to be undesirable by gentiles, or to a Jew who tries to pass as a gentile.

DURKHEIM'S RESPONSE

Where does Durkheim stand over the issue of assimilation? His position is not easy to establish. Some of the facts might be mentioned briefly. He rejected Judaism as a religion on the grounds, I think, of relativism. The Jewish God was held to be universal, yet he did not reveal himself in the same way in each society (Pickering 1984: 10). Davy (1919) holds that by the time Durkheim went to the École Normale in 1879 he had abandoned all Judaistic practices and had therefore cut himself off from the religion of his forebears. Something of the personal implications of this comes out in a contemporary writer, Bernard Lazare, himself a Jew. He wrote:

> As soon as a Jew rejects the ties of ritualism, when he ceases to practise dietary laws, when he abandons the sabbath laws, nothing more remains in him: no troublesome residue litters his mind . . . [but from Jewish scholars he remembers] to exercise reason and always to call upon it.
> (Preface to Alphonse Lévy, *Scènes familiales juives*, 1902, Paris. In Marrus 1971: 193)

There is the story told by Étienne Halphen, that his (Halphen's) great-grandfather, Moïse Durkheim, wrote to the Director of the École Normale Supérieure, asking that his son, Émile, should be excused lectures on a Saturday – a request which was refused (Halphen 1987: 7). This would seem to point to the fears of the rabbi-father that his son would be forced to tread the road of assimilation. But giving up Jewish beliefs and practices is one thing: embracing some form of Christianity another. There is another, better-known story that Durkheim, while at school, might have become a Catholic due to the influence of a female teacher (Davy 1919: 183; Pickering 1984: 6) .[4] Probably it was an adolescent, mental flirtation. He always admired Catholicism, as is evident in his writings, but he was nevertheless critical of it (Pickering 1984: 427–34). Protestantism did not seem to attract him at all and it is questionable whether he really understood it (ibid.: 435–9). There seems little reason ever to question the fact that he remained an agnostic, and at times an atheist, all his adult life. Incidentally, Durkheim's daughter, Marie, brought up her own children, it is said, 'completely without religion'. Two sons married Catholic girls and converted to Catholicism; the third son, who married a Jew, was later remarried to a Catholic; but he himself has not become a Catholic (personal communication from Étienne Halphen; and see Meštrović 1988: 28). Of all Durkheim's brothers and sisters, and their offspring, only one, Céline Durkheim, a sister of Durkheim, was religiously devout (personal communication from Mrs Claudette Kennedy. See note 1).

Many Jews who were contemporaries of Durkheim rejected all concepts of God and had little place for religion in their personal lives or in their academic endeavours. Not so Durkheim who, as I have argued elsewhere, in so many respects exhibited religious qualities (Pickering 1984). Yet it is remarkable that, despite his great interest in the sociology of religion, which extended to the fact that he saw religion as the key to the understanding of social life, he seldom referred to Judaism. People will doubtless point to references to Jews and the Jewish way of life in his early book on suicide (1897a), and there are passing references in other books, particularly to Jewish law, in his thesis of 1893, *The Division of Labour* (1893b). It is strange, therefore, that with his personal knowledge of Judaism which he must have imbibed as a child when he was instructed in the synagogue and at home, he never wrote a book or article exclusively devoted to the subject or which referred to it extensively. He seems to have almost deliberately shunned it. Nor are there any indications that he planned to write about it. When he wrote a short but revealing piece on anti-semitism he said he had done no research on the subject and wrote only from personal impressions (1899d: 59; see Appendix).

As is probably known, all Durkheim's papers and manuscripts were lost during the Second World War when the Nazis threw them all into the street from the home of the Halphens. By a strange turn of fate the Nazis turned the Paris house into a place of interrogation and torture (Halphen 1987: 9; see also Meštrović 1988: 19–20). Whether the papers contained any accounts of Durkheim's own religious attitudes we shall never know. The fact remains that we simply have no knowledge of his personal beliefs, apart from the one which is generally known, which centres on the death of his son, André, to whom he was deeply attached and who was killed in the First World War. In a letter to Xavier Léon he said that nothing in all the religious wisdom and ritual that he had studied consoled him in the great loss which had befallen him (see Lukes 1973: 556).

To be sure, Durkheim never denied his Jewish background and indeed was prepared to declare openly that he was a Jew. He said so when he contributed to the inquiry into the subject of anti-semitism conducted by Henri Dagan at the time of the Dreyfus Affair (1899d). In it he also said that he experienced anti-semitism first-hand in eastern France during the 1870 war, living as he did then in Lorraine. He married a Jewess, Louise Dreyfus, and so did not break the basic boundary-making requirement for Jews. He supported the Jewish organization, Comité Française d'Information et d'Action auprès des Juifs des Pays Neutres (Davy 1919: 193). In the middle of the First World War there was an upsurge of anti-semitism in France and Durkheim was accused of being a German agent and was attacked in the Senate in 1916. This was despite his writing anti-German pamphlets (1915b; 1915c; and later, 1916a; and see Appendix, Introduction to 1990a). His ardent patriotism was emphasized by leaders of the government of the day who spoke strongly in his defence (Lukes 1973: 557; Pickering 1984: 17). In the war he was also put on a commission to examine the patriotic attitudes of Russian refugees around Paris. He was the vice-president and helped compile an objective yet sympathetic report which has just come to light (see 1990a in Appendix).

His response to the Dreyfus Affair is well known. He quickly became a Dreyfusard not on account of Jewish loyalties, it is said, but on moral grounds and in support of the Third Republic (Lukes 1973: 333 n.49; Meštrović 1988: 30). The assertion is difficult to prove but it is known that he attempted to influence important intellectuals to join him as a Dreyfusard and he organized and was an official of the Bordeaux branch of the Ligue des Droits de l'Homme et du Citoyen over against which stood the Ligue de la Patrie Française (see Lukes 1973: 347ff.). In opposition to the more subtle right-wing attacks against certain trends in French society, which arose out of the Dreyfus Affair, Durkheim wrote his important article, 'Individualism and the Intellectuals' (1898c). In it he maintained an ethical defence of individualism over against egoism and upheld the cult of the individual as the religion of the future. Such themes were constantly in his mind, as can be seen from his writings on morality and other subjects. He supported Jewish issues when he thought Jews were unjustly dealt with (see items in Appendix). However, he appeared to avoid being involved directly in Jewish issues of the Affair when he rejected an invitation to give a lecture on its religious aspects made by a rabbi of Bordeaux (see Cedronio 1989: 52).

To what degree was Durkheim assimilated into French society? He was certainly not incorporated into it, either positively or negatively. He never deliberately and irrevocably cut himself off from all his Jewish roots and connections. As we have seen, he did not convert to Christianity nor did he remain completely aloof from attendance at the synagogue, though it was obvious that he only attended on rare occasions, when, for example, he was in Épinal (see below). Without any shadow of doubt Durkheim wanted to be seen as a Frenchman, as an unqualified patriot. In one way this is not so surprising since it has recently been asserted that in the mid-nineteeth century urban Jews in Lorraine had become integrally French (Caron 1988: 22–3). As is well known, Durkheim coupled his patriotism with a great admiration for the Third Republic. It would seem that he hoped his sociology might come to be seen as a theoretical undergirding of the Republic. A striving after identification was not accomplished by means of an open denial of his Jewishness but as far as possible by keeping it silent or hidden. He therefore distanced himself somewhat from the Jewish community but never cut himself off from it. When it came under threat, he always loyally supported it (Derczansky 1990: 157).

An incident is reported, which recalls his wish to keep his Jewishness hidden. It occurred when he was in Épinal and went to the synagogue at the request of his mother. He was said to have been embarrassed when the rabbi, seeing him in the congregation, referred to him personally and indicated that the presence of a great professor from Paris was proof that Judaism was still a flourishing religion (Filloux 1970: 301; Pickering 1984: 12).[5]

There is another interesting account which underpins Durkheim's apparent wish to keep his Jewish roots covered. His nephew and colleague, Marcel Mauss, was said to be fond of talking about his family background, not least that he was descended from a rabbi (Clifford 1982: 153). By contrast his uncle, from such evidence as we have, remained virtually silent on the subject.[6]

Let me repeat what I have written elsewhere. Durkheim's wish for hiddenness might also be seen in the fact that he, who was named David Émile, chose always to be known as Émile rather than by the more Jewish name of David (Pickering 1984:18).[7] Derczansky suggests that this may have been due to his mother who encouraged him to use the name Émile. Jewish mothers, he argues, were in the vanguard of assimilation (1990: 16n.1). But we have no evidence to show that Durkheim was influenced by his mother in this respect. And to what extent was his mother, the wife of a rabbi, so keen on assimilation? Maybe what she and other Jewish mothers strove for was accommodation.

In brief, Durkheim 'presented himself not so much as a Jew, who had guiltily rejected the faith and practice of his forebears, but as an enlightened intellectual liberal' Frenchman (Pickering 1984: 18). To such a position Jewishness was held to be quite irrelevant. Durkheim's position with respect to assimilation thus approximates to what I have referred to as accommodation. He half abandoned his Jewishness to demonstrate his French citizenship.[8]

FACING INSECURITY[9]

In view of the sometimes fragile balance between emancipation and upsurges of anti-semitism in France, the question arises concerning the individual and corporate response of Jews to aggressive outbursts. The same issue is crucial in the understanding of the attitudes and actions of European Jews in the years which immediately followed Hitler's rise to power.

One reaction of Jews to persecution is that they do not want to know that it has broken out, or is on the point of breaking out. They are meekly prepared to accept whatever suffering comes to them and never complain about it. Thus the Jewish writer Bernard Lazare declared in the 1890s:

> There are a great number [of Jews] who have retained the
> deplorable habit from the old persecutions – that of receiving
> blows and of not protesting, of bending their backs for the

storm to pass, and of playing dead so as not to attract the lightning.

(Lazare, 'Contre Antisémitisme', Le Voltaire,
20 May 1896. In Marrus 1971: 182)

Péguy, not a Jew but a great Dreyfusard, wrote in *Notre Jeunesse* that the great majority of Jews fear war, and continued: 'They fear trouble. They fear unrest: more than anything perhaps, they fear, they mistrust simple inconveniences. They prefer silence and servile calm' (1910: 76; see also p. 80).

Léon Blum, Jewish writer, socialist and leader of the Popular Front, in reflecting in 1935 on the Dreyfus Affair, made the point:

> They [Jews] did not talk of the Affair among themselves; far from raising the subject they studiously avoided it. A great misfortune had fallen upon Israel. One suffered with it without a word, waiting for time and silence to wipe away the effects.

(Souvenir sur l'Affaire, Paris, 1935, pp. 25–6.
In Marrus 1971: 212)

This kind of attitude explains the saying that 'It is doubtful whether Dreyfus would have ever been a Dreyfusard'. It is said that most French Jews refrained from involvement in the Affair (Sharot 1976: 121). And there was no large-scale Jewish organization to combat anti-semitism (ibid.) But it might be argued that Jews have acquired these attitudes directly from anti-semitic ideas and actions. This position is in keeping with Sartre's analysis which asserts that anti-semitic actions have brought about obviously not all, but many modern Jewish traits (1954: 176/t.1948: 120). And there is an old Jewish saying which runs something like this: 'As Christians do, so does the Jew'.

One hope of guaranteeing protection rests with the law.[10] But the law may be both protector and opponent, giving both the hope of protection and the fear of annihilation. Above all, those with the shadow of persecution hanging over them want to know where they stand and what their rights are. It is generally the law which gives them the answer. Those who are actually or potentially subject to persecution very frequently defend themselves by demonstrating, for example in the courts, that they are law-abiding citizens. It is common knowledge that minority groups, especially those subject to persecution, are, as a rule, law-abiding groups, save in the matter of religious faith. And the law is often their protector against attacks by mobs and hostile factions. Knowing the law means that the persecuted know when they can appeal to it. By contrast, they are uncertain of their position when their protection rests on the whims of kings and despots.

For Jews the rule of law is particularly pertinent for the simple reason that Judaism is very much a law-based religion. The Torah – laws found in the Jewish Bible – was coupled with other books on Jewish law derived from the Torah, for example, the Talmud. Brought up with the notion of the Torah, Jews most likely appreciated societies where carefully codified laws tended to determine the parameters of people's behaviour. It may be that Jews saw societies with codified law as being in some way an extension of the structure of their own religion.

To what degree are these 'social facts' reflected in Durkheim's personal and academic thought?

The most obvious connection is the emphasis in his sociology which he gave to society viewed as a stable entity. Further, he fostered the concept of social cohesion, as in trying to explain how cohesion comes out of diversity. This is most obvious in the *Division of Labour* (1893b). (One Jew told me that when he read the *Division of Labour* for the first time he was struck by the Jewish character of Durkheim's notion of mechanical solidarity. And it is true that in it Durkheim refers frequently to Jewish law.)

The other side of the coin is that Durkheim is often accused of paying little or no attention to social change. This charge is patently false but at the same time it cannot be denied that he gives the impression of being much more concerned with the stability of societies and the forces of coherence than with those endemic of change. Nor should it be overlooked that he accorded to society almost divine status (see Pickering 1984: ch. 13).

One cannot fail to see the association here with the history of Judaism itself. The Jews have maintained their identity for 4,000 years. During all this time factors of continuity and cohesion have been greater than those of change or innovation (see Scharf 1970: 162). What is striking, says Scharf, is the persistence of Judaism from the ninth to seventeenth centuries in being free from assimilation, syncretism or schism (ibid.: 159).

It should be emphasized that not all Jewish history has been so characterized. From the time of the Diaspora to about AD 1000 there was much instability and change. Further, if one examines Judaism in India and in Islamic countries there has been a far greater tendency towards acculturation and even syncretism, one imagines, than in Judaism in European countries. There is a strange paradox in the role of Christianity here. On the one hand, terrible Christian persecutions, as in Spain in the fifteenth century, decimated the Jewish populations. Yet on the other hand, because Christianity was based on well-defined beliefs, it forced Jews to create religious and social boundaries, just as Christianity itself created boundaries. This prevented syncretism and gave strength and cohesion to Judaism.

The alleged stability of preliterate societies and their relatively small populations have led such a scholar as Tiryakian (1979) to see a connection between Durkheim's Jewish background and his deep interest in such societies. Tiryakian pointed to the Arunta, who formed the centre of Durkheim's great *Elementary Forms of the Religious Life* (1912a). The argument is wrong in suggesting that Durkheim sees the Arunta in terms of the Jewish people and that by studying them in detail Durkheim rediscovers his ethnic roots (Tiryakian 1979: 111). It seems that there is little evidence that this was the case, or that Jews in Durkheim's time searched for their lost roots. Such a quest might be seen as mainly a North American phenomenon.

In connection with Durkheim's concern for social stability, witness his distancing himelf from, if not horror of revolution. He supported gradualism – indeed, he strongly advocated reforms of the Third Republic, especially those connected with education and those which put the ideals of democracy and a *laïque* state into practice. Anything more radical he would not countenance. He was convinced that lasting changes were not made through revolution but came gradually in and through the solid tradition of a well-established society (see 1925a: 156/ t.1961a: 137). Tiryakian is probably right in stating that Durkheim's optimistic view of the state as an institution which can protect the individual from particular forms of oppresssion comes from his Jewish background (reference unknown). His distance from, yet concern for socialism in its several manifestations and parties, which were supported by many Jews, has been an aspect of his life much commented on (see Lukes 1973:

542–6). Durkheim's temerity over socialism lost him support, even during his lifetime. Certainly his type of sociology, which appeared to gloss over change, received more than its share of criticism.

Why was there this fear of revolution and radical change? Can it be correlated with the feeling that in a revolutionary situation the position of Jews was likely to be uncertain? As has been indicated, their emancipation and their new sense of freedom were dependent on state legislation. A revolution which might have right-wing or extreme nationalist overtones could rescind such legislation. Who knows, persecution and pogroms could well follow from the uncertainties of a revolution. Further, much distance had been covered along the road of Jewish emancipation in France. Jews had become socially accepted and many were economically prosperous. It was an ideal country for Jews to live in (Rabi 1962: 105). And at a personal level, Durkheim's leading position in the university world was well assured. Would not revolution with its uncertain consequences suddenly revoke all this? Before we proceed to examine such a question, it goes without saying that there have been Jews who have been advocates of revolution, notably of course Karl Marx. But our position is that a dislike or fear of revolution has been the dominant attitude of Jews.

As we have noted, at the height of the Dreyfus Affair in 1899, Durkheim wrote a piece for an inquiry on anti-semitism which had been initiated by Henri Dagan (1899d. See Appendix for the English translation and for additional comments). Durkheim's argument was that a deep social malaise had descended on France and it was this which had given rise to anti-semitism. It is possible to argue, however, that anti-semitism was itself part of the malaise. The effect is thus in reality the cause or one of the causes. None the less at one level Durkheim's argument – that France's ills are held by some people to be due to the presence of the Jews – is essentially a scapegoat one. He rejected the idea that the religion of the Jews and likewise their particular cultural characteristics were prime factors. And he continued: 'Jews are losing their ethnic character with extreme rapidity. In two generations the process will be complete' (ibid.: 61). Durkheim developed a very simple and logical solution to anti-semitism: eliminate the social malaise and hostility against the Jews will disappear.

Something must be said at this point about Judaism in Paris. Towards the end of the nineteenth century, many Jews, propelled by the German occupation in the east, migrated from Alsace to Paris, which soon became the centre of French Judaism. Here Jewish life began to acquire a number of well-marked traits. It became largely secular; it attempted to find an acceptable place in Parisian society. And not only was it liberal in politics and to some degree socialist, it was particularly optimistic about the future of French Jewry. France was seen as another promised land. There was, therefore, no need to worry unduly about anti-semitic aggression. Even the Dreyfus Affair might be seen as little more than an unfortunate hiccough. The prayer for the country in the synagogues of Paris contained the words: 'France is of all countries the one you [God] seem to prefer because it is worthy of You' (in Sharot 1976: 86). The intellectual, secular Jew dovetailed easily into French society, which had no established religion, despite its Catholic heritage. To be accepted did not mean having to declare oneself a member of a national Church, as, for example, was the case in England.

Not surprisingly, Durkheim is ambiguous about the situation. On the one hand, he seems worried about the Affair, seeing it as part of the contemporary social malaise, as his letters of the period show (for example, to Bouglé of 22 March 1898). But publicly he reflects uncritically the liberal, optimistic attitude to both anti-semitism and the future of Jews in his country – an attitude which was not shared by Theodor Herzl and others who founded modern Zionism. Could one really believe that the Dreyfus Affair was an attempt to blame the Jews for the social malaise, as was Durkheim's argument? But more importantly, was it widely agreed that a malaise did exist at the time? The defeat of 1870 was attributed to many causes, including France's lack of concern for science in its schools and universities. Also, the government of the day recognized the existence of social problems (Nye 1983: 134). A series of social problems which every industrial society faces does not constitute a crisis or even a malaise. It is strange that if the social malaise were of such overriding importance in France, not more has been written about it by sociologists, not least by way of defining it. Durkheim neither described it systematically nor analysed it. In books and articles and in, as far as we know, correspondence, the notion of a social malaise was not given prominent attention or even mentioned by other members of the Année Sociologique group, who were disciples of Durkheim and who assisted him in the publication of the journal, *l'Année sociologique*.

Intermingled with a secular optimism, there was also in Durkheim, it seems, a feeling of insecurity. This inner fear might have arisen from what he saw as the social and moral malaise in society, and this might have put a question-mark over the social stability of France. Throughout the nineteenth century there had been the rise and fall of governments, empires and republics, coupled with periods when individual freedoms were restricted and ideals of democracy denied. And at the turn of the century the Third Republic was not of long duration. The future did not seem assured.

One might describe Durkheim's basic position as follows. He saw himself as a member of a minority group which had been emancipated and he wanted to see the emancipation persist unchallenged. It was all the more likely to endure under a secular, republican state, which continued the policy of the French Revolution. Jews of Durkheim's ilk wanted political stability in which they could prosper and 'be themselves'. Any threat of a revolution would be counterproductive, since its outcome would be uncertain: worst of all, it might allow right-wing Catholicism to assume power. Hardly surprisingly, Durkheim supported the separation of Church and State, which finally came about in 1905.

In a letter, recently come to light, which Durkheim wrote to Henri Hubert on 22 February 1898, he indicated that he did not admire the then proposed title of the Dreyfus League – La Ligue des Droits de l'Homme et du Citoyen. He proposed instead, La Ligue pour le Respect de la Légalité et la Défense de l'Honneur National (*RFS*, 1987: 488). He said that the proposed title would attract the so-called nationalists. One might add that it also smacked of the ideology of the French Revolution. By contrast, Durkheim's title emphasizes the importance of law and order and the implied necessity for respecting it. There are considerable problems in grasping Durkheim's attitude to nationalism (see Chapter 6). On the one hand he was an ardent patriot and nationalist, yet he was opposed to a right-wing militant nationalism. There were correct and wrong types of nationalism (see Chapter 6). The opposing right-wing league, the Ligue de la Patrie Française, was started slightly later and appealed to that form of nationalism which Durkheim opposed. Any reference to the rights of man, which some might see as relating to social justice, is omitted in Durkheim's proposed title, although the League was concerned with justice based on republican ideals. For Durkheim, rights are not intrinsic to man but are determined by society (see 1950a: 153–4/t.1957a: 122–3).

One might mention in passing that Durkheim's gentle approach to contemporary Judaism is to be contrasted with the gentile verbal violence of another, later *philosophe*, Jean-Paul Sartre. Admittedly his *Réflexions sur la question juive* was written in 1946 with the evils of Nazi Germany and the Pétain government much in mind. There is nothing to indicate that anti-semitism was merely the outcome of something akin to a social malaise. For Sartre, the gentile, anti-semitism is an appalling evil which must be eradicated. By contrast, is there not in Durkheim something of the passivity to be seen amongst Jews, which was mentioned a little earlier on? This is suggested in the gentle way he proposes that anti-semitism should be counteracted in France, namely, by asking the government to show 'how odious such a crime is' and 'to enlighten the masses as to the error in which they were encouraged' (1899d: 62).

When the outcome of the Affair had been assured for the Dreyfusards and the forces of anti-semitism had been dispelled or at least quietened for a time, Durkheim could point to the events themselves as constituting a time of effervescence (Pickering 1984: ch. 21.2). Durkheim saw the Affair, which divided many families, as an episode which raised the social and political climate of France and so overcame what he saw as a certain coldness and indifference permeating society before the Affair. One wonders if the coldness was the same as the social malaise just referred to.

But his optimism can be seen in another light. It is no less than one which reflects his own wish to be assimilated or incorporated into French society. 'Two more generations, and the process is complete' (1899d: 61). Other Jews, such as Theodor Herzl, were not so convinced. For them anti-semitism was endemic in Christian culture, and therefore to live in a Christian society meant to live in a society which could always threaten Jews with hostility and hatred. The pessimists seemed to be right and Durkheim was shown to be a false prophet – witness the upsurge of anti-semitism in France during the First World War, the Nazi holocaust, Pétain, and to this day Le Pen, Monseigneur Lefevre, and the recent desecration of Jewish cemeteries. Fears of the past still linger on and are not eradicated despite the present social stability. Interestingly enough, Durkheim commented on the attack made by Germany and the United States against strong anti-semitic feelings in France in 1915. He did this in his capacity as chairman of a government commission on Russian immigrants, mostly Jewish, in the department of the Seine (see 1990a in the Appendix).

Durkheim's persistent optimistic liberalism is associated with the cult of the individual. Although he rejected the concept of progress, it is quite clear that for him the growth of rational human values was evidence of progress for mankind (see Pickering 1984: ch. 26). Perhaps because of that, Durkheim did not wish to see any gross interruption of the liberal, humanist dream, launched by Saint-Simon.

Finally, a less important point. Reference has already been made to the Année Sociologique group. One of Durkheim's greatest achievements was the creation of this team of brilliant young scholars, some of them Jewish, who applied the basic ideas of Durkheim's sociology to so many academic areas. Durkheim claimed to see in his group the parallel in scientific research where teams of workers make discoveries by mutual aid and interaction. He showed a great reverence for numbers: society is always superior to the individual; many are better than one. Does this indicate a certain insecurity? A fear of isolation? Loneliness? An oppressed minority often wants to have a group working within it to give it strength. Was this in some way a driving force which made him favour the collectivity and refer to the 'we' (see 1925a: 274/t.1961a: 240)? Here are echoes of Jewish mutuality and group identity, emphasized in a minority situation or when the group is faced with hostility.

VARIOUS TYPES OF FRENCH JEWRY: THE ASHKENAZI INFLUENCE ON DURKHEIM?

The Jews of France were expelled in 1394. Later they gradually returned and began to form two distinct groups. The Sephardim settled mainly in the south-west, around Bordeaux and Bayonne. Having originally spent several centuries under Islamic domination, these immigrants from Spain and Portugal fled to France in the sixteenth century on account of severe Christian persecution. They became fluent in French and were the first to write about Jewish affairs in that language. They never acquired civil jurisdiction over their members and they limited internal control to religious and charitable affairs. The reason for this was that they arrived in France as *marranos*, that is, they were outwardly Christian but remained cryptic Jews. (*Marranos* is a word of abuse of Spanish origin meaning swine.) Slowly they shed the Christian cloak and openly declared themselves to be Jews. In the course of time some leaders became deists and broke the ritual law. Not surprisingly this group had moved in the direction of assimilation and became relatively accepted by society before the Revolution of '89 (see Hertzberg 1968: 189ff.).

The other group consisted of Ashkenazi Jews who settled in Alsace-Lorraine, also in the sixteenth century, but who came from Central Europe. They spoke virtually no French but kept to Yiddish and Hebrew, even at the time of the Revolution. They had some wealthy members and some who were semi-Westernized intellectuals but in the main and in contrast to the Sephardim Jews in the West, they were relatively poor, were generally hated by their neighbours and were culturally distanced from them (ibid.: 1 and 314). The Ashkenazi Jews had themselves set up courts of law and attempted to regulate their own affairs through such courts. They wanted to be free, and were encouraged to be free of civil authorities. They also looked after a growing number of poor Jews. This had the consequence of making Ashkenazi Jews culturally isolated, and they tended to be more removed from the general run of French society than were the Sephardim. Self-government ended with the French Revolution but the cultural isolation of the Ashkenazi Jews persisted for some time. In many ways they became leaders in accommodating Judaism to the modern world and were the originators and leaders of Zionism. They originally settled in the countryside but as a result of poor agricultural conditions, began to drift into the towns. Metz, from the early days, became their centre. Much later, in the 1870s and 1880s, many migrated to Paris, which then became, as has been noted, the focal point of French Jewry.

Derczansky maintains that Durkheim's father stood in the tradition of Lithuanian Judaism which had come from Eastern

Europe. It was strongly juridical and stood aggressively opposed to every form of messianism and mysticism (1990: 158). Not all Ashkenazi Judaism had the characteristics of Lithuanian Judaism, but the latter found a place in the rabbinic school in Metz. Some might wish to see the influence of this particular form of Judaism on Durkheim's personal and family life which has been marked by such characteristics (Pickering 1984: 18–20). Durkheim had a cold, stoical and ascetic demeanour (ibid.: 19). He was no lover of the arts. His personal predilection for restraint was a reflection of his admiration for his mentors, Boutroux and Renouvier, who were imbued with similar virtues (Derczansky 1990: 158). But his notion of social morality was not only one of restraint, it bordered on asceticism.[11] And Durkheim's rejection of mysticism and his lack of interest in types of religion in which the individual claims to have an immediacy of divine experience might also have come from Ashkenazi Judaism.

INFLUENCE OF JEWISH DOCTRINES: INTRODUCTION

Durkheim has been described as the Moses of sociology. If that is the case, then he might be said to have led uncertain followers into a land of intellectual milk and honey together with promises of academic success (see Pickering 1984: 551; *RFS*, XX: 304).

In a somewhat different vein it might be argued, and indeed has been, that the whole of Durkheim's thought is essentially Jewish. One could go further and assert that just because it was Jewish, he regarded it as unnecessary to write on Judaism as such. However absurd that claim might sound, it is true that Judaism was seldom written about either by him, or even by members of the Année Sociologique group, some of whom were Jews, as we have already noted.

The thesis that all Durkheim's thought is shot through with Jewish ideas is to assume too strong a position. It disregards what was so crucial to Durkheim's intellectual position, namely, philosophical and scientific thinking arising from the Enlightenment.[12] What one does see, however, as has often been maintained, is that a number of his concepts have a parallel with Jewish ideas of a social and religious kind (see Filloux 1976; Prades 1987: 301–6).

Nevertheless, some people would not want to press home such

connections or make much capital out of them. Interestingly enough one such person is his grandson, Étienne Halphen, who wrote recently that Émile Durkheim was emphatically areligious and that 'all those who have wished to sense in his work the mouldy smell of Judaism were taking a wrong path' (1987: 6). Although M. Halphen would admit he is no Durkheim scholar he is not alone in holding such opinions, perhaps expressed less strongly. In his now famous intellectual biography of Émile Durkheim, Steven Lukes speaks a great deal of the influences on Durkheim's thought in terms of individual thinkers. But there is no reference at all to the influence of Judaism.[13]

ENDLESS POSSIBILITIES

For those who would argue that Durkheim's sociology has been influenced by what he was taught from the Jewish Bible and Talmud, the list of candidates is endless. For what it is worth I present the following possibilities in note form and at random. Some are so obvious as to be naive. Some have been mentioned by scholars before: others are proposed for the first time (see Bois 1914: 364ff.; Filloux 1976).

1 An anti-aesthetical approach to life, which was against dilettantism and was suspicious of the arts, especially the visual arts. Real life was viewed as *la vie sérieuse*.

2 His use of dialectical thinking derived from his rabbinic family background.

3 His emphasis on teaching and education.

4 The position of importance given to ethics, seen as the object of education in preparing a person for a dutiful place in society.

5 His emphasis on the concept of God as law-maker.

6 The importance of the notion of impurity, especially with regard to blood, as in the essay, 'The Prohibition of Incest and its Origins' (1898a(ii)).[14]

7 The central place of justice in his notion of social ethics.

8 His doctrine of man as homo-duplex – two natures, the individual and the social.

9 His concern for the group, people, the nation, the totality, as the basis of sociology. Particularly his notion of mechanical solidarity.

10 Religion defined in terms of a group.
11 Concept of the sacred, including that of the holy and pure, compared with the notion of the profane.
12 His contribution to a theory of sacrifice.
13 Concepts of sin and expiation.
14 Emphasis on social solidarity.
15 Society being both of this world and quasi-divine, akin to the immanence and transcendence of God. In this way it is *sui generis*.
16 An overall essentially practical outlook and not one which was utopian or idealistic. His rejection of philosophical speculation: a greater concern with what he saw as social reality.
17 His position with regard to sexual morality.
18 A high level of identification and integration in minority religions.

CONCLUSION

So, do Durkheim's sociology and his basic thought bear a distinctly Jewish stamp? In trying to answer this, one fact must first be acknowledged: Durkheim himself would surely have been the last person to have agreed with the claim. For him the academic goal was not to create a sociology that contained distinctly cultural ideas and concepts but one based on objective and universal knowledge, that is, scientific knowledge. During his time, and indeed after it, there was the hope that sociology could in some way follow in the path set by the natural sciences. Anything which pointed in another direction was greatly abhorred. To admit a Jewish base for his sociology meant that his claims for the discipline would be vitiated.

Even if sociology is not a Jewish science, as some people have suggested, can Durkheim's sociology be thus branded, irrespective of how he might or might not have viewed it?

Before that question is answered attention should be turned briefly to another world where a similar issue arises, the world of music.

One of the few nineteenth-century Jewish composers was Ernest Bloch, born in Switzerland in 1880, and who died in the United States in 1959. He gained the reputation for being 'a Jewish composer'. Scholars agree that his work was inspired by

Jewish music. Yet if this was the sole criterion for such an assessment, one might falsely deduce that Prokofiev was Jewish on account of his well known overture on Jewish Themes. On the other hand, Mendelssohn, who was of Jewish extraction, seems to stand very much within the nineteenth-century classical musical tradition with no suggestion of any Jewish overtones in what he composed. And to what extent has Kurt Weill been influenced by the music of the synagogue or by Jewish folk songs? Perhaps hardly at all. Where there are Jewish themes in the music people have composed, as in the case of the recently deceased Leonard Bernstein, the influence of his ethnic background stands out clearly and he deliberately used Jewish religious themes. But one cannot characterize the whole of Bernstein's music as being Jewish. And perhaps not all Bloch's compositions were shot through with Jewish themes. But what of Mahler, Berg, Schoenberg, or Darius Milhaud, who incidentally said, 'I am a Frenchman by birth; Jewish by faith'? How Jewish was their work? There is no alternative but to rely on internal evidence and judge each work of a Jewish composer on its own merits. Generalizations about Jewishness have to be made with great care and it is the criteria for making the judgments which raise acute problems.

What then of Durkheim? If it is difficult to draw conclusions with music, it is equally, if not more, difficult with sociology. We have shown a number of parallels between Durkheim's sociological thought and modern Jewish political problems on the one hand, and Biblical concepts on the other. From such data three points emerge.

1 It is extremely hard, if not impossible, to prove the direct influences at work on Durkheim's thought, unless such influences are admitted by Durkheim himself. Correlations have to remain correlations without any immediate or necessary connection between them. To go beyond the stage of correlations involves debatable methodological and logical assumptions.

2 It may seem obvious that a particular Jewish doctrine has influenced Durkheim's thought but in all likelihood the doctrine will have had a long history and be subject to various interpretations and developments. One must therefore be careful in stating more precisely the doctrines which are to be used in making correlations.

3 The problems involved are compounded by the fact that such religious doctrines are not exclusive to Judaism. Many of the Jewish religious doctrines are also to be found in Christianity, for the simple reason that they have been taken over into Christianity and subsequently modified or developed. Further, it might well be argued that Jewish thought in Europe has taken on board Christian ideas or Christian interpretations of certain Jewish doctrines. This but serves to emphasize what was said in the previous paragraph.

Let us look briefly at some of the evidence for suggesting that Christian rather than Jewish influences were at work on Durkheim's thought. First, Félix Pécaut, the liberal Protestant thinker, held that Durkheim's doctrine of man, which has obvious parallels with both Jewish and Christian doctrines, was more Christian than Jewish (1918: 3). The reason for this view was that the Jewish doctrine, based on the Jewish Bible, is much more vague than that which was formulated by Christian theologians from the time of St Paul onwards, where man is said, in fairly dogmatic terms, to have a body and soul. Durkheim adopted this dualistic nature of man in many places, not least in a well-known paper he gave in 1913 entitled 'The Religious Problem and the Duality of Human Nature' (1913b). Second, Durkheim's assertion that society is *sui generis* and sacred is clearly related, as we have already noted, to the Jewish notion of a chosen or holy people. But it is also associated with the Christian doctrine of the Church as a divine society. Christians all down the centuries, whether Orthodox, Catholic or traditionally Protestant, have referred to their membership of the one Holy Catholic and Apostolic Church. They have differed and still differ about the actual identity of such a body, but they would never deny that one exists either in this world or in an unseen world. Durkheim's definition of religion, as in *Les Formes Elémentaires*, is closely associated with these ideas, where he employs the notion of a Church – a word which is absent in the Old Testament. The nearest Jewish concept is people – the people chosen by God, that is, the Jews. The Christian doctrine of the Church in the New Testament speaks of a 'called-out' or gathered society, over and against a 'natural' society into which people are born. The Jews see themselves as a 'total' society, where there is no contrast between the people and those who are of a distinct religious persuasion. That fits in better with Durkheim's concept of society as a whole being sacred and with his notion of religion within a primitive society. Yet Jews acknowledged that there were other peoples created by God, that is, the gentiles. Third, Schoenfeld and Meštrović have recently argued, with a great deal of force, that Durkheim, in his concept of justice as the basis of social morality, was far more influenced by Judaism than by Christianity (1989). They suggest that Durkheim, in establishing a base of social morality, rejected the notion of charity as portrayed in the New Testament and upheld the idea of justice based on the concept of a covenant. Such a notion dominates Jewish religious thought. While there are obvious correlations between Durkheim's thought on these matters and basic Jewish ideas, the argument is difficult to sustain. The authors fail to take into account many intertwining influences which operated in the development of Durkheim's thought, especially those of the philosophers of the Enlightenment, and also the way in which Christian and Western thought as a whole has dealt with the issue of social justice. That social ethics should rest on justice is not unique to Judaism. Can one really say that Durkheim's thought was more influenced in the matter of social justice by Jewish ideas than by those of Kant or of his teachers, such as Boutroux or Renouvier – Durkheim openly declared the influence Renouvier had on him – who were all gentiles?

The difficulty in all this lies in the fact that Judaism and Christianity are not distinct religions which, in terms of certain basic ideas, are easy to disentangle. A great many Jewish doctrines were taken over by the early Church, while others were modified. And that is hardly surprising as the early Church was nothing more than a Jewish sect. Furthermore, Durkheim did not inhabit a Jewish ghetto culturally isolated and well insulated from the rest of France. He lived openly in a France which was constitutionally secular and pluralistic and which had a long Catholic history. Within the *mélange* of ideas which permeated Durkheim's mind, it is virtually impossible to compartmentalize which of them came from Jewish sources and which might be labelled Christian. A quotation from Sartre confirms these kinds of difficulty. He said that he was told that when Jewish atheists questioned the notion of God, what they were really rejecting was the notion of God which they had learnt from Christianity (1954: 80/t.1948: 55).

In this chapter I have deliberately emphasized historico-social situations which confronted Durkheim and other French Jews and which were perhaps reflected in his thought. While it is true that the direct influence of these responses is also difficult to prove, they have at least one advantage over ideas derived from religious doctrines, in that they are not so ambiguous as to make it doubtful whether such ideas were of Jewish or Christian origin. On political issues the researcher is on more clearly delineated ground, even though it may in the long run turn out to be a marsh rather than firm rock.

There is a further and yet more important factor. If the point of reference is external forces influencing Durkheim's thought, those of an historical nature have pre-eminence. In considering the question of Jewish background, one has to take into account the facts that Marx was violently anti-religious, that Raymond Aron, who held the chair of sociology in the Sorbonne, was openly hostile to Durkheim's thought, and Brunschvicg, the leading French philosopher of the inter-war period, poured scorn on Durkheim's work. The position of these Jewish academics has to be taken into account. What differentiates them from Durkheim can be related to their attitudes towards different historical situations which faced them. At the same time it should not be forgotten that Jewish intellectuals do not close ranks in the face of academic opposition to one of their members, the open debate is very much in the rabbinic tradition and is one of the gifts which Jewish intellectuals have passed on to modern society.

But I go back to the beginning, which is also the end. Assuming the legitimacy of the inquiry, perhaps what I have said may be seen as off the mark,[15] and if so, it may be that only someone steeped in Jewish religion and culture can solve the enigma of Durkheim's Jewishness. But the enigma is for all to see and is, strangely enough, symbolically engraved on Durkheim's tomb in Montparnasse cemetery in Paris. In the right-hand corner there are some Hebrew words which have been so weathered as to be indecipherable.[16]

NOTES

1 One point should be noted which is contrary to what Lukes has written, which was based on a personal communication from Étienne Halphen. It would seem that Durkheim did not attend a rabbinical school in Épinal as Lukes holds (1973: 39). Meštrović has shown that there was no such school in Épinal at the time (1988: 28). However, Mrs Claudette Kennedy, one of Durkheim's great-nieces, has stated in a personal communication that it was said in the extended family of which she was very much part that Durkheim had been sent to a rabbinical school and that he had rebelled and had refused to continue his studies. It is possible that he went to Metz where there was a rabbinical school. The issue has still to be resolved.

2 Childhood studies in general have been enlightened by the work of another Jew, Sigmund Freud, so that in psychoanalytical studies of Durkheim, one Jew has been used to 'explain' another. The work of Greenberg (1976) in which he compared the early years of Durkheim with those of Bergson, another Jew, are not particularly convincing, largely because insufficient biographical or autobiographical material is available. Similarly Lacroix fails to substantiate psychoanalytical hypotheses (1981). A more common-sense approach to the early days of Durkheim's life has been advanced by Lenoir (1930), and more recently, by Filloux (1977; see also Filloux 1976; Meštrović 1988: 26ff.). But they all inevitably suffer from the same problem – a lack of information about Durkheim's early years and the influence that events might have had on his subsequent life and thought. Insofar as no further material is likely to come to light, for the 'patient' is dead, and first-hand knowledge about his emotions, personal attitudes, and early experiences is unlikely ever to appear, no detailed analysis is possible. However, it may be that a large batch of letters by Durkheim to Mauss, now held in the Collège de France, may reveal something of a pychological nature which relates to his Jewishness.

3 Gordon's notion of assimilation with reference to structural assimilation is more complex than the way in which I have used the term here.

4 Interestingly enough, those living today who are direct descendants of the Durkheim family know nothing of this story, which has been handed down by Georges Davy.

5 Mrs Kennedy has pointed out an inconsistency in the account given by Henri Durkheim and reported by Filloux. Émile Durkheim's mother, Mélanie, died in 1901 in Épinal. The son did not become a professor in the Sorbonne until 1902. But how was Durkheim received generally by Jewish authorities in France? One answer comes in looking at the Jewish press at the time of his death (see Anon, 1917a and 1917b). The obituaries noted with regret that he was not a practising Jew, that, alas, as the son of a rabbi, he did not know the religion of his ancestors, that as a sociologist he did not

appreciate the social character of Judaism, that as a learned teacher he caused other Jewish intellectuals to distance themselves from Judaism. Yet, although he was a non-practising Jew and was really at the edge of Judaism, he remained a Jew at heart, openly supported oppressed Jews and extolled the virtues of Judaism. And, with France at war, it was noted with satisfaction that: 'M. Durkheim s'était consacré avec un zèle inlassable à la propagande patriotique' (1917b: 294).

6   In this respect he was totally unlike the person with whom he is often contrasted, Karl Marx. Marx had been forcibly baptized by his father in the Lutheran Church. The son not only repudiated whatever vestiges of Christianity he might ever have entertained, but also openly attacked Jews in various books and articles. Another interesting example of a Jewish social scientist is that of Claude Lévi-Strauss. Like Durkheim, he was the son of a rabbi and he, too, did not convert to Christianity. We are informed that also, like Durkheim, he made very few references to his background, even going so far as wanting to deny it. He was fortunate to get out of France just before the Germans arrived.

7   Durkheim's wish to be identified as a Frenchman is also manifested in the tradition in his family that the name should be pronounced 'Durkhem' with a short 'e' and not 'Durkheim' with its German connotation. It is believed that in Épinal today both pronunciations are used. According to Mrs Kennedy, Durkheim's great-niece, this was not so in Durkheim's day. It was 'Durkhem' only. That the pronunciation should be 'Durkhem' is validated, she says, from the student song at the École Normale:

Adorons le totem
Que le Maître Durkheim
Prêcha parmi nous

After the 1870 war, what Frenchman would wish to have his or her name pronounced in a German fashion? Needless to say, descendants of the Durkheim family still insist on the more French pronunciation.

8   Except for his first year, Durkheim lectured in the University of Bordeau on Saturdays between 5.15 and 6.15 in the evening. Obviously this raised no problems for him teaching on the Sabbath. One assumes he was not forced to teach on that day. They were public lectures on subjects in sociology. (See university dossier on Durkheim. My thanks to Philippe Besnard for this point.)

9   I owe some of the points raised in this section to Professor Uri Almagor of the University of Jerusalem.

10 All persecuted groups, especially those with a long history of persecution, seek security against oppression which might be secured by protective laws. An alternative is to seek out nations or patrons who will guarantee freedom from harassment in the face of their persistence in holding to a particular way of life. The history of an Anabaptist sect, the Hutterites, amply bears this out in their

wandering from country to country in Central and Eastern Europe
in order to escape, first from Protestant persecutors and then from
more protracted and severe persecution at the hands of Catholics,
notably those of the Jesuits. In the face of hostile laws they sought
the patronage of individual nobles sympathetic to what they stood
for.

11 For example, in his lectures on socialism and in supporting the
contention of Saint-Simon, he said in connection with individual
desires: 'A moral power is required which cries out "You must go no
further" (1928a: 292/t.1958b: 200). And in much the same vein in
Suicide he held that society must 'set the point beyond which the
passions must not go' (1897a: 275/t.1951a: 249).

12 Within a wider context one could argue that sociology was an
outcome of the industrial revolution. Or, it was a product of France
and of the '89 Revolution. Its 'inventor', certainly of the word itself,
was Auguste Comte. But might it not also be said that in its more
developed stage, it was strengthened by Jewish thought, although it
was hardly a Jewish science? In line with this argument, not only can
one point to Durkheim, but to writers such as Georg Simmel
(1858–1918), who was a contemporary of Durkheim, and Karl
Marx, not to mention others who contributed earlier to the subject.
One might also mention less well-known sociologists such as Ludwig
Gumplowitz (1833–1900) and Eugen Ehrlich (1862–1922). Both
studied in Vienna and both became nominal Christians (*EJS* 17/2:
'Why Jews invented sociology'). Subsequently there were many
other academics and university teachers in sociology who were Jews,
for whom the social sciences seem to have had a particular attrac-
tion, but also let it not be forgotten that in sociology's earlier days in
North America, many sociologists were Christian ministers of one
denomination or another. Nevertheless, rightly or wrongly, sociology has been dubbed a Jewish science.

13 In a conversation I had with Steven Lukes several years ago, he said
he did not tackle Durkheim's Jewish background and its influence
on his thought because it was something he felt he could not address
partly due to the sheer lack of evidence. It was a topic very difficult
to grasp.

14 Mary Douglas in a personal communication thinks this is a direct
influence of Old Testament ideas. This is probably true but it does
assume a central place in his thought.

15 I should like to thank Steven Sharot, David Sorkin, David Feldman,
Étienne Halphen, Steven Lukes, Mrs C. Kennedy and others, along
with members of various seminar groups, for their comments on the
paper.

I would raise a question-mark over this whole enterprise.
I wonder what is the merit or advantage in speaking of someone's
work as being Jewish. That there is some virtue in it arises in part
from the academic quest to discover what influences are to be
seen in someone's thought. So it is argued that Durkheim was influenced by reading Robertson Smith, or, again, by being taught by

Renouvier. It is a way of trying to discover how original or dependent on other people the thinker was. By extension, one can postulate the degree to which Durkheim was influenced by the Judaism of his day. Nevertheless we are not accustomed to talk about the Christian background of Descartes or Kant. Such a background does not seem significant. And the reason no doubt is that they were brought up as Christians in a Christian society. The Jewish background of Durkheim is more interesting because it is that of a minority religion. But in pointing to the background of Judaism, is there not the danger of fuelling anti-semitism on the one hand, or of being overtly pro-Jewish on the other? Sartre would have none of this. Because of his hatred of anti-semitism, he felt that the only solution was to bring the issue into the limelight.

16 Durkheim was buried in a Jewish section of the cemetery. The tomb was originally that of his wife's family. Her father, Henri Dreyfus, died in 1903. It is virtually impossible to decipher the Hebrew letters which are located just above Emile Durkheim's name.

Chapter 2

Primitive Classification
The argument and its validity

N. J. Allen

Among the works of Durkheim and his close collaborators, *Primitive Classification* (I deliberately use the English title rather than the French) is one of those that anglophone social anthropologists are most likely to read and even to own. But what do they make of it? Some of the students to whom I set the text find it almost entirely baffling, and it is indeed extremely rich. Now that it is so common for anthropologists to incorporate autobiography into their ethnography, perhaps I can do the same with a topic that belongs to anthropological theory and intellectual history.

It is October 1965, the second tutorial of a complete beginner in the subject. My supervisor, Rodney Needham, has published his translation of Durkheim and Mauss (1903a(i)) two years previously (when he was about forty). He assigns it for my weekly essay and encourages me to buy it. Nearly a third of the book consists of his forty-two-page Introduction, which is in four parts (Needham 1963). Part I is about the need for a translation: classification is the prime and fundamental concern of social anthropology and this pioneering essay on the subject has been neglected. Part II presents what the translator sees as the essence of the argument, together with its defects – logical, methodological and general. The judgment is severe: the Frenchmen's argument is logically fallacious, methodologically unsound, and very possibly, devoid of any validity whatever (ibid.: xxix); indeed, the entire venture is misconceived (ibid.: xxvi). Nevertheless, Part III proposes that the essay retains some value: historically, it has been influential; methodologically, there is *something* to be said for it; above all, theoretically, it draws attention to the notion of classification. The notion is a vague one, but if anything, this seems a virtue to the translator. Part IV deals with translation, both generally, as a worthwhile activity for academic social anthropologists, and specifically, as regards the problems raised by this particular text.

The whole introduction is written with great verve, radiates self-confidence, and refers to an impressive and useful range of anthropological literature. No doubt at the time I assumed that it was authoritative. Perhaps I felt, as possibly some students do today, that after such an introduction, it would be a waste of time to do more than skim the text itself, densely packed as it is with confusing details about Australian Aborigines, Amerindians and Chinese. One already knew that the argument was all wrong, and that the central lesson to be drawn from it was that anthropology was about classification.[1]

Over the years, while remaining grateful for having been introduced to the work, I began to have doubts about the mode of introduction. In a general way, as students should, I came to recognize that no supervisor is likely to be right about everything. Fieldwork contributed, for an unelaborated notion of classification, though it marked some of my early papers (for example, Allen 1972), seemed to carry me only a limited distance in understanding Hinduizing Himalayan tribes. Moreover, my various more theoretical endeavours seemed in one way or another to suggest that Durkheim and Mauss might have been on the right track after all. I shall mention three of these lines of work, the first two rather briefly.

First, comparative work on Himalayan kinship and social structure led me to an abstract theory which is explicitly world-historical in scope. This has perhaps given me a greater-than-average sympathy for the evolutionist style of discourse that was normal when *Primitive Classification* was being written.

Second, many reasons led me to a special interest in Mauss. Among them were the help he can give to kinship theorists (Allen 1989a: 53), and the acknowledged influence he exercised on Dumont, whose work on the Hindu world seemed destined to remain a landmark for a long time to come. Reading all Mauss's collected works, I developed an immense respect for him, being particularly fascinated by his essay on the person. This led, via a conversation with Michael Carrithers one lunchtime in Wolfson College, to a paper (Allen 1985) in a collection devoted to that essay. But Mauss's essay strongly resembles

Primitive Classification. So was the latter really as misconceived as its translator had claimed?

Third, over the last decade, I have been trying to carry forward the work of Georges Dumézil. In the early 1920s Dumézil embarked on the study of comparative mythology under the influence of Frazer but, as he himself recognized, his work only 'took off' in the late 1930s after his contacts with Mauss and with the sinologist Granet. So far as I know, he never cited *Primitive Classification*. It is above all Granet that he acknowledged, though he found it difficult to formulate the exact nature of his intellectual debt (1981: 21; 1987: 64; cf., di Donato 1983: 402–3). However, the matter is perhaps not entirely mysterious.

It was in 1934 that Dumézil started attending Granet's lectures, and it was in the same year that Granet published *La Pensée chinoise*. The latter might almost be called *Chinese Primitive Classification*, so obvious and so explicit is the debt to *Primitive Classification*: 'Chinese notions belong to a system of classification which it is entirely legitimate to compare with (*rapprocher de*) "primitive classifications" ' (1934: 28). On the next page comes the oft-cited footnote 22 to the effect that *Primitive Classification*'s few pages on China 'ought to mark a date in the history of sinological studies'.[2] So we have two explicit connections: *Primitive Classification* influences Granet, and very soon afterwards Granet influences Dumézil. It does not *necessarily* follow that *Primitive Classification* lies behind Dumézil's significant work; but the evidence within that work is suggestive.[3] If so, someone who aspires to build on Dumézil has reason to look at *Primitive Classification* with a sympathetic eye.

But if from one point of view Dumézil is probably indebted to *Primitive Classification*, from another he more than repays the debt. As I hope to show below, Dumézil's work gives considerable support to the argument of *Primitive Classification*. Yet its own cogency lies internally, in the quality, quantity and interconnectedness of the analyses of Indo-European material, and is not dependent on its (hypothetical and indirect) source of inspiration. My argument therefore begins with Dumézil. Having looked to Saussure for theoretical assistance, it then turns to *Primitive Classification*, especially to its ethnographic core, before returning to Needham. I have no space to react individually to the other commentators, in particular Lukes (1973: 446 ff.), who in this context essentially follows Needham.

DUMÉZIL AND SAUSSURE

Out of Dumézil's vast *œuvre* I am concerned only with his analyses of manifestations of the three 'functions' within the Indo-European speaking world. I shall have to be very curt, apologizing to any who may be encountering this line of research for the first time. The results of trifunctional analyses can usefully be expressed in tables having the form of Figure 2.1: each row and each column has a label which expresses its unity, and each box in the matrix has at least one entry. The label for a *row* refers to the context or domain from which the entries have been abstracted, while the label for a *column* is one of the three functions. A function is a cluster of ideas, whose unity was presumably 'felt' by the earliest Indo-European speakers (or their ancestors), and was recognized by Dumézil on the basis of his comparisons between different domains from different Indo-European cultures. Sympathetic readers of Dumézil soon learn to re-create for themselves this sense of the identity and coherence of each function.

The rules for making entries in the table are quite strict. Within their original context (say, a certain ritual), the potential entries in a *row* must be solidary, homogeneous, distinct and exhaustive; simultaneously each entry must unambiguously fall under Dumézil's definition of the function associated with its *column*. In practice, Dumézil, being a comparativist, typically juxtaposes analyses drawn from different areas of the older Indo-European world, for instance a triad of gods from the Scandinavian pantheon with another triad from the Roman. But there is nothing to stop one assembling and tabulating all the analyses bearing on a single culture, say ancient Rome. Each row would now refer to a different domain within that culture. Thus, in Figure 2.1, *efg* might refer to a distinct segment of the king list, *klm* to the modes of marriage recognized in Roman law, *qrs* to the group of priests called *flamines maiores*; and other rows would refer to yet further contexts or domains, perhaps to certain triads in the pseudo-historical narratives – the three tribes who originally came together to form the Roman people, a particular set of symbolic objects, the alleged causes of a certain event, and so on. If one wishes, the individual rows can be grouped under headings such as pseudo-history, law, religion.

I believe that there are very many more rows yet to be

	F1	F2	F3
D1	e	f	g
D2	k	l	m
D3	q	r	s

(F = function, D = domain)

Figure 2.1 Abstract form of Dumézilian trifunctional analyses

identified in the Roman material (as indeed elsewhere), and also, more fundamentally, that we need to add two more columns (not necessarily filled in *every* row), one on either side of Dumézil's block of three (cf. Allen 1991). However, neither of these points is crucial to the comparison with *Primitive Classification*, which turns on the abstract properties of the schema.

This brings me to Saussure and, more precisely, to his contrast (1985: 170ff.) between syntagmatic and associative (nowadays 'paradigmatic') relations.[4] These exist within a language (*langue*) regarded synchronically, and (at least in the words of his editors) correspond to two forms of our mental activity. First, the meaningful units of language unroll over time, as it were along a line, and the relations that exist along this notional line of discourse are syntagmatic. They are relations *in praesentia*, because the units between which they hold are effectively co-present. Second, any particular meaningful unit is associated with a whole constellation of other units with which it shares some feature or other. These associative or paradigmatic relations are *in absentia*, since they link a unit which has been selected for use with others that have not been. Saussure saw these latter relations as existing in the (normally unconscious) memory.

Dumézilian analyses are usually based on indigenous texts (only rarely on artefacts), and a typical context is thus a stretch of text. It may happen that the entries in a row of a Dumézilian schema appear as an uninterrupted sequence of words in the text, for example the triad of gods Jupiter, Mars, Quirinus. In such cases the relationships between units are obviously syntagmatic; but the situation would scarcely be different if the three gods were abstracted from a larger stretch of text, a myth perhaps, in which each of them played a comparable role.

Saussure goes further (1985: 172). Syntagmatic relations hold not only between co-ordinate elements but also hierarchically, between co-ordinate elements and the superordinate totalities which they form. *Contremaître* ('overseer') is related syntagmatically to *contre* and *maître*, since wholes and their parts are equally co-present in the line of discourse, albeit on different analytical levels. The analogy in the Dumézilian case is between the individual entry (the part) and the label for the row (the whole), for example between a particular *flamen* and the three *flamines* regarded as a group.

So, are the relations between the entries in a column paradigmatic? Certainly they are, generally, *in absentia* – the stretches of text in which we encounter the F1 original tribe are different from those in which we encounter the F1 mode of marriage, the F1 king, etc. (see Figure 2.1). But by the rules of the method, the entries in a column are necessarily related *at least* insofar as all pertain to the cluster of ideas that defines one function (though the relation may of course be closer than that). All the entries in the F2 column relate somehow to physical force or war. However, the idea that these relations exist in the subconscious memory of individuals is problematic here. Occasionally one row is linked to others in a way which is obvious: the relation between the three *flamines* – *dialis*, *martialis* and *quirinalis* – and the canonical triad of gods must have been no less obvious to the Romans than it is to us. But in general one simply does not know how much awareness there was of the 'vertical' associations recognized by the analyst, or how far such awareness could have been induced by judicious questioning. Very likely it was often nonexistent by the time our evidence entered the written record, but present at some (unspecifiable) period in the more distant past.

In spite of this difference, two further points justify us in describing the vertical relations as paradigmatic. First, I quote Saussure (1985: 174): 'Whereas a syntagm immediately calls to mind the idea of an order of succession and a fixed number of elements, the terms in an associative [i.e. paradigmatic] family do not present themselves either in a definite number or in a fixed order.' This applies precisely to our case, and we shall find it useful later. Consider the number of entries in a Dumézilian row. This is not always three, for there may be more than one entry per box; but the number is always fixed (and, one might add, usually fairly small, very seldom reaching double figures). Second, it is characteristic of manifestations of the three functions (though not invariable) that the texts present them in the order of the functions. In contrast, the number of rows one could write for Roman culture is not fixed;[5] and the order in which they are presented is arbitrary, that is, chosen by the analyst with a view to expository convenience or rhetorical effectiveness.

Regarding rows, we argued, following Saussure, that the relation between entries and label is syntagmatic, so what can we say regarding columns? The analogy between language and Dumézilian schema is not immediately helpful here, since a particular linguistic unit is related paradigmatically not to a single set of units such as could be written in one column, but to multiple sets. Starting from *enseignement* (teaching), Saussure's diagram shows separate sets radiating in four directions and consisting respectively of other derivatives of the verb, of semantic neighbours such as *éducation*, of other words with the same suffixed morpheme, and of words which merely rhyme. Nevertheless, the relation between a function and its manifestations is one of likeness *in absentia*, and must be classed as paradigmatic.[6]

So far we have been looking at the Dumézilian schema synchronically, as a summary of aspects of early Roman culture. What can we say about it diachronically? Presumably, if we could trace it back in time, we should find both greater pervasiveness of the three- or four-functional organization through the various domains of social life, that is, more rows, and a clearer apprehension by the people themselves of the conceptual links between entries in a column. But this is only inference. What about the subsequent history, which we can document? In general, as the centuries pass, each domain becomes transformed in different ways. With the coming of Christianity, the old triad of gods with their *flamines* becomes obsolete, as does the old legal triad of modes of marriage. The narratives about ancient kings and about the original tribes of Rome become precisely 'ancient history', irrelevant to all but scholars, unknown to the wider public unless fragments of them appear in school textbooks or can be used by the tourist industry. *And the new institutions and*

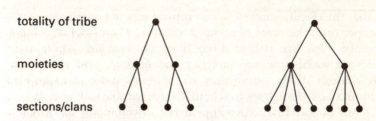

totality of tribe

moieties

sections/clans

Figure 2.2 Stylized depiction of Australian social structure

narratives do not fit into the schema. For modern Italian culture a Dumézilian schema of anything like comparable scope is out of the question. The style of cognitive ordering embodied in the schema has simply dissolved.[7]

PRIMITIVE CLASSIFICATION

With these ideas in mind I turn to *Primitive Classification*. I start not with the 20 per cent of the essay which make up the Introduction and Conclusion, but with the remaining 80 per cent. We shall see that much of what Durkheim and Mauss are saying can be summarized in schemata comparable to the Dumézilian one; and I hope to show that the analytical language we have been developing helps to clarify their argument.

The ethnographic core of *Primitive Classification* has four parts. Part I starts with Australia, which the authors think offers the humblest classifications on record. Before coming to particular tribes, they generalize about aboriginal social structure. A typical tribe is divided into two moieties, each of which is subdivided in two cross-cutting ways: it is split into a certain number of clans, each associated with a totem, and it is also split into two marriage classes or 'sections'. Here we can ignore the rules of marriage and recruitment which define these social units, but it is worth illustrating the two structures in branching diagrams (Figure 2.2).

Straightaway we have a classification: members of society are allocated unambiguously to moieties, clans and sections. What is more, we have, in our terms, a two-level hierarchical classification, moieties being superordinate to clans or sections. Now comes an important italicized phrase such as one regularly finds near the start of *Année sociologique* texts. The thesis which Part I will try to demonstrate, and which has not been stated previously, is that the classification of things reproduces the classification of people (into the units of social structure). The evidence comes mainly from five tribes: three from Queensland, where the relevant social units are moieties and sections, and two from New South Wales, where they are moieties and clans. Can we summarize the analyses in schemata comparable to Figure 2.1?

Units of social structure appear not uncommonly as rows in Dumézilian schemata; the obvious example is the list of *varna* categories so salient in accounts of traditional Hindu social order. In the Australian case, comparable lists of sociostructural units were presumably elicited by the ethnographers when they questioned their informants. The units in such lists could reasonably be described as solidary, homogeneous, distinct and exhaustive; and I suspect that they were often enumerated in a standard order. In any case, one can envisage a domain labelled 'society' and consisting of units related syntagmatically.

A problem which rarely arises in the Dumézilian case is how to show the multi-level nature of the socio-structural classification in a two-dimensional diagram. 'Levels' are normally shown vertically, as in Figure 2.2, but we shall need the vertical dimension of the page for paradigmatic relations. One solution is to envisage the branching diagram as lying in a third dimension, on a plane extending backwards behind the page. We need not actually try to draw this third dimension, but can distinguish superordinate groupings from their subordinate units by using thicker lines to separate the former.

If it is true that the classification of things reproduces that of men, is the relation between a class of the one sort and a class of the other paradigmatic? The relation is *in absentia* since, in general, it is in the mind, rather than in a spatio-temporal context, that natural species and objects of various kinds are associated with units of social structure. Moreover the species associated with a particular unit are indefinite in number and come in no fixed order (unless one wants to say that the totem itself comes first).

When we draw the relevant diagrams (Figure 2.3), we need only two rows, one for the humans in their social units, the other for the rest of the contents of the cosmos. The aborigines could obviously have distinguished different domains within the cosmos, but the sources used by Durkheim and Mauss say little about this. Thus, as regards number of rows, the extreme

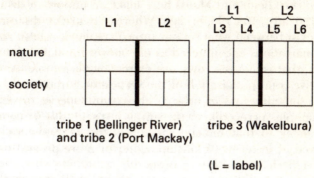

Figure 2.3 Queensland tribes

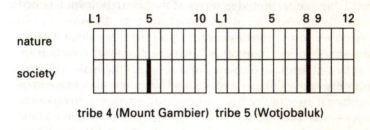

tribe 4 (Mount Gambier) tribe 5 (Wotjobaluk)

Figure 2.4 New South Wales tribes

simplicity of the first set of diagrams is misleading. The labels L1 and L2 are in the one case 'male' and 'female', in the other Yungaroo and Wutaroo, and they apply both to the moieties of society and to the two halves of nature into which everything else is classified. Tribe 3 is only slightly more complex. If the original ethnographic data and the interpretation are reliable, the two-level classification of society into moieties and sections applies also to nature. The authors emphasize the pervasive relevance of the classification to various cultural contexts – to dietary rules, ritual, divination, and the use of message-sticks.

The New South Wales tribes (Figure 2.4) classify nature according to their totemic clans. In both cases the clans are distributed into two named moieties, but it is only in tribe 5 that this is relevant to the classification of nature. In both cases the species or entity used as totem provides a category label both for the other natural species in its column and for the members of its clan. Durkheim and Mauss here make an important distinction (1903a(i): 16/t.1963b: 20). Whereas clear-cut discriminations exist between what (in our terms) are entries *within* rows, the demarcations encountered as one moves up and down the schema, that is, *between* rows, are extremely permeable. As for the native conceptualization of the vertical or paradigmatic relations, sometimes (as in tribe 3), the natural species or object (for example, a crocodile or the sun) is just said to *be* Yungaroo or to *belong* to that moiety; sometimes the relationships are conceived of in terms of kinship, closer or more distant, or in terms of 'flesh', friendship or property.

Part II of *Primitive Classification* asks how widespread such classifications are in or near Australia. The ethnography cited here does not give rise to such clear-cut holistic schemata as in Part I, but is interpreted in terms of historical derivation from or incomplete reflection of such schemata. In Mabuiag (Torres Straits) we have moieties called respectively 'small' and 'great', and linked with certain other binary oppositions, as well as with totems and associated species or artefacts. The main difference from previous configurations would lie in the punctate or fragmentary nature of the rows, whose entries might perhaps better be shown as blobs than as boxes. A systematic classification of the contents of the cosmos gives way to what looks like the relics of one. Similarly, Australian astral mythology is viewed as an expression within one domain of present or previous systematic classifications. Part II is interesting particularly for its emphasis on diachrony, on the transformations to which the classificatory schemata are liable. Thus the Aranda, who have more than fifty-four totemic groups, prompt discussion of segmentation, that is, of the splitting of social units, and of their *émiettement*, their disintegration or crumbling into fragments.

Part III, the longest, deals with the North American Zuñi and with some Sioux groups, before returning to the Australian Wotjobaluk (our tribe 5). The Zuñi resemble the tribes of Part I in that their classification of the universe is in principle exhaustive and systematic. The account starts with what we have been calling the column labels, which in this case are the cardinal points plus zenith, nadir and centre. Under these headings the whole cosmos is parcelled out – seasons, elements, animal species, social functions, colours, *and* (here we encounter the second recourse to an italicized statement) the eighteen

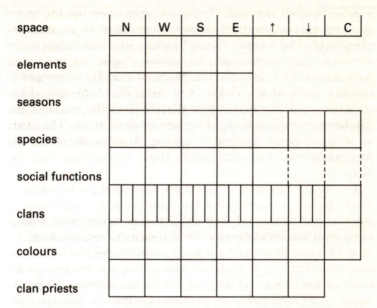

space	N	W	S	E	↑	↓	C
elements							
seasons							
species							
social functions							
clans							
colours							
clan priests							

The 'natural' or 'normal' order for listing is as shown, but in some contexts the centre can be 'first as well as last' (Cushing 1896: 369–73).

Figure 2.5 Zuñi (New Mexico)

matrilineal clans, organized in groups of three (Figure 2.5). A clan has direct paradigmatic links with a region of the *pueblo*, a colour and a totemic species (from which it takes its name), and also, in a qualified sense, with a social function.

As for the history of the schema, Durkheim and Mauss suggest that the nineteen clans derive by segmentation from seven proto-clans. They see traces of an even earlier phase in a grouping of six priests associated with six of the clan totems, and perhaps in the six recognized classes of wild game which are linked with six of the regions; the last region to be added would have been the centre. Finally they raise the possibility of an even earlier four-fold phase when the clans were arranged in two moieties, as suggested by a creation myth referring to two pairs of eggs.

The original title of the essay (abbreviated in the translation) is 'Of some primitive forms of classification'. The authors have now recognized two main forms or types (they use the terms interchangeably). In the Australian type the labels for columns are provided by totems or units of social structure, while in the Zuñi type they are provided by regions of space or, in another formulation, by oriented clans. Much of Part III is devoted to arguing, on evidence drawn first from the Zuñi, then from elsewhere, that the second type derives from the first, that the gap between them is bridged by intermediate forms. The Sioux as it were point backwards to the Australians, while the Australian tribe 5 is typologically closer to the Zuñi than the Sioux are.

Among the Sioux, the Omaha are treated at greatest length. Their highly segmented totemic patriclans are organized in moieties and associated with social functions and with a large number of species and entities. When the tribe sets up camp, the units of social structure have fixed positions relative to the line of march. Thus social units *are* related to space, but only to the space of the camp and only relative to the direction of move-ment – not absolutely to cardinal points. In contrast, the Wotjobaluk clans are related absolutely to fixed portions of the horizon, that is effectively to cardinal points, even though no link is reported between the cardinal points and categories of nature. Comparable linking of social structure and directions occurs in Mabuiag at the level of moieties (leeward/windward), and at Aranda tribal gatherings. Part III ends by modelling the transition from the Australian to the Zuñi type.

Part IV deals with the authors' third and last form of primitive classification. Whereas in the first type social structure itself virtually provided the column labels, and in the second it oper-ated at one remove, via space, in the third type, best exemplified by China, it is no longer part of the classification. The various more or less conflicting schemata, which are of extreme com-plexity, embrace nature, or much of nature, and various orders of time, but they do not embrace society (Figure 2.6). Having searched (unconvincingly) for direct evidence that the animals in the duodenary cycle were formerly totemic, the authors look briefly at the similarities between Taoism and early Greek thought, especially in the context of divination. Systems of divi-nation depend on classifications not unlike the tribal ones, and so do mythologies, for example those of the Indians or Greeks: well-organized pantheons share out nature among their mem-

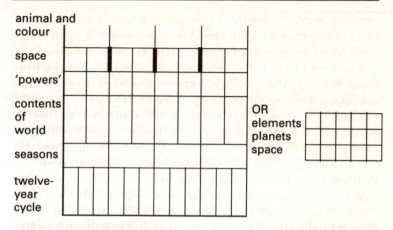

Figure 2.6 China (simplified)

bers, just as do totemic social structures. The discussion of 'developed mythologies', which lie behind not only the rise of monotheism, but also that of philosophy and science, perhaps suggests a fourth type of classification, the mythological type, in which the columns would be headed by a hierarchically organized pantheon with henotheistic tendencies. In any case, these allusions to the gods of Greece and India bring us back to the Indo-European world of Dumézil. So let us now try to view the essay as a whole.

The Introduction proposes that the construction of logical and scientific classifications, with their clearly delimited taxa, is not an activity naturally inherent in the individual human mind, but a social institution which has developed over a long history. Even in the contemporary West, domains such as folklore and religion retain a prescientific cognitive style.[8] In archaic literate cultures this style pervaded a larger number of domains, while among the simpler tribes it was basic to conceptions both of man and of nature.

In the main body of the text the authors reverse direction, and start with tribes. The different types of organization form an evolutionary sequence. In the simplest case, the units of social structure, the totems which represent them, and the associated components of nature all form a close-knit unity. In the second type, the link between social structure and the rest of the classification passes via the conceptualisation of space in terms of

cardinal points. In the third type, social structure and the classification of nature have cut loose from each other. The third type
leads on to the genesis of scientific classifications in Greece.

The Conclusion is too rich for easy summary, but the main
point for us is the typological contrast between primitive and
scientific classifications. Both types are hierarchically structured
philosophies of nature,[9] but they differ in their relation to
society. In the primitive type one should think of society as
having originally provided, not only the model or inspiration for
the classification, but also its actual *cadres*, its framework and
dividing lines. Moreover, the assimilations and differentiations
that constitute any classification were originally based not so
much on purely intellectual judgements of sameness or difference as on the affective attitudes and evaluations that permeated
social life. This was a major obstacle to the emergence of scientific classifications.

CRITICISMS

Among Needham's many criticisms of the essay, one concerns
causation. The criticism is foreshadowed in his Part I, with
reference to the prevailing neglect of *Primitive Classification*: a
certain publication devoted to the interdependence of social
relations and cosmological ideas fails to mention the essay's
attempt to demonstrate 'a constant causal connection between
the two' (1963: x). The point recurs in his Part II as one of two
general objections applying to the entire argument: 'There is no
logical necessity to postulate a causal connexion between society
and symbolic classification, and in the absence of factual indications to this effect there are no grounds for attempting to do
so' (ibid.: xxiv).[10] The following page refers to 'the strength of
[the authors'] preoccupation with cause', which leads them to
present the facts as if society were the cause of the classification.
They are 'explicitly concerned to propound a causal theory'.

But how much of this can be accepted?

1 The relation between social relations and cosmic classifications is not presented as constant, but as differing in the
Australian, Zuñi, Chinese and modern cases.

2 Durkheim and Mauss do not explicitly characterise their
theory as a causal one, and seldom use the vocabulary of cause
and effect (not once in their Introduction). What they are most

obviously propounding is an *evolutionary* theory – both the first and last paragraphs of *Primitive Classification* use the word *genèse* (genesis), and the authors' central interest is surely in origins. Origins and causes are not unrelated, but the *preoccupation* with causes seems to be the translator's.

3 Insofar as they do discuss cause and effect, one can distinguish claims relating to the long term and the short term. In the former case they talk of influences: they suggest that distant influences (spanning millennia) have left behind as an effect contemporary habits of mind which constitute the very framework of all classification (p. 72, t. 88). But Needham's criticism relates to the short term. Here the authors use a variety of expressions: the classification of things is 'modelled on' social organization, there is a close relationship (*rapport étroit*) between abstract ideas and the corresponding social organization (1903a(i): 72/t.1963b: 88). In the one passage where they do talk explicitly of causation, their causal arrow is not solely *from* society *to* classifications of things. When introducing the notion of segmentation (ibid.: 25ff./32ff.), they propose that once a classification of nature has come into being, it can act back on (*réagir sur*) its cause (that is, on the society which served as its model), and contribute to modifying it.

4 In any case, whatever use is made of notions of causality, *Primitive Classification* clearly presents social organization as primary or prior to the classification of nature, as the prototype or basis on which the latter is modelled. Needham implies that there are no grounds for such an attribution of priority. Is this true?

To start with, Durkheim and Mauss are clearly not propounding a mechanistic synchronic law valid at all times and places. They know, as well as we do, or better, that the nineteen clans of the Zuñi have not generated nineteen regions of space, that the indefinite number of Chinese clans has not generated an indefinite number of columns in the Chinese schemata. They do not claim that the classification of things *always* reproduces that of men, or that reproduction is so exact that moieties in society are *inevitably* accompanied by binary divisions of nature. The issue of a straightforward causal arrow only arises really clearly at the beginning of their evolutionary scale. It is here that we may try to choose between three possibilities. Were classifications of men extended so as to constitute classifications of nature (the

Durkheim–Mauss view)? Or, was society modelled on a classification of nature (the view which they attribute to Frazer and which Needham finds tempting)? Or, should we simply envisage the set-up coming into being as a whole, and abstain from ascribing priority to either of its components (the view which Needham ultimately settles for)?

The topic is too large for satisfactory discussion here, but one line of argument can be sketched in support of *Primitive Classification*. It is not unreasonable to argue that incest prohibitions mark the emergence of humans from prehumans. If one also accepts that such rules can be subsumed in the rules of marriage and recruitment which define social structures, then the latter are fundamental to humanity in ways that systematic classifications of the contents of nature are not: an early human society lacking a unified cosmology is a possibility, one lacking a social structure is not. Moreover, there are serious arguments for putting section systems similar to the Australian near the start of a sociostructural evolutionary scale (cf. Allen 1989b: 182). In the absence of strong arguments in favour of the rival hypotheses, Durkheim and Mauss's remains the best of the three.[11]

Needham's lack of interest in envisaging the genesis of classifications of nature goes together with an unsympathetic attitude towards the whole undertaking and, in particular, a tendency to gloss over the world-historical thrust of the argument. Thus much weight is laid on the charge that Durkheim and Mauss repeatedly make unevidenced assertions. But insofar as it deals with archaeologically invisible aspects of non-literate societies, any evolutionary argument *has* to envisage changes which cannot be historically documented. The charge is not wrong, but it is not helpful. In this sort of discourse statements about change imply in the subtext a phrase such as 'In the light of our theory it looks as if . . .'

Similarly, the italicized statement at the start of Part I of *Primitive Classification* is criticized (1963: xiv) as a *petitio principii*: to assert that the classification of things reproduces that of people is to assume what needs to be proved. No, it is simply to announce the hypothesis in the light of which the evidence will be assembled and interpreted.

As for the fact that in many societies the correspondence between social structure and classification does not exist, or exists only partially, this was of course entirely obvious to Durkheim and Mauss. It is presupposed in their Part II, and it opens their Part IV. It is therefore pointless to demand that they test their thesis by demonstrating concomitant variation (p. xvi), or that they pay special attention to negative instances. It is rather like asking Dumézil to devote a book to the absence of trifunctional patterns in the plays of Terence. What is interesting, and calls for explanation, is that some peoples *do* possess classifications embracing men and nature in a single simple schema; everyone knows that others do not.

The insensitivity to the world-historical aspect of the argument is illustrated by a reference to the Chinese case. This, says Needham, 'may be disregarded, since it exhibits no correspondence at all [between society and classification], and its only value is that it shows that such classifications [i.e., of nature] are not confined to simple societies' (1963: xxv). But its value for the argument of *Primitive Classification* is much more than this. Because of its richness and pervasiveness in social life, the Chinese type of classification serves to bridge the large gap which would otherwise exist in the sequence leading from the Zuñi type to the Greek and scientific types.

Needham's opening criticisms (ibid.: xii) concern Durkheim and Mauss's references to 'confusion' and lack of differentiation in the thinking of tribal people, and their suggestion that this sort of thinking survived in contemporary religious thought and folklore in the form of notions such as transubstantiation and metamorphosis. The phraseology of 1903 is clearly antiquated, indeed regrettable and misleading. No one nowadays would say that a Bororo or an Australian 'confuses' a human with an animal. But the problem Durkheim and Mauss were alluding to has not disappeared, and we still lack a satisfactory analytical language in which to discuss it. In most societies, in some contexts, people do associate, or link, or identify elements from different domains in ways that scientists do not, and what is needed is not denunciation of 'gratuitous and implausible elaboration' (ibid.: xx), but an attempt to rephrase the problem in more appropriate language. It is here that the terms syntagmatic and paradigmatic may be helpful. Elements placed in the rows of our schemata and related syntagmatically are never confused with each other; on the contrary, their heterogeneity is perhaps even more emphatic than in scientific classifications. The 'confusions' relate to elements placed in columns, that is, to the paradigmatic relations.

Let us look more closely at two aspects of this issue. First, Durkheim and Mauss think that belief in transmutations could not arise if things were represented in the form of well-delimited concepts (1903a(i): 3). Needham objects in effect (1963: xii) that to conceive of *x* being transmuted into *y* presupposes distinct concepts of *x* and *y*; thus the Frenchmen are guilty of a logical flaw. But these men were trained philosophers: were they really being so stupid or careless? Their point is that to a modern and scientific mind a man and a parrot are classified in two quite separate domains, which are so sharply delimited from each other that the two entities cannot possibly be linked by physical continuity or transmutation. Other points of view or other societies no doubt see things differently: whereas a man of one clan is sharply delimited from a man of another, and a parrot is sharply delimited from a hornbill, in some contexts man and parrot, rather than being sharply delimited, 'participate' one in another (to use Lévy-Bruhl's term). It is as if the boundary between the concepts of man and parrot were somehow fluid. The syntagmatic boundaries are unambiguous, the paradigmatic ones are not.

Second, under the heading of method and use of evidence, Needham (ibid.: xxii ff.) objects to the couple of pages on sentiment in the Conclusion of *Primitive Classification*. He sees in them the abrupt and gratuitous introduction of a factor for which the previous text has provided no justification; and he finds it difficult not to recoil in dismay. However, this negative reaction neglects the discussion in Part I (1903a(i): 19ff./t.1963b: 23ff.) of how the Australians, or more precisely the Wotjobaluk, conceive of the relations between the groups composing their classifications. They do so, *tout d'abord*, in terms of closer and more distant kinship, so that the beings attributed to ego's moiety are his flesh and his friends, while his sentiments towards beings of the other moiety are quite different. More generally, one might comment, if classification is related to social structure, the latter, especially in Australia, is interwoven with kinship, and kinship in turn is a matter of emotional links as well as genealogical ones. Thus when in their Conclusion the authors raise the obvious question of how the contents of nature came to be allocated to the particular columns in which we find them, they have already prepared us for their answer, namely that the allocation involved sentiment as well as logic. The concepts of tribal peoples, they suggest, have strong affective connotations, positive or negative; the northern region of space is not merely an abstract direction, a compass point, but has qualities of its own, values or associations which will have a bearing on how it fits into the classification. These affective associations will contribute to the paradigmatic inter-domain linkages, helping to maintain the permeability of the divides. Perhaps their idea raises more questions than it answers, but it is not obviously gratuitous. *Would* it be enough to seek purely cognitive explanations, and ignore the affective?

Needham's most fundamental criticism, the one supposedly showing up the entire venture as misconceived, concerns Durkheim and Mauss's concept of mind. They subtitle their essay 'Contribution à l'étude des représentations collectives' but, Needham says, when they talk about categories or about the classificatory function, their concern is really with the innate ability of the human individual, a topic belonging essentially to cognitive psychology. The charge is that their confusion on this issue invalidates the attempt to explore the origin of classifications.

No doubt Durkheim and Mauss could be clearer both in their concepts of mind (does not this apply to most of us?) and in their language, but the general orientation of the essay seems clear enough. It is indeed, primarily, about *collective* thought, about the prehistory of scientific classification, regarded as a social institution. They are not concerned with individual psychological capacities, but with the use to which these capacities are put in societies. Indeed, I suppose that, had they been questioned, they would have agreed that even animals possess the cognitive ability to make pragmatic classifications in the sense of 'rudimentary distinctions and groupings' (ibid.: 5/7): a dog classifies some humans as friends, others as needing to be barked at or bitten. In any case, at no point do the authors even hint at any development in inborn cogitive capacities in the course of human history (incidentally they remark on the intelligence of one of Howitt's informants (ibid.: 50/t.61)). The essay is about philosophies of nature, and the issue of inborn capacities only arises because philosophers and psychologists suppose (wrongly) that such capacities are a sufficient explanation for the logical and scientific notion of a taxonomy.

Primitive Classification is far from perfect. Although many of Needham's most emphatic criticisms turn out to lack substance, others are fully justified. Carelessness in the bibliographic citations and sheer misrendering of sources are of course to be deplored (1963.: xlvi ff.). Some of the speculations are indeed tendentious, or even totally unjustified, for example those about marriage rules in Siam. The authors do seem to contradict themselves on whether primitive classifications are primarily of practical or speculative significance (ibid.: xiii n.3).[12] Moreover, the final paragraph contains a particularly unfortunate formulation, which may have been responsible for some of the misreading:

> We have already had occasion to indicate, in the course of the argument, how even ideas as abstract as those of time and space are at each moment of their history in close relationship with the corresponding social organisation.

No. They have tried to demonstrate this for a number of the tribal societies they have considered, but the statement does not apply to the literate ones. Three years later, at the end of his essay on the Esquimos, Mauss (1906: 129/t.1979: 80) was a little more precise, though his language has dated: *Primitive Classification* had shown how the mentality [world view] of *lower* tribes directly reflected their anatomical constitution [i.e. social organization].

However, far the greatest weakness of *Primitive Classification* seems to me to relate to the 'technological classifications', treated in a brief note (1903a(i): n.225/t. 1963b: 81 n.1). What are they, and how do they fit into the argument? Possessed by mankind from earliest times, doing no more than express aspects of the praxis in which they are embedded, they are mere distinctions or divisions between ideas, not systematized, not constituting classificatory schemata (*tableaux*). Presumably they resemble the fragmentary distinctions and rudimentary groupings attributed to young children (ibid.: 5/7). This suggests the following scheme:

evolutionarily ancient
- (A)   primitive systematic philosophies of nature
- (B)   technological classifications

modern
- (C)   Scientific classifications
- (D)   children's classifications (unsystematized adult ones?)

The contents of B are left shadowy. The only concrete suggestion is a classification of components of the diet according to
techniques of appropriation, for example of animal foodstuffs
into fish, birds and land animals. But what about the subdivision
of these taxa? Surely mankind always distinguished different
species of land animal. But this already implies a taxonomic
hierarchy, which is supposed to be a feature of A, not B. No
doubt, in 1900 very little was known about folk classifications of
plant and animal species (ethnotaxonomies), but even at that
time the question could have been raised. As we now know, such
classifications may indeed be hierarchical, and they may have
little to do with totemistic conceptions of the cosmos; moreover,
they exhibit world-historical trends (for example, Brown 1984
– part of a body of work which might be called 'lexical
evolutionism').

The obscurity surrounding B and its relation to A has important consequences. An initial disclaimer (1903a(i): 6/t.1963b: 9)
recognizes that *Primitive Classification* will not exhaust the question of how humans come to classify, and the opening of the
essay (ibid.:1–2/t. 3) emphasizes that mental operations, faculties
and functions may have a diversity of roots, being built up
laboriously from the most heterogeneous components. Thus 'all
sorts of foreign elements' may have entered into the development of the function they are concerned with (ibid.: 6/t. 8). This
foreshadowing of the notion of *bricolage* (characteristic of Mauss,
cf. Allen 1985: 37–8), may have been intended simply to pre-
pare the reader for the heterogeneous contents of A (animals,
cardinal points, etc.), for the authors are explicitly concentrating
on the relationship A–C (1903a(i): n.225); but it seems to leave
open the possibility of an input of B into C. Insofar as B can be
construed as embracing ethnotaxonomies, the authors would
surely have been wise to leave this possibility open – cf. Atran
(1990), who is scarcely interested in A at all. To reduce the
history of scientific classification to the history of the decline of

the element of social affectivity (1903a(i): 72/t.1963b: 88) is certainly to oversimplify.

CONCLUSION

So what *is* the value of the essay? It does much more, I think, than draw attention to a vague and indefinable notion of classification, worthwhile though that might be. In the first place, it establishes the notion of a primitive classification, which is a *specific* way of articulating a world view, or at least considerable portions of that scarcely graspable totality. What characterizes this particular type of classification (though the authors themselves do not use such terminology) is that it can be expressed in a schema made up of rows and columns, these alignments consisting of entities ('entries') linked respectively by syntagmatic and paradigmatic relations. By virtue of this property it contrasts radically with the type of world view to which we are accustomed.

One way to envisage the relationship between the two is to imagine that, as the paradigmatic links between rows cease to be felt as 'real', the domains cease to be aligned vertically, and drift on to a single plane or line. It is not that, say, animals and metals cease to be related at all. They cease to be related paradigmatically, for the scientific world-view offers no support for vertical links; all that is left to the animals and metals is a remote syntagmatic relationship resulting from their respective places within the animate and inanimate branches of a single hierarchical classification of nature. In this sense the world becomes 'flattened'.[13]

Second, the value of *Primitive Classification* lies in the relation it posits between this type of world-view and social structure. It recognizes three main phases in the relation. Originally, the social structure generates the classification of things. Subsequently, the predominance of social structure declines, and the two elements interact. Finally, the link is broken, and the primitive world-view itself declines, though survivals may linger in spheres such as religion, magic and folklore.

In trying to clarify the argument of *Primitive Classification*, I have neglected relevant issues such as the relation of the essay to the intellectual milieu in which it was written, its place within the *œuvres* of its two authors, and its use of the anthropological material then available. But clarifying the argument is in any case only a first step towards the question of how far the authors were *right*. Here my main point has been that a large body of relevant evidence is now available in the work of Dumézil and his followers. The only reasonable explanation for these findings is that the speakers of proto-Indo-European, who were of course non-literate tribesmen, possessed a primitive classification. As for its origin, in spite of the cautious agnosticism of Dumézil's mature work (cf. Dubuisson 1991), the best explanation would seem to be Durkheim and Mauss's. Typologically, in view of the correlations it makes between, for example, social functions, colours and types of priest, the Indo-European classification most closely resembles that of the Zuñi, and indeed one of the many consequences of recognizing a fourth function is that it increases the resemblance, enabling one to include cardinal points and centre in the schemata for at least certain Indo-European cultures (cf. Allen 1991: 149; and in press). As for millennial trends in the Indo-European case, consider the increasing separation between social structure and the rest of the classification, and the lingering dissolution of the functional pattern in the latter. Are not such findings precisely the sort of thing that Durkheim and his nephew were predicting in their astonishing essay ninety years ago?

NOTES

1 The influence of this view lives on – cf. Chapman *et al.* (1989: 17) – who talk of classification as 'an area of expertise that anthropology has made its own'.

2 By omitting 'ought to' (*devraient*) Needham (1963: xxii n.1), followed by Lukes (1973: 449n.79) and Freedman (1975: 19), altered the force of Granet's remark. My translations do not always repeat Needham's.

3 I have noted elsewhere (1987: 38 n.2) the remark in Dumézil's 'breakthrough' article from 1938: 'It is rare, among the semi-civilized, that the classification of one category of concepts is not solidary with other classifications.' The use of the term *cadre* (framework) in the three sources might also repay study (Durkheim and Mauss use it at least eighteen times). Might the lack of reference to *Primitive Classification* be related to Dumézil's lack of enthusiasm for Durkheim, whom he regarded as too much a philosopher (1987: 48)?

4 A note on the history of ideas. Though influenced by Durkheim in some respects (Doroszewski 1933), Saussure here drew on the short-

   lived Polish linguist Kruszewski, who himself drew on British associationists (Jakobson 1971: 719). Dumézil (1987: 117) denies any direct influence from Saussure's *Cours*. For myself, I probably owe a debt to the papers of Edwin Ardener (see Ardener 1989, which is an important collection of essays), though my own use of the syntagmatic/paradigmatic contrast is narrower than his.

5 This is not only because further research is likely to result in new rows, but also because the number of rows one thinks it worth extracting from a single context may be a matter of judgement.

6 In the final analysis it is the duality of the axes that matters, not the names one gives to them or to their labels. It may be worth noting Saussure's discussion of the two factors involved in the notion of value (1985: 159ff.). A five-franc coin can be *compared* with like objects (one-franc coin, etc.), and can be *exchanged* for unlike objects (loaf of bread). One thinks of the differential social values attached to the functions or their manifestations and expressed in their numerical labels. Moreover, the one franc is subsumed in, and in that sense co-present with, the five francs, and Saussure envisaged the coin axis horizontally, the exchange axis vertically (Engler 1967: 259ff.).

7 Presumably this *partly* explains the incredulity with which so many scholars react to Dumézil's findings: the type of cognitive order he discovered lies outside their experience.

8 In discussing Durkheimian texts, one may be torn between trying to breathe new life into their dated phraseology and trying to update it, thereby necessarily introducing anachronisms. The problem is of translating from 1900 to 1990, no less than from French to English. 'Cognitive style' is not in the original, but I use it deliberately, hoping to imply the relevance of *Primitive Classification* to recent debates about, for instance, 'modes of thought' or 'rationalities'.

9 Cf. the phrase 'primitive philosophies' as used by Powell (1896: lvii).

10 Durkheim and Mauss do not talk of 'symbolic classification' or its French equivalent. They usually talk simply of the classification of things, or (once (1903a(i):3/t.1963b: 5)) of 'symbolic correspondences'. The English phrase was used as the title of a book which includes a summary of the earlier critique of *Primitive Classification* (Needham 1979: 25–7).

11 Needham's initial preference for a reversed direction of causation is based on the consideration that 'forms of classification and modes of symbolic thought display very many more similarities than do the societies in which they are found.' If this is so, as the China-Zuñi comparison might suggest, then within an evolutionary perspective it implies only that social structures tend to change faster than cosmologies.

12 And so on. However the Introduction is not always accurate on details. Durkheim and Mauss do not claim regarding tribe 5 that 'a classification by clans preceded one by spatial regions' (1963b: xx), nor do they refer to the prey animals as 'mediators between the Zuñi and their gods' (ibid.: xiii).

13 Perhaps the metaphor could cause confusion, since hierarchies are so often imaged by using the vertical dimension as in Figure 2.2. However, in the imagery used in the other figures here, they lie behind the page, at 90° to it.

Chapter 3

A fresh look at Durkheim's sociological method

Mike Gane

Durkheim's methodological writings still contain many enigmas. In this chapter I attempt to discuss some of the crucial issues concerning his approach to method, his attitudes, some subtleties, and some remaining problems.

I

The Rules of Sociological Method (hereafter *Rules*) was first published as a collection of articles in *Revue Philosophique* in 1894 (spread over four issues); and then published as a book in 1895 with some alterations and corrections (1895a); another edition was published in 1901 with some further additions. There are two English translations (1938b and 1982a).

The *Rules* stands at a crucial period in Durkheim's intellectual career, between the *Division of Labour in Society* (1893b) and *Suicide* (1897a) and the first volume of *L'Année Sociologique* (1897–8). But in fact it is quite possible to argue that the first version of the *Rules* is the section of the Introduction to the first edition of the *Division of Labour in Society* – an introduction that Durkheim later omitted in the subsequent 1901 second edition, this omitted section appears as an appendix in the first English translation (t.1938b) and the beginning of the cut is noted in the main text (1893b: 41), whereas the second translation (t.1984a) not only ignores the text of the first Introduction, but no note at all is given in the text for the place or content of the excision.

Some writers (such as Steven Lukes 1982: 1–27) have claimed that Durkheim altered his actual methodological practice after the *Rules* but never faced up to providing an adequate revision of his methodological procedures. Many projects were left in-complete at his early death, including the analysis of pragmatism which promised to be a new look at issues of truth and the conception of science and its methods (Durkheim 1955a). But around 1901 he did envisage a new, joint work on methodology together with Marcel Mauss and Paul Fauconnet (see Besnard 1983: 150–1). The proposed book was never realized but some of the collaborative work was published, notably 'Sociology in France in the Nineteenth Century' (Durkheim 1900b), 'On the Objective Method in Sociology' (Durkheim 1901b), 'Sociology and the Social Sciences' (Durkheim and Fauconnet 1903c), and 'Sociology' (Fauconnet and Mauss 1901) – this last essay is de-scribed by Mauss as having the status, along with the *Rules* itself, of being a 'manifesto of the school' (see Besnard 1983: 151). By this time Durkheim was the principal agent in an established school of sociology for which he provided both a sociological theory – a specific methodological orientation – and an outline of a large research programme. However, Durkheim's own proj-ects all appear to have treated the methodology of the *Rules* far more as a first statement of a general argument than as a definitive, inflexible set of constraints. In fact, they form a context against which later methodological orientations were to be debated and developed; for Durkheim liked to invent and discover, even to reverse the order of his methodological pro-cedures if the case required and as the actual investigations unfolded.

Some of these reversals were so dramatic that commentators appear to have had great difficulty in realizing what Durkheim was doing: for example in *Suicide* (1897a) Durkheim seems to have been unable to use the method of establishing classificatory types by the 'external signs' or characteristics of the social fact in question (as demanded by his rules). Thus, anticipating argu-ments that he had not been faithful to his method, he said that the 'mode' of suicide 'has nothing to teach us' about the cause of suicide, this 'was discovered by a wholly different study' (1897a/t.1951a: 293). This 'different' study is explicitly described as the 'reverse' of the method recommended in the *Rules*, though it is perhaps very close to another method described there as a second-best or supplementary method. He thus proceeded not by rational work on 'external' characteristics, but by identifying specific causes from which he went on to 'deduce the nature of the effects' (ibid.: 147). Soon after *Suicide* had been finished and published, Durkheim's attention turned to other projects which presented methodological problems, yet the methodological writings of 1901–3 show little, if any, recognition of the practice of the methodological improvisation of the works of the intervening period of 1895 to 1900. To the end of his life Durkheim continued to work in relation to the terrain established formally by the *Rules*, even if every work in some way modified his actual practice rather than remaining close to the letter of its formulations.

After a long period following Durkheim's death in 1917, during which the *Rules* was either ignored or regarded as Durkheim at his weakest, there has recently been a renewal of interest in the work. Examples are the important study by Stephen Turner, *The Search for a Methodology of Social Science* (1986), my own book on the *Rules* (Gane 1988), and a new French edition with J.-M. Berthelot's introduction (1988). Berthelot tried to indicate the changes Durkheim introduced between the 1894 and 1895 versions. Thus, after a period in the 1970s and early 1980s, when reaction to the book was most critical because it was presented as a classic but thought at best a 'negative heuristic', recent discussion has tended to show that Durkheim's position was more interesting and subtle than it was usually thought to be. Certainly it was now seen to be in line with the mainstream of French epistemology and philosophy of science in the twentieth century.

I want here to pose some new questions about this text, questions which relate to the issue of the nature of the rules and to their elaboration and use. In a sense these are focused around the question, why did Durkheim need rules, and why these rules? It is also necessary, I think, to ask questions about how to read Durkheim (and indeed how Durkheim read Durkheim). This will tend to help situate some of the crucial questions in the context of contemporary discussions of social epistemology and theory. In this context my objectives are to look at some of the ways in which Durkheim might provide instruments for following through certain current problems and issues of modernity and post-modernity. Some of these issues might then feed back into an understanding of Durkheim's approaches.

II

First of all, it is crucial to note Durkheim's own rather rudimentary but important comment that it is essential to take into account all the significant caveats and qualifications in his texts. His demand is really a call for a holistic reading on the hand, with its demand that judgment on issues always be delayed until the exposition of full and complex positions is fully registered (1895a/t.1982a: 31). This is absolutely necessary in this form of writing which attempts to introduce new terms, but especially where old terms are carefully redefined. Because Durkheim regarded his specific contribution to sociology to be at a relatively early stage in its development, much of his analysis is concerned with a first rational critique of the principal ideological notions of its objects. It is clear from the *Rules* that Durkheim even believed in a strictly logical critique of ideology, that is, a critique not founded on any new empirical basis, which could provide valuable new knowledge in its own right, but on the condition that it proceeded with the correct method (ibid.: 97–103).

Second, it is important to notice at the beginning that such reading has, as it were, a technical requirement. It is formulated in the sense that reading must apply the principle of 'methodical doubt' (1893b/t.1933b: 36) in order to understand the balanced totality of the argument. But there is something else as well. Durkheim at various points says he 'believes' in his project and he often encourages his readers to have 'faith' in the scientific enterprise. Indeed he has a view of the relatively privileged position of French intellectuals, because they have, as a result of the respected position of rationalism in French culture, a freedom both from empiricism and mysticism, which he thought had dogged British and German theory respectively. He refers constantly to the unique possibilities of the French contribution to the science of society (given that it rises from a simple to a complex rationalism) (1938a/t.1977a: 334–48), which is to some extent related to the development of a necessary attitude, involvement or orientation. It is linked also to a special conception of the idea of progress and progression (he criticized Montesquieu for not developing this notion). He also believed that the emergence of sociology was itself a 'social fact' which seemed to parallel the emergence and development of socialism and some radical religious movements, but that it had to complement these movements, and had a unique role to contribute in the attainment of higher levels of objectivity of analysis. This was why sociology had to be located in the university rather than in a party or the Church: the university had its own specific social basis, a hard-won relative independence and forms of allegiance in the division of labour. For Durkheim science represented a hard, extremely demanding intellectual and practical discipline, quite different in principle from any aesthetic pursuit (1925a/t.1961a: 267ff.).

Scientific movements and institutions are social forces and social relations which Durkheim never really considered at length. Equally important is the connection of scientific knowledge and social or human values. It is clear here that Durkheim thought there was no absolute separation between them, and he believed there were important practical objectives embodied in the scientific project. Durkheim was aware that adequate reading was not simply a rational process. There was something else involved as well. Developing a Durkheimian term from *The Elementary Forms* (1912a), this might be called a 'ritual attitude'. It seems clear that Durkheim wanted the reader, whom he probably thought of as masculine, to adopt the following ritual attitudes (see Gane 1992: 123ff.):

i   an optimistic faith in science, in its practices, its methods (1895a/t.1982a: 32).
ii an optimistic faith in critical secular rationalism more generally (1938a/t.1977a: 77).
iii an optimistic faith and involvement in university autonomy in the social division of labour (ibid.: 75–87) and a recognition that:
iv a belief in the idea that (a) much of the energy for sociology comes from movement in society as a whole (the debt) (1928a/t.1958b: 283–5); (b) for sociology should also pay its debt to society (1893b/t.1933b: 406–9) through: (c) the scientific discovery of the law of history (ibid.: 126) which as Durkheim saw it would form the basis of the law of the advanced society (ibid.: 23–31).

Thus the *Rules* is written both for a general audience and one which might either agree spontaneously with these attitudes or might be willing to adopt and practise them. It points to a particular engagement and a particular type of optimism and seriousness. It tends to play down the idea that each intellectual should find a unique course of investigation and it suggests that the true scientific mode is that of a group or team effort.[1] It is clear that Durkheim wanted to work as a member of a group of colleagues and to benefit from the critical discipline and energies produced within it. The *Rules*, then, is in this perspective, a school book, or rather it is the prospectus for a new intellectual collectivity, an intellectual movement, in close competition with both neo-religious and Marxist intellectual programmes, which carried the same degree of social responsibility (1928a/t.1958b: 284–5).

If this is the case it is open to us to investigate such work as a kind of movement rule-book. To be a sociologist is to practise these rules. Durkheim does not present them in the personal mode, but in the impersonal mode. It is as if in wanting to be a sociologist he is saying, 'I am going to found this club: I submit myself to its rules.' But what is the nature of this club and therefore of these rules? It is obviously only given meaning by the intellectual vigilance of its members: there is no other policing of the rules (unless the club becomes part of a bigger formal institution, like a university, with disciplinary powers), and Durkheim did not envisage sociology becoming a state-controlled ideology, indeed the independence of the university was essential to his conception of institutional socialism (Gane 1992: 137–64).

Today, it might be possible to say that the author himself, who constructed the rules, would be in an authoritative position to promote and defend them; and that the school itself would relate to these rules as a particular conception of its intellectual discipline, its *conscience collective*. It is highly likely that, having written on the evolution of morals and sanctions, Durkheim should also have considered intellectual morals, disciplines and sanctions. In a sense, his relation to the question of rules of method is one of his own contributions in this field.

This sphere of rules and intellectual discipline is not directly that of the demand for intellectual honesty (that is, a critique of falsification of materials, evidence, arguments, etc.) which is essential to the moral milieu of the university.[2] It is rather that these rules form part of a practical and strategic enterprise in social science. They are in one sense Durkheim's *utilitarian* rules of practical procedure in the intellectual realm, for Durkheim's actual programme of research is not directly outlined in *Rules*, it is only indicated by instances, by inventories of possible topics, by examples and illustrations. It would be possible to say, following the discussion on constraints in the *Rules* (1895a/t.1982a: 51), that intellectual constraints are bounded by questions of whether or not they work in a technical sense, rather than moral or political ones, and that is their necessity. But if they do work it is because they establish a certain form of impersonal objectivity and intellectual obligation: truth is established (or as he latter wrote, created (1955a/t.1983a: 84–5)) as law – a theme to which he was to return many times. This position thus seems to call for a particular orientation of ritual attitude.

v   the ultimate value is that of scientific laws or truths (1895a/ t.1982a: 163; 1955a/t.1983a: 88).
vi   the approach to method should in essence be practical and always devoted to the discovery of such truth which can only be beneficial for society.

It is clear that in Durkheim scientific truth is not determined democratically. It is determined through theoretical and empirical science and finally and irreversibly established in its forms of demonstration, validation and proof. In an important sense, therefore, the *Rules* is an attempt not only to say how sociological work should proceed, but also, by implication, to state how to recognize sociological truths. Thus there is a further assumption that:

vii sociological truths are to be judged valid only if they correspond to scientific and sociological reason (1892a/t.1960b: 55).[3]
viii only sociologists are valid judges of sociological truth established in the framework of the larger set of scientific disciplines (1895a/t.1982a: 162).

The *Rules* also implies not only a kind of sociological reasoning but also a notion of its role and value. It is undoubtedly the case that Durkheim thought this was in line with what all the sciences accepted as their own practice and intellectual sphere: regional autonomy and specialization (the intellectual division of labour) meant special spheres of intellectual competence and control within a larger framework. Thus, when we consider the question

of reading the *Rules* it is really a question of the ritual attitudes
adopted in such a reading as well as the nature of the technical
process employed. From the *Division of Labour* we know that
Durkheim believed the ensemble of sciences were in a perilous
state bordering on the anomic, and that it was essential to
establish conscious forms of intellectual discipline across the
whole sphere of scientific inquiry.[4] We also know from the *Rules*
that Durkheim thought science a revolutionary form and, from
its modern inception in the renaissance, has demanded the
displacement of the dominance of dialectic and rhetoric by a
new and absolute method of objectivity (1938a/t.1977a: 340).
Sociology is situated very consciously within the context of the
progression of the scientific movement, and for Durkheim is
essential for the long-term success of that movement. Here
Durkheim is strictly Comtean and it is no accident that not long
after the *Rules* he proposed a new role for 'general sociology'
which would articulate the intellectual organization of the social
sciences (1903c/t.1982a: 175–208) and thus contribute decisively to resolve a drift into intellectual anomie. In the final
analysis it might be possible to suggest that the development of
such ritual attitudes could be given a scientific justification
through sociology itself, and this would provide the basis for a
new scientific ideology: the belief that:

ix   sociological knowledge provides the rationale for the adop-
     tion of scientific ritual attitudes. The cycle is completed (see
     Conclusion to 1912a: 30).

III

Do these scientific but ritual attitudes really make such a difference? Can they be justified by sociology itself?

To answer this it is only necessary to compare two sets of ritual
attitudes. Let us take an imaginary 'anti- or post- modern' reader
for example. This reader would not readily accept the fundamental point that the highest value is *scientific* truth, or that
reality can be understood as being veiled, so that rational efforts
should be undertaken in order, through penetration, to reveal
underlying truths. Curiously this view can be translated into
Durkheimian terms. Put in its most dramatic form, the argument is this: the very conception of 'reality' in modern science

and art is a product of a certain type of breakdown of essential social balance in a period of political absolutism. Science corresponds to a relatively recent change in the social conception of nature as definitively separated from us and which can be completely mastered. It is perhaps a method which has pathological ambitions in itself but this is even more strikingly visible when the object of mastery is society itself. But whereas Durkheim shares the ritual attitudes associated with such absolutism in relation to the object, he does not, or only in part (and later than the *Rules*), see that this is an abnormal form (1938a/ t.1977a:157–60, 225). (Indeed, this line of criticism can be extended as, in Nietzsche, so as to embrace the whole project of the rationalist tradition which stresses the pre-eminence of reason, logic and objectivity.)

To express this another way one might say: from what critical position is the reader reading? Some post-modernists read from a position which is expressly pre-Cartesian, outside the set of rationalist assumptions (for example, the writings of Baudrillard). This is useful since, by contrast, it throws light on the position from which Durkheim himself reads, which is now revealed as very remote from a neutral position in relation to things. In some versions it can be understood as a religion of nature comparable with that of Spinoza (1895a/t.1982a: 82), a position cultivated in recent French Marxism, by Althusser and others. Durkheim's position is perhaps also an intensification of that of Spinoza, in the sense that here God is not nature, but society transfigured. What marks the audacity of Durkheim's position, which goes beyond Comte's pseudo-catholic sociolatry, is that society is held to worship itself: it knows itself now, not through superstition, but through a genuine and adequate knowledge, that is, through sociology. It produces an intense paradox (also found in Spinoza) between a view of the universe as completely determined, because for Durkheim society infinitely determines us, and one in which at the same time we are *encouraged to act* in a certain manner and to correct or complete nature. Here Durkheim begins to hold a theory of abnormality over one of immorality. The solution to the human condition is to align action and faith (see the Conclusion of 1912a) with that which is known to be necessary. In Durkheim, as in Marx, this appears as a kind of voluntaristic, highly active and transformative and scientifically founded fatalism. In much of postmodernist thought there is on the other hand a fatalism that tries to recover – not, as with Durkheim, the lost guild society of the Middle Ages – but the society of the gift and reciprocal symbolic exchange. A neo-Maussian reading would hold that both Marx and Durkheim remain within the field of the capitalist forms of the abnormal division of labour and culture (Baudrillard 1993: 1–5).

To return to the *Rules*. They are often read either as a strict if complex logic (see Berthelot 1988), or as a completely frivolous conceit, a crudely formulated gloss on preconceived theses. They can be read as a suggestive and exploratory essay full of enthusiasm for the new perspectives of sociology, and therefore a treasure-house of ideas, which are not strictly method or theory. Durkheim himself, probably and characteristically, wanted something more than a logic and a treasure-house. Further, he wanted something more than discipline, although discipline had its own pay-off in social relations, that is, as long as it was not stifling (intellectual education and discipline as a complement to his lectures on *Moral Education*). He wanted to avoid initiating a completely incoherent series of studies. But on the other hand he wanted inspired studies and not ones deduced entirely mechanically or determined by methodological fiat. These rules are not laws of method – are not of the same order as scientific laws, which admit of no exception – they are somewhat provisional, are practical and strategic and are designed to facilitate ways of investigating and assessing phenomena. They have all the attributes of preparation for a journey: they chart a route. But this route is envisaged as taking place over terrain little or completely unknown. Thus, the preparation has to be characterized as a piece of advice, hopefully prudent, wise, and open. He says in effect: 'nature has produced this landscape, some of the terrain is impassable, so don't go there; go another way'. Nature itself will provide some fundamental assistance, just as Spinoza had argued. However, in relation to these rules Durkheim tends to want to use exactly the same kind of language that he uses to describe scientific laws. But when he discusses the notion of proof he then adopts the Saint-Simonian term, the 'administration' of proof. Of course Saint-Simon used the term in a different context, when in politics government will be replaced by administration.

This is how Durkheim phrased the idea of the project for the book in the short Introduction to the *Rules* published in 1895:

> The very nature of things has therefore led us to work out a better defined method, one which we believe to be more exactly adapted to the specific nature of social phenomena. It is the results of our practice (*pratique*) that we wish to set down here in their totality and submit to debate. They are undoubtedly implicit in our recently published work *La Division du Travail Social*. But it seems to us to have some advantage to single them out here, and formulate them separately and accompany them with proofs, illustrating them with examples culled from that book or taken from work as yet unpublished.
>
> (1895a/t.1982a: 49, translation modified)

It seems then that Durkheim may have envisaged the aim of the *Rules* as providing new 'proofs' for his method, and indeed he does use the word 'proof' in this sense in the text (for example, ibid.: 141, etc.), as well as the word 'illustration'. Durkheim also frequently talks of the 'verification' of his arguments and even of the correctness of his 'definitions'. Thus, the well-known conception of the *social fact* which opens the *Rules*, is presented as a definition which can be 'verified' (ibid.: 53) – a process quite different from 'illustration' through numerous 'inventories'. He says of this particular verification that it is enough for anyone to 'observe' certain processes (a direct appeal to the reader's common sense). When it comes to his 'fundamental rule' of the sociological method (to treat social phenomena as things), he explicitly avoids deducing it from any attempt to 'philosophize' about the nature of social phenomena (ibid.: 69); again, it is not arbitrary or taken up at will, for it is something which 'forces itself upon our observation' as datum (ibid.). Durkheim inverts the relation of sociology to philosophy in order to develop a sociology that is critical of philosophical definitions. As he was to argue later, this was not in any way to attempt to annihilate philosophy, but rather to rejuvenate it – for 'science is destined . . . to provide philosophy with the indispensable foundations which it at present lacks'(ibid.: 239). His evidence for his proofs, therefore, includes appeals to necessary observation, to 'sense-perceptions', not to subjective concepts (ibid.: 81), not to philosophically grounded presuppositions, or ideological *idola*.

When Durkheim proceeds in the important chapter, chapter 3

of the *Rules*, to consider the problem of normal and pathological social phenomena, not only does he feel the need to verify the rules but 'to verify' the very idea and terrain of social pathology. In fact his argument for a social pathology is strictly utilitarian: sociology is founded on the further discipline that it must be useful (ibid.). Most of the discussion concerns itself with practical difficulties of the sociological analysis of pathology. First, Durkheim is not slow to admit that if societies are considered in terms of species – and pathology should, if the analogy with biology holds, be relative to species – not only is it difficult with few individuals in a species to establish an average, it is even difficult to 'know how to determine approximately the moment when a society is born and when it dies' (ibid.: 90). After briefly considering the possibility of deductive and descriptive reasoning, Durkheim shrugs off this difficulty. Abstractly the normal must, he says, outlining the primary method, be defined by what is average or generic, relative to the species and the stage of development of the species. Yet this may, he adds, lead to serious errors where the cycle of the social species is incomplete. In this case the generality of a phenomenon may simply mean that a redundant social institution continues to survive through 'blind habit' (ibid.: 95). A second supplementary method must come into play. 'Having established by observation that the fact is general, [the sociologist] will trace back the conditions which determined this general character in the past and then investigate whether these conditions . . . have changed' (ibid.). The latter analysis may confirm the former analysis. Phenomena found in the average case should be 'verified' as being normal with analysis which shows that they are bound up with the 'conditions of the collective life in the social type' (ibid.: 97). This second method seems very close to what Durkheim calls the 'reverse' method used extensively in *Suicide* (as noted above). He had a strong interest in these questions since he had already argued in the *Division* that there are important aspects of modern societies that are generalized *but are also* pathological.

It is at this point of the argument in the *Rules* that Durkheim provides his famous analysis of normal and pathological crime. It is presented not as a proof of the method but as an illustration of the dangers of not applying sufficient methodological sophistication. The effect of this discussion is to draw attention to the normal sphere and function of crime, to the immediate success of his primary method of observation, and tends to draw a veil over his view that crime rates, like suicide rates, were abnormally high. He does not get involved in any temptation to use his supplementary method at this point. At the end of the chapter he returns to the question of the centrality of the study of pathology in a tight tautology – 'the principal purpose of any science of life . . . is in the end to define and explain the normal state and distinguish it from the abnormal' (ibid.: 104) – if it is not possible to define the normal, or if the normal is doubted 'what use is it to study facts?' he asks (ibid.: 103). Out of this dilemma he again appeals to the function of the study of normal and pathological facts as imposing external regulation on both action and thought. The discipline of sociological method encloses a circle and provides a rationale for itself. The implication is clear. Without this tight discipline of the pressure of real problems the scientific search for knowledge can itself deviate from truth.

When the exposition reaches the next and central chapter, called 'Rules for the Constitution of Social Types', Durkheim suggests that sociological definitions which establish social species and social varieties find a way out of the philosophical confrontation between nominalism and realism, just as in a later work, he argues that there is a way out of the opposition between rationalism and empiricism (1912a). But the actual argument for rules of classification is barely outlined as Durkheim gets involved in a discussion of crucial experiments and the nature of the experimental method, since he wants to reach a point where he can classify without waiting for a complete inventory of the elements of all societies. Thus against empiricism he argues that the crucial experiment, if carefully done, will provide a knowledge of the facts which are general in a social species, even though only a small number of examples, perhaps only one, are known (ibid.: 111).

Durkheim's rules of classification at this point in the *Rules* follow those of Herbert Spencer, but with one crucial addition. Durkheim criticizes Spencer's notion of the basic form of the most simple social structure which can be the base for a systematic classification by degree of complexity of structure. Again against the empiricist assumption, the single social segment is not defined in relation to any known society. Durkheim thus

adopts a purely hypothetical, formal, structural type of classification. Yet even here it is not altogether completely secure in its
terms. Between the versions of *Rules* for 1894 and 1895 he
replaced the term 'species' and wrote 'varieties' when formulat-
ing the way to classify societies. He wrote: 'according to the
degree of organization they manifest . . . within these classes
different varieties will be distinguished . . .' (ibid.: 115). It was
only in the 1901 edition that Durkheim confronted (then indirectly) the Marxist classification by economic form. Durkheim
wrote simply but again with practicality in mind, 'the economic
or technological state, etc., presents phenomena which are too
unstable and complex to provide a basis for classification' (ibid.:
118). And related to this, unlike Marx, Durkheim opted for a
specific kind of morphological not aetiological social classification (although his study in *Suicide* chose the latter over the
former).

The final chapters of the *Rules* concern the explanation of
social facts (chapter 5) and the administration of sociological
proofs (chapter 6). In the first of these Durkheim examines
more closely the question of the relation of morphology to
other social structures and forces, and concludes that, although
morphology is the basis for social classification, sociological
explanation has to be made in the light of the fact that the
crucial determinants of any social phenomenon lie in the 'inner
social environment' of the living society. This can be analysed,
he suggests, as a combination of two characteristics, its 'volume'
(number of social units) and its 'dynamic density' (intensity of
interactions and networks). It is to this milieu sociology turns for
its basic determinants which are causal (these must be isolated
first) and functional. In a striking and important observation, he
suggests, analysis must be synchronic. It is because the causal
process is not chronological, and, he notes significantly, as it
seems to contradict his idea of a 'law of history', 'the stages
though which humanity successively passes do not engender
each other' (ibid.: 139). Durkheim's radical ahistoricism here
appears to move away from his own position in *The Division of
Labour* and against that of Comte. Indeed logically, he rejects
brusquely Comte's law of the three stages as a true evolutionary
law (ibid.: 140). He outlines a notion of a 'genealogical tree of
social types' (ibid.: 115), and this does not, he insists, imply
any direct historical causation of social progression, or any

determined temporal sequence of social development. Durkheim represents this discussion of the crucial role of the 'inner social milieu' as again a 'proof' of the necessity to establish indirect classification on 'the mode in which the social aggregates come together' (ibid.: 141) and not of the immediate causes of such articulations.

This observation is elaborated and clarified in the discussion of sociological proof, which is described as the experimental or the comparative method. The discussion begins in a typically practical manner with an attack on Mill. Since Mill allows different effects to follow from the same cause, or the same effect to follow from different causes, the end-result will be confusion and an inability to establish 'precise laws'. Durkheim appeals directly to the correct practical and theoretical ritual attitude, to the 'principle of causality as it arises in science itself' (ibid.: 150). Crucial elements of the method are introduced with another reflection of causal processes. The aim, he says, is to discover laws or the invariant connection of a cause and an effect. The problem in sociology is that when two phenomena are found to appear and disappear together it may appear that this conjunction is absurd and confounds other laws. If this occurs the comparative method must seek to investigate the nature of the link between the two orders of facts and to investigate the existence of a 'third phenomenon on which the two others equally depend or which may have served as an intermediary between the two'. (ibid.: 152). Suicide and increased education can be found in conjunction but can only be related theoretically through the analysis of 'the weakening of religious traditionalism'. Thus, what might be called this complex comparative method requires its own process of 'interpretation'.

Durkheim raises, it seems, the most ambitious perspectives: not a universal history, but an even more complex version of abstract evolutionism; that is, a 'genetic' analysis of all institutions. This analysis is not strictly historical or synchronic since it has as its object the complete, if formal, explanation of a social fact through following 'its entire development throughout all social species' (ibid.: 157). It is identified as 'a new series of variations beyond those which historical evolution has produced' (ibid.: 154). Durkheim felt the need to add a new paragraph to the text in 1895, in which he tries to specify the nature of this type of evolutionary law. The key formulation is:

What must be done is not to compare isolated variations, but a series of variations, systematically constituted, whose terms are correlated with each other in as continuous a gradation as possible and which moreover cover an adequate range. For the variations of a phenomenon only allow a law to be induced if they express clearly the way in which the phenomenon develops in any given circumstances. For this to happen there must exist between the variations the same succession (*suite*) as exists between the various stages (*moments*) in a similar natural evolution. Moreover, the evolution which the variations represent must be sufficiently prolonged . . . for the trend (*sens*) to be unquestionably apparent.

(ibid.: 155)

Having reached this point Durkheim has to achieve a remarkable feat: to show that there are diachronic or genetic laws which are quite unlike historical trends or Comtean sequences.

In his discussion he isolates three cases which might be grouped in terms of his concept of the 'range' of analysis undertaken. The first is an analysis of social facts within one single society which can show the variations according to milieux, for example, suicide, which varies with sex, age, etc., supposing there are sufficient detailed statistical data. Second, if the object of analysis is an institution which can be identified as established and functioning across a number of societies, the analysis must also range across the relevant societies of the same kind. If this is attempted it would be possible to compare the evolution of a particular institution across different cultures. Third, going beyond the purely evident comparison of institutions there is, says Durkheim, the important effect of the transmission of materials from one society to another across time. So, he notes, 'society does not create its organization by itself alone', after all, it 'receives it in part ready-made from preceding societies' (ibid.: 156). And as a rule, 'the higher the social scale, the less importance [of] the characteristics acquired by each people as compared with those which have been handed down' (ibid.: 157).[5] Thus, the complete analysis, he claims, is 'at one stroke the analysis and the synthesis of the phenomenon . . . . It would show us in a dissociated state its component elements by the mere fact that it would reveal to us how one was successively added to the other' (ibid.). We have then a number of possible kinds of comparative analysis going from the most specific concrete analysis within a given society, through to an abstract elaboration of all formal types. Durkheim's ultimate aim seems to be something which follows not a history but an analysis which establishes through 'abstract' evolutionary schema, its range as a 'natural evolution' of one specific culture. This is dominated by synchronic analyses relative to each stage (or social species), then completed with genetic analyses which reveal the inherited materials out of which these societies were able to develop – all in a framework of universal evolution.

IV

The impressive and curious unity and close, even closed circularity of the argument of the *Rules* is now apparent, as indeed, is its enormous ambitions. It tries to establish the domain of sociology not through an appeal to philosophical foundations but the necessary character of social data. It establishes a logic of explanation and proof that is at the same time oriented towards practical intervention. It rejects as mysticism the notion that science cannot establish norms and goals. It gives priority to synchronic social comparative analysis. At the same time it emphasizes the genetic, diachronic analysis of the social transmission of social materials and resources. It establishes a structural form of social classification that avoids the excesses of teleological reasoning. It rejects the primacy of individual agency while at the same time providing sociology with a practical aim. It seeks to avoid aligning itself with Marxism, yet curiously in effect it establishes the means for an analysis which, in the last analysis, is more radical than that of Marx. Durkheim tries to show that the condition of modern economic life is abnormal, and that this abnormality can only be remedied by restoring the system of occupational guilds in a way appropriate to modern conditions. It is in fact institutional socialism.

Crucially, Durkheim has considerable difficulty in defining a single satisfactory direct method for demonstrating his basic ideas. What he wanted to investigate was his hunch that there was a basic flaw in the structure of modern societies, particularly that of France, to which could be related a whole series of abnormal phenomena. His joint aims were therefore to found a scientific sociology, and to reveal that this science could demonstrate the abnormality, both morphological and functional, of current social structure. The great obstacle which lay in his path was the apparent contradiction in wanting to define the normal by reference to the objective generality of the phenomenon under consideration in the relevant social species. At the same time he wanted to acknowledge that a specific morphological abnormality was itself general. In contemporary societies it was the general absence of the guild structure, as it still is in capitalist societies of the West. Durkheim was, therefore, forced to add to his preferred method a supplementary one which could take care of this problem. It required the sociologist to demonstrate the 'general character of the phenomenon is related to the general conditions of collective life in the social type' (ibid.: 97). This was especially necessary where the development of the social type was incomplete. Durkheim argued that *despite* the generality of economic anomie, this anomie had reached pathological dimensions. It is pathological since modern society is of the same species as medieval guild society, where this degree of anomie did not reign.

It is perhaps difficult today to realize the extent to which Durkheim took his notion of social pathology. It is difficult because it centred on one major thesis, namely, that contemporary societies had a fundamental anatomical flaw. But his view that the abolition of the guilds in the eighteenth century had left a void in the social body continued to have the most pernicious consequences. Shortly after the *Rules* was published Durkheim gave lectures on Saint-Simon in which he argued that one of the first consequences of the abolition of the guilds was the French Revolution. In some lectures he delivered in the later 1890s Durkheim argued that the whole structure of modern voting should be linked not to territory but to occupational structures (1950a/t.1957a: 96–109). In his book *Suicide* he argues that the abnormally high rates of suicide can only be prevented through the introduction of counterbalancing institutions, such as the guilds (1897a/t.1951a:373–84). The case was featured at length once more by Durkheim as the new preface to the second edition of the *Division of Labour in Society* of 1901 entitled 'Some Remarks on Professional Groups'. In this preface he argues that social organization progressively moves to function away from territorial bases, and that in politics, as in other areas of moral life, it is the reintroduction of occupational organization which is destined to restore normality to social structure.

It is not very surprising, then, that after his death Durkheim became identified as an intellectual precursor of totalitarianism or corporate states, although there is considerable material in Durkheim's works to reveal a continuous critique of political tyranny (see Chapter 6). What is perhaps more surprising is the gradual appropriation of Durkheim to American consensus conservatism and sociological functionalism in the 1940s and 1950s. In that period, with one or two notable exceptions, the whole critique of the abnormality of such a society was simply expunged from Durkheimian sociology or rewritten as an exercise in normal social deviance. Curiously, today, with the historical demise of Marxism and state-dominated corporatism, Durkheim again appears radical, and perhaps it will not be long before the Durkheimian category of social pathology will make its reappearance in sociology. But the problem of the apparent contradiction between the key Durkheimian theses concerning social abnormality and methodological preferences for defining norms through generality remains, and has become even more difficult to unravel. It is therefore easier to see how after one hundred years the famous Book III (on abnormal forms) of the *Division of Labour in Society* would be brought up to date than chapter 3 of the *Rules* (on the distinction between the normal and pathological). It is clear that most Durkheimians prefer to take the option simply of forgetting about chapter 3 of the *Rules*, thus reproducing what I suggest might be called a specific genre of Durkheimian revisionism,[6] a Durkheimian sociology without a heart.

NOTES

1 See Durkheim's discussion in 1955a/t.1983a: 91–2. In countering ideas of homogenization of thought in scientific activity he suggests that 'intellectual individualism . . . becomes a necessary factor in the establishment of scientific truth . . . it simply means that there are separate tasks within the joint enterprise' (ibid.: 92).

2 Occasionally Durkheim pointed to explicit textual falsification, for example, Durkheim (1913a(ii): 15).

3. Durkheim later wrote in the conclusion of the *Elementary Forms*:

Ever since the authority of science was established, it must be reckoned with; one can go farther than it under the pressure of necessity, but he must take his direction from it. He can affirm nothing that it denies, deny nothing that it affirms, and establish nothing that it is not directly or or indirectly founded upon principles taken from it.

(1912a/t.1915d: 431)

4 Durkheim (1893b/t.1933b: 356–7); and see Fauconnet and Durkheim, in Durkheim (1895a/t.1982a: 202–6).
5 A comment which links with Durkheim's observation that 'there are social facts . . . which are produced not by the society but by already formed social products', in Durkheim (1924a/t.1953b: 32).
6 This comment is, in part, offered from a Comtean perspective.

Chapter 4

Durkheim and social facts[1]

Margaret Gilbert

INTRODUCTION

Chapter 1 of Durkheim's classic *The Rules of Sociological Method* is entitled 'What is a social fact?'[2] The text that follows this title has been a source of some puzzlement. When all is said and done, what *is* a social fact?

Durkheim gives us several examples of social facts, including law, custom, the beliefs and practices associated with particular religions, systems of currency, and professional codes of conduct.[3] He also gives two famous alternative definitions of a social fact, neither of which tends to provoke the 'Eureka!' response.[4] In addition to the examples and the definitions, there are numerous pregnant characterizations. But how are we to deliver their meaning?

Take the following quite trenchant claim: 'What constitutes social facts are *the beliefs, tendencies, and practices of the group taken collectively*' (Durkheim 1895a/t.1982a: 54. Emphasis added). It is evident from the surrounding text that Durkheim means to make an important conceptual contrast between a belief that every group member has and something else. But what precisely is the something else? It is clear what Durkheim supposes it *not* to be, but not so clear what he thinks it is.

Durkheim makes some claims that may simply seem suspicious, such as the idea that a society is a *sui generis* synthesis of individuals.[5] 'Synthesis? How can that be?' one might say, echoing John Stuart Mill. 'When people come together to form a social group, they are not converted into another kind of *substance*!'[6] Or one might echo Max Weber: 'I am a social being just insofar as I orient my own actions towards other people.

Membership in a group such as a family may involve *feelings* of 'belonging together'. But group members do not literally compose one 'thing'; certainly they do not compose a thing which *thinks* and *acts*. 'There is no such thing as a collectivity which *acts*.'[7]

These reactions are understandable, and there are certainly both puzzles and obscurities in Durkheim's text. Nonetheless, it can be interpreted in such a way that what he has to say about social facts is quite plausible.

That was my conclusion towards the end of a project that Durkheim himself might not have approved.[8] This concerned a set of vernacular concepts involved in everyday thought and talk about social groups, that is, about groups such as families, discussion groups, unions, tribes and so on. These concepts included those of a social group itself, and the concepts of a group's belief, of a social convention, and of a group's language. The aim was to articulate as far as possible the structure of these concepts.[9]

As it turned out, the resulting analyses cohere quite strikingly with Durkheim's account of social facts. The analyses also show how that account can be filled out. They provide a justification for the claims that social groups are syntheses *sui generis*, that groups may, with point, be said to have beliefs and attitudes and perform actions of their own, and so on. Finally, they indicate that there should be no problem in accepting the reality of social facts as Durkheim characterizes these.

In this chapter I shall first explain what I take Durkheim's conception of a social fact to be. I refer at all times to the conception expressed in the *Rules*, focussing on chapter 1 and the first and second edition prefaces. Though this text is of course extremely well known, some explanation of how I myself understand Durkheim's statements is called for. At the end of this discussion I turn to the particular case of collective belief and consider how Durkheim's account of social facts in general (as I understand it) applies to this case. I then argue for and sketch my own analysis of what I take to be the basic vernacular notion of a group's belief and indicate how I have elsewhere analysed a number of related notions. It is easy to show how well Durkheim's characterization of social facts in the *Rules* fits our vernacular conceptions.

I. DURKHEIM'S CONCEPTION OF THE SOCIAL FACT[10]

When an original thinker such as Durkheim attempts to express a new vision, multiple interpretations of the relevant text are likely to be forthcoming. Fundamental, new perceptions may not get the primary focus in the text but rather form a background of sketchily indicated presuppositions. The perceptions may not be expressed clearly or with the utmost felicity. They may be expressed in many different ways, leaving the reader to wonder whether one particular way is to be taken as canonical, or whether the author is perhaps confused. Ideas are not so much being expounded as being formulated for the first time. A reader may find signs of reaction to rival theories and to critics, and question whether these have given rise to rhetorical exaggeration or to slips made in the heat of intellectual combat. A blander, easier, more conventional interpretation may be preferred to one which, if it were accepted, would force the reader to change his or her own outlook in fundamental ways, or consciously to acknowledge disturbing truths. There may be changes between one book and a later work. Scholars may wonder whether and in what way later statements throw light on what was meant earlier: have the author's views altered, or simply become clearer? A great work of sociology is like a great painting: there is much to be found in it, and people will differ as to what they find. To change the figure, it will provide grist for many different mills.

I do not attempt to offer a 'definitive' interpretation of Durkheim's discussion of social facts, even when that is limited to key sections in the *Rules*. Rather, I wish to show that one way of interpreting Durkheim coheres with the results of a different project, and allows what he is saying in this text far more plausibility than it is sometimes granted.

The obvious place to start, if not to finish, is with Durkheim's two famous definitions of a social fact. Durkheim wrote:

> A social fact is any way of acting, whether fixed or not, capable of exerting over the individual an external constraint; or: which is general over the whole of a given society, whilst having an existence of its own, independent of its individual manifestations.

> (*Ibid.*: 59)

In short, the first definition is in terms of 'external constraint', the second in terms of 'generality-plus-independence'.

In both cases a social fact is said to be a *way of acting*. I take it that 'acting' here is short for what throughout the preceding discussion Durkheim refers to as ways of *acting, thinking, and feeling*. Similarly I shall generally use the phrase 'way of acting', and the term 'practice' in a generic sense.

Let us first consider 'external constraint'. Durkheim stresses that social facts have 'coercive *power*': they are *capable of* exerting an external constraint over the individual. At one point he uses lively anthropomorphic language, saying that, when 'I' break the law 'the rules of law react against me.' In reality one is taken into custody, or tried, and punished, by human beings acting *by reason of the fact that the law has been broken*. The case is similar with transgressions of social convention and established morality. So there is reason to take Durkheim's basic thought here as this: certain ways of acting have a special status such that when I deviate from them other people will *take themselves to be justified* in reacting against me. This interpretation takes the focus off the 'coercive or punitive reaction' and puts it on the question: what is the special status of the practices in question?

Let us now turn to the second definition. Here a way of acting which is a social fact is said to be general 'over the whole of a given society'; at the same time it 'exists in its own right, independent of its individual manifestations'. The characterization in terms of independence may seem to be in conflict with that in terms of generality: it suggests that the existence of a particular *collective* way of acting is *not* a matter of that way of acting's being generally conformed to in a given group at the individual level. Is this construal of independence simply wrong, so that there is not even the appearance of a problem here? Or can it be argued that, in Durkheim's view, generality is not strictly necessary for social fact-hood while independence is?

There is good reason to think that generality is not part of Durkheim's core conception of a social fact, in spite of its appearance in his second definition. At many points in the preceding discussion he himself downplays its importance. Thus we read: 'It is not the fact that they are general that can serve to characterize sociological phenomena. Thoughts to be found in the consciousness of every individual . . . are not for this reason social facts' (ibid.: 54). He warns against confusing social facts with 'their individual incarnations'. He goes on:

> What constitutes social facts are the beliefs, tendencies and practices of the group taken collectively. But the forms that these collective states may assume when they are 'refracted' through individuals are things of a different kind.
>
> (ibid.)

Again, he writes that, where a collective practice is at the same time common to all the members of a social group 'if it is general, it is because it is collective . . . It is a condition of the group repeated in individuals because it imposes itself upon them. It is in each part because it is in the whole – not the reverse' (ibid.: 56). This way of putting things suggests that it may be possible, in Durkheim's view, for a way of acting to be collective without being general at all.

At this point it is natural to ask why generality is alluded to at all in Durkheim's second definition. As Durkheim himself later argued, in giving his definitions he wanted to note ways in which the sociologist could discover particular social facts. Generality, like public censure, is a good, observable *sign* that there is a social fact in the offing. This could explain why it is included in one of the so-called definitions of a social fact.

So far we have the following: social facts are ways of acting with a special status in a particular social group such that members of the group feel justified in censuring other members for non-conformity; general conformity to a practice does not make that practice collective. Collective practices are independent of their 'individual manifestations'. (This is still quite obscure.) A collective practice is a 'condition of a group'.

This last remark surely is quite crucial, though it has no *explicit* part in the 'definitions'. Its centrality to Durkheim's conception of the social fact is shown by the following key passage. Speaking of the ways of acting he has in mind, Durkheim writes:

> To them must be exclusively assigned the term *social*. It is appropriate, since it is clear that, not having the individual as their substratum, they can have none other than society, either political society in its entirety or one of the partial groups that it includes – religious denominations, political and literary schools, occupational corporations, etc.
>
> (ibid.: 52)

From this I take Durkheim's *basic conception* of a social fact to be as follows. It is the conception of a *way of acting whose substrate is a social group*. Alternatively (and equivalently) it is a way of acting which *inheres in* a social group.[11]

It is possible to make a few clarifying comments on this conception following an important passage in the second edition preface (written after the first edition material had been duly exposed to criticism). Here society is characterized in a telling way, the notion of inherence in society is connected with a notion of *production by* society, and Durkheim expresses the provocative idea that social facts are external to individual *consciences* (usually translated with the rebarbative term 'consciousnesses').

> If, as is granted, this *sui generis* synthesis which constitutes every society gives rise to new phenomena, different from those which occur in consciousnesses in isolation, one is forced to admit that these specific facts reside in the society itself that produces them, and not in its parts, that is to say, its members. In this sense therefore they lie outside individual consciousnesses (*consciences individuelles*) considered as such.
>
> (My translation of Durkheim 1895a/1901c: xvi–xvii.)

This is by no means crystal-clear. Nonetheless, what Durkheim says here suggests the following expanded version of his basic conception of a social fact, which can be expressed in terms of four theses.

1 *The synthesis thesis:* Human social groups are syntheses *sui generis*: they involve a unique kind of synthesis of individual human beings.
2 *The productiveness of groups thesis:* A social group as such gives rise to a set of ways of acting, thinking, and feeling.
3 *The newness thesis:* These 'ways of acting, thinking, and feeling' are 'new' phenomena. In particular, they are of a genus different from that of the ways of individual human beings. For example, *collective beliefs* are of a genus different from that of the *beliefs of individual humans*. Given all these things, 'one is forced to admit'
4 *The inherence thesis* (which we have already met): collective ways *inhere in* social groups, they have a group as *substrate*.

In sum, the *expanded basic conception* of a social fact goes like this:

a social fact is a way of acting, thinking or feeling of a special, 'collective' kind; it depends on and inheres in a special kind of entity: a particular social group.

Clearly this still leaves many crucial questions unanswered. One is this: how do a set of individuals create a group? What is the relationship between an individual group member and the collective ways of acting? If a group has a belief, how if at all does this fact connect with the beliefs, and more generally the minds of the group members?

At this point it will be useful to confront explicitly the thought that collective ways of acting '. . . lie outside individual consciousnesses . . .' (see the last quoted passage). I shall call this *the externality claim*. It may seem to go too far.

Consider again the idea of a group's belief. If we say that such a belief exists 'outside individual consciousnesses' it may look as if we are committed to the existence of a 'suprapersonal' group mind, that is, *a mind in no way constituted by or through the minds of individual human beings*. Such a conception may well seem absurd. How are we to construe Durkheim here? Is he in fact saying something absurd?

Here is what Steven Lukes suggested in his book on Durkheim:

> Social facts, Durkheim wrote, 'exist outside individual *consciences*'. Durkheim here perpetrated an important ambiguity . . . Social facts could be 'external' to any given individual, or else to all individuals in a given society or group: to speak of them as 'outside individual consciences' leaves both interpretations open. *He obviously meant the former, but he frequently used forms of expression which implied the latter.*
>
> (Lukes 1973: 11–12. Emphasis added)

Given the obscurity and diverse tendencies within Durkheim's text, it is hard to say what he 'obviously meant' at any point. He does indeed at times make the point that a given person is born into a ready-made society, a society whose institutions are thus external to her in the sense that they existed before she did and can survive her death. These remarks accord with Lukes's interpretation of the externality claim.

But the passage from Durkheim most recently quoted suggests that the ambiguity referred to by Lukes is *not* really what is at issue. It suggests a deeper and more interesting reading of the externality claim. On this reading it emphasizes a central aspect of the notion of *inherence in society*: social phenomena inhere in social groups as opposed to the individuals who are the groups' members.

We can reasonably ask for some elucidation of what is meant by *inherence in a social group* as opposed to its individual members.

Recall that Durkheim conceives of a social group as a special kind of synthesis of individual human beings. I take it that this means that by associating with one another in certain special ways, and only thus, do individuals come to form a social group. Now Durkheim evidently conceives of the social group as a causal prerequisite for the occurrence of the 'new' phenomena that constitute social facts. These simply cannot occur outside the context of a group as such. This is how we can make sense of the idea that these phenomena inhere in the group as opposed to the individuals who are its members.

Now, to inhere in a social group is, of course, to inhere in something constituted by individual human beings in association. Hence in a sense no phenomenon inhering in a social group is *totally independent of* or totally *external to* individual human beings. However, it is proper and perspicuous to insist that a special and significant relation *to a group as such* is involved, if the existence of social facts depends so strongly upon individuals being 'synthesized' in precisely the relevant special way.

As Mike Gane has rightly stressed, Durkheim's writing is often very carefully qualified and nuanced.[12] So, in the passage that I am focussing on, Durkheim does not baldly state that social facts 'exist outside individual consciousnesses'. What he actually says is, '*In this sense*, therefore, they lie outside individual consciousnesses *considered as such*.'[13]

In the context it is clear that he means something like this: they are dependent on individual consciousnesses or persons-with-minds only insofar as these are combined together into a social group. Social facts are best construed precisely as *group* facts.[14]

In the next section I shall focus on collective beliefs. So let me apply what I have said so far about Durkheim's social facts to collective beliefs in particular.

In Durkheim's view, collective beliefs are phenomena of a type that can only occur when there are social groups. They are, we might say, essentially group-involving. A social group, more-over, is a phenomenon *sui generis*, something that arises when individual humans are associated in *a unique* way. The generality of a belief throughout a group is not enough for that belief to count as the group's belief. Its generality may not even be necessary. If the belief is indeed general, that will be *because* it is collective. Finally, there is the matter of coercive power. Following my earlier proposal, the claim of coercive power is the claim that collective beliefs have a special status such that if particular group members do not behave in some appropriate corresponding manner, other group members will feel justified in uttering reprimands, and so on. In other words, they will feel justified in imposing pressure to behave appropriately.

In at least one place Durkheim explicitly equates the collective with the *obligatory*.[15] He tends to stress coercive power rather than obligatoriness, as in his definition. However, his clear suggestion is that reprimands will be seen as in place for the reason that collective beliefs, for example, are seen as having normative implications. That is, when there is a certain belief in their group, members will understand that they now *have a reason to act in a particular way*. More specifically, some forms of behaviour are now *obligatory*: the reason in question takes the form of an obligation. One aspect of the obligatory nature of the behaviour in this case is that others are entitled to complain when there are deviations. Thus we can read Durkheim as suggesting that the 'coercive power' of social facts stems from their more fundamental 'obligatoriness'.[16]

Applying this idea to collective belief, it runs as follows: if a group has a certain belief, that imposes upon the members certain obligations. If a given member defaults on these, the others will have grounds for complaint.

The claims about social facts in general and collective beliefs in particular that have been presented in this section do not tell us all we need to know. What thought is it that allows people to justify reproaches to others for speaking or behaving in a certain way? What, in other words, is the perceived source of the obliga-toriness intrinsic to collective belief and other collective ways? What sort of synthesis is a human collectivity? How is this synthesis necessary to the existence of a collective way of acting? Is the nature of the synthesis relevant to the obligatory nature of collective beliefs? If we take Durkheim's statements at all seriously, we need to address these questions to see if they can be answered satisfactorily. Otherwise the plausibility of his account of social facts remains unclear.

As I shall show, the questions just noted can be answered in a way that gives us a complete and consistent model of collective belief. Whether or not Durkheim would himself endorse the answers I have in mind, I do not know, but they show that there is at least one way in which his claims as a whole can be justified. To put it another way, they provide a basis for accepting all of his claims.

II. COLLECTIVE BELIEFS: THE JOINT ACCEPTANCE ACCOUNT

In everyday speech people often ascribe beliefs to groups. Thus people say things like 'The union believes that giving in now would set a dangerous precedent', 'Our department thinks it important for students to be taught in small groups', 'That couple over there believes that it is important that household chores be shared', and so on. How is such vernacular talk of a group's belief to be understood? What is it for a group to believe something according to the concept at issue?

In the *Rules* Durkheim expressed great scepticism about the use of pretheoretical conceptions in the new science of sociology. He had in mind the uncritical use of both common-sense beliefs and vernacular concepts. He argued that sociologists must approach phenomena with their spectacles unfogged by pre-scientific concepts or claims of fact.[17] To my knowledge Durkheim did not consider the idea of carefully analysing vernacular concepts so as to understand their structure. Insofar as he decried their use rather sweepingly, he might well have dismissed such a project had it been suggested to him. At the same time there is a great difference between spontaneously using a concept without careful investigation of its meaning and implications, and using it when armed with a clear and conscious understanding.

It is evident that in writing his chapter on the nature of social facts Durkheim was himself relying to some degree on what is sometimes referred to by philosophers as 'pretheoretical intuition', that is, on judgements made in the light of everyday concepts as opposed to scientific theory. I am not saying that his sense of the 'external signs' of social facts came from this. Rather, his sense of what social facts are in the first place was dependent on his appreciation of what the label '*social*' means – or would best mean, if it were limited in a scientifically fruitful way.[18] This was presumably derived from the vernacular concept expressed by the French term '*social*' and related terms, such as '*société*'.

What the conceptual analyst is doing, in effect, is bringing to consciousness the content of pretheoretical intuition, marking the contours and inner structure of the concept under scrutiny. Once this is done, we can ask how the vernacular concept can serve us in our theoretical phase, when we try to describe the world as it is. Before this is done, we are hardly in a position to judge a vernacular concept's worth for the purpose of understanding the world and its workings.

There is a rather different point in favour of the analysis of vernacular concepts from the point of view of social science. This is perhaps more in the spirit of Max Weber than of Durkheim. To investigate vernacular collectivity concepts is to investigate concepts that deeply inform social life itself: these are the concepts *in terms of which social life is lived*. Whether or not there is something unscientific or unpromisingly 'practical' about them, therefore, they should surely not be ignored by the social scientist. If human social life is the topic of study, the scientist will need to have some understanding of what people think they are doing, and thus to understand what their concepts amount to. If one lacks this understanding, one will have a very impoverished view of the terrain under study, insofar as it is constituted by thinking things, indeed, by rational animals.

The analysis of vernacular collectivity concepts, in sum, may be expected to be of use to social scientists in more ways than one. They will have a set of newly articulated concepts at least potentially of use in their own descriptions of society and in theory construction. They will also have an articulate understanding of the concepts in terms of which social life, the object of study, is lived. We do well, then, to ignore any antipathy to such a project that Durkheim's own strictures could help to generate.

Let us consider, then, what it is for a group to have a belief, according to our vernacular concept. Possibly there is more than one relevant concept here. Certainly different people use terms in different ways, and a variety of different phenomena could be given the label in question without this being completely bizarre. Be that as it may, if we look at certain pretheoretical judgements on cases, and take these to fix the contours of our vernacular concept of collective belief, it emerges that this is a complex concept that picks out an undoubtedly important range of phenomena. More to the point is the fact that the phenomena in question fit Durkheim's description of social facts remarkably well.

In the rest of this section I sketch an account of group belief that copes well with a number of challenging pretheoretical judgements. Before presenting this account I discuss critically two other accounts that might be proposed. Both of these are what I shall call 'summative' accounts: they assume that *in order for a group to believe that p, the belief that p must be general within the relevant group*, that is, most members of the group must believe that p.[19] (Here and in other such formulations the letter 'p' does duty for whatever proposition is in question.[20])

I start with what I shall call the *simple summative account*: a group believes that p *if and only if* most members of the group believe that p. In other words, in order that a group believe that p, the belief that p *must* (as a matter of logic) be general within the relevant group, and that is *all* that is required. This is the account that most people are inclined to come up with off-the-cuff if an account of group belief is demanded of them.[21]

This account seems not to be adequate. Suppose an anthropologist were to report, 'According to the Zuñi tribe, the north is the region of force and destruction.'[22] Suppose now that the writer went on to describe how it is with the Zuñi as follows:

> Each member of the tribe secretly believes that the north is the region of force and destruction, but each one is afraid to tell anyone else that he believes this; he is afraid that the others will mock him, believing that *they* certainly will not believe it.

I suggest that if this description were correct, we would not normally think it appropriate to sum things up by saying that *the Zuñi tribe* has this belief about the north. Nor would it be felicitous to say, '*The Zuñi* have this belief.' We would much more properly say, 'Every member of the Zuñi tribe has this belief.' Of course if the belief is a very unusual one, if, in particular, it is unique to the members of this tribe, it will be reasonable to look more closely at Zuñi society to explain the belief's generality within that society. Perhaps some facts could be revealed that allowed for the ascription of this very belief·to the group. The question here, however, is whether *all* that is needed from a logical point of view for a group to believe something is the generality of the relevant belief.

Let us leave the simple summative account of collective belief there for the moment and consider a related account. This still keeps a belief that most members have individually as the core of collective belief. It adds what philosophers and economists nowadays tend to call a 'common knowledge' condition. Many writers have attempted to give rigorous accounts of the phenomenon of common knowledge.[23] For present purposes let us use the following partial characterization: if it is *common knowledge* in a certain population of people that p then (a) the members of the population know that p and (b) the members of the population know that (a). To give an example, if Professor Fine is currently presenting a paper at a conference, it will (presumably) be common knowledge *among the people in the room where he is speaking* that he is indeed speaking in that room at that time. Everyone in the room will know that he is speaking and everyone in the room will know that everyone in the room knows he is speaking. (As this example indicates, common knowledge may obtain among people who do not know each other as individuals. Those in Professor Fine's audience may well not know exactly who is in the room. They may also be quite vague as to the number of people present.)

According to the imaginary report 'quoted' above, each member of the Zuñi tribe believes a certain thing but also believes that the other Zuñi do not believe it and that they are likely to mock him for having such a strange belief. If a common knowledge condition were added to the condition on group belief laid down in the simple summative account, one could not conclude from the imaginary report that the Zuñi tribe itself had a certain belief – apparently a desirable result.

For this and other reasons one might think that the main problem with the simple summative account of group belief is that it does not require that there be common knowledge that the belief in question is generally held by group members.

Common knowledge of any fact is clearly an important, consequential phenomenon. Similarly, of course, the mere generality of a belief will be consequential: it will probably lead to a convergence in behaviour. Important as both the generality of a belief and common knowledge of that generality are, there is reason to believe that our vernacular concept of a group's belief concerns a phenomenon different from either of these.

Here is a case which provides an argument against both the simple summative account and what we can call the complex summative account, which adds a requirement of common knowledge.

Five women regularly meet together with a psychotherapist. Each of them is primarily concerned to work on problems of her own, yet these five form an informal group of sorts. One day the therapist asks each of them to think for a moment and then summarize her personal belief with respect to the possibility of an egalitarian marital relationship. She goes around the group asking each one in turn to state her position. Each does so, clearly drawing on her previous personal reflection and uninfluenced by what the others have just said. It turns out that each of them believes that an egalitarian relationship is impossible. This is now, we may assume, common knowledge.

If these were all the facts, it would not, I think, be appropriate linguistically for one of the members to report to a friend, 'Our therapy group thinks that an egalitarian marriage is impossible.' There would be something off-colour about this, something not quite true to the facts. In contrast, if she said, 'All the members of our group thought that . . .' or 'We all thought that . . .' this would be impeccable. One can see this in advance of understanding what the problem is, that is, in advance of knowing what it is that would allow a group member appropriately to declare, 'We thought . . .' as opposed to 'We all thought . . .' or to claim, 'The group thinks . . .' as opposed to 'The group members think . . .'.[24]

In the situation envisaged, then, the conditions of the complex summative account of group belief are fulfilled, but the relevant group belief statement is not clearly appropriate. It appears, then, that neither the simple nor the complex summative account of group belief can be correct as a general account of group belief. In particular neither gives *logically sufficient* conditions for group belief in the general case.

Do one or both of these accounts at least give necessary conditions for group belief? In particular, does group belief require that (along with whatever else) most members have the belief in question? In other words, will an acceptable general account of group belief be a summative account of *some* kind? I shall now present an example that suggests a negative answer to this question.

Consider the following case. Suppose that certain Fellows of an Oxford college are meeting informally to consider a number of college matters, including the current state of the cuisine at their High Table, which is addressed first. Someone produces eight copies of the previous week's menu, one for each member, and these are handed out and carefully scrutinized. 'We have meat every lunchtime!' someone observes rather indignantly. 'We have potatoes at almost every meal!' says another wryly. Dr Lean, the most senior member present, speaks up in an emphatic and summarizing tone: 'Clearly there's too little variety! Someone had better speak to the chef!' He looks around him briefly. There is a pause. 'Shall we move on to another topic?' No one demurs. Given some such scenario, it would seem to be appropriate for a member subequently to report to a friend, 'Our group thought that High Table meals are flawed.'

Now, when the meals were being discussed, only three of the eight members actually spoke out against the meals. Let us assume that they genuinely believed the meals were flawed. Let us also suppose the following: two of the others had no strong opinions either way. Another was too shy to state her contrary view. A fourth thought the meals quite adequate, but was anxious not to cross one of the critics. A fifth attempted to deny that the meals were flawed, but gave up trying to gain the others' attention. Perhaps it was common knowledge among the members that this was the disposition of personal views. Even assuming all this, it seems that as long as the discussion proceeded more or less as described, one could subsequently say that the group thought the meals were flawed. If this is so, then it is possible for a group to believe that p even though it is not the case that most members believe that p. It may not even be necessary for a single member to believe that p.[25]

Let us continue on a little with the story of the Fellows' group. The discussion of High Table meals has concluded, and the members have moved on to discuss the Fellows' Garden. Without apparent sarcasm, Professor Blunt remarks: 'In contrast to our excellent High Table meals, the Fellows' Garden leaves much to be desired!' Dr Lean objects: 'But I say, old chap, we judged the meals to be quite flawed!' He implies that there was something *in*appropriate about Blunt's referring baldly to 'our excellent High Table meals' in the context of a presumed group belief to the opposite effect.

This implication seems correct: there is something conceptually inappropriate about Blunt's comment in its context. Blunt might have done better had he said something like this: 'I realize that the group thinks otherwise, but personally I have always found the meals to be quite satisfactory. As to the Fellow's Garden, however . . .' He would then make it clear that he was speaking *in propria persona* and not in his capacity as group member.

To generalize from the discussion of Dr Blunt's intervention, the following seems to be true of group belief. Once a particular group belief has been formed, each member of the group has an obligation not baldly to deny that belief or to say things that presuppose its denial in their ensuing interactions as members of the group. If someone does say something which implies rejection of the group view, he is obliged to give some sort of explanatory preamble, perhaps making it clear that he is speaking personally. A violation of these obligations is understood to be grounds for rebuke by other members of the group.[26]

I believe that the concept of group belief at issue in this case is a central component of our vernacular conceptual scheme, permeating even transient encounters and brief conversations. Thus in a casual encounter one person may say, 'Lovely day, isn't it?' Another may respond, 'Yes, indeed', in which case a group belief that it is a lovely day is established. The other might have responded, 'Isn't it a little hot?', leading the original speaker to respond, 'On second thoughts, you're right. It is too hot!' establishing a quite different view as the group view.[27] In neither case does there seem to be any conceptual requirement that the group view correspond to the personal view of one or other of the participants. In both cases once the group view is formed it would be odd to express the contrary view in the course of the same conversation without some special preamble.

In sum, there appears to be a vernacular concept of collective or group belief for which a group belief that p does not require that most of the group members personally believe that p: at the limit, no member need believe that p. Once such a belief is

formed, it is understood that the members are under an obligation not baldly to deny it. A violation of this obligation is
understood to be grounds for rebuke by other group members.

What model of group belief would explain these aspects of
group belief? Under what conditions does a group have a belief
according to the vernacular conception at issue? The account I
have developed elsewhere can be presented in more than one
way. What follows here must necessarily be rather brief and
schematic. Since I shall introduce a number of new terms, it is
worth stressing that I do not take myself to be inventing new
concepts but rather making explicit the structure of concepts
already in operation.[28]

I have elswhere referred to my account of collective belief as
the 'joint acceptance' account, since it can be stated briefly thus:

> *A group G believes that p* if and only if the members of G jointly
> accept that p.

This statement needs a lot of unpacking. What is *joint acceptance*? In order for members of a group G jointly to accept that p
it must be common knowledge in G that each of the individual
members of G has openly expressed a conditional commitment
jointly to accept that p together with the other members of G.

The phrase 'conditional commitment' as I use it here needs
explanation. The process that I envisage is *sui generis*, as is its
outcome. The aim of the mutual expressions of conditional
commitment is a state I refer to as *joint commitment*.[29] Given a
joint commitment, each of the parties has an unconditional
commitment to do what they can to fulfil the joint commitment.
The participants understand that they can achieve a joint commitment only if *each one* expresses his or her willingness to be
jointly committed. Thus what each one must express can be
described as a 'conditional' commitment: what is expressed is
sufficient to produce a joint commitment provided only that
everyone else also expresses it (in conditions of common knowledge). To illustrate this process with a simple example, if a man
approaches a woman at a party and says, 'Shall we dance?' he
expresses his willingness to be jointly committed to their dancing
together. If she replies, 'Yes,' then the joint commitment is in
place. What he expresses is not that he is unconditionally committed to doing his part in their dancing together, but that he
understands that he will be so committed if she responds appro-

priately: they will then both be unconditionally committed through the resulting joint commitment.

An important feature of joint commitment is this: once people are jointly committed in some way, they have a set of obligations and entitlements towards each other. These obligations are a function of the joint commitment itself: they are 'creatures of the will'. The joint commitment constitutes, in effect, a 'contractual' bond.[30]

In the case of collective belief there is a joint commitment with a specific content. The parties are jointly to accept that p, for some proposition, p. This could be amplified as follows: they are to accept that p *as a body*. A primary obligation for each party is to act as is appropriate to the members of a body with the belief in question.

The foregoing account of group belief accords with a number of pretheoretical judgements. It also ties in with similarly warranted accounts of other collectivity concepts such as the concept of a shared or collective action, and the concept of a social (or societal) convention, as I have argued elsewhere.[31] It is possible to say more about this account by way of both explication and defence, but some of that discussion must be waived here.

I see the account just presented as an account of the *basic case* of group belief. It does not fit a rather common type of case in which beliefs are ascribed to groups. However, as I shall explain, I believe that such cases can best be understood in term of the joint acceptance account.

I have in mind cases exemplified by such statements as 'Russia believed it was pointless to remain in Afghanistan' or 'The University is of the opinion that the number of foreign students must be limited.' Such statements may be made without anyone thinking that all or most members of the relevant groups in question have even contemplated the opinion in question. Russia could have believed it was pointless to remain in Afghanistan, even though most Russians did not know of the existence of Afghanistan. In these cases, the group in question has an administration or leader of some kind, and we ascribe the view of the administration or leader to the group as a whole.

Even small, relatively simple groups may have acknowledged leaders. One can imagine a deferential spouse asking his better half: 'What do we think about that, dear?' One obviously needs an analysis of some basic sense of group belief in order to analyse this sort of case, for we need to understand what the deferential spouse means by 'we think'.

What the deferential spouse is doing, I suggest, is expressing his willingness *jointly to accept the dominant spouse's view as the view jointly accepted by the couple*. Her not demurring to such talk may be enough to constitute her own matching expression of willingness: she is willing to be the source of *their* views.

On the 'deferred authority' model of group belief, then, there is an underlying joint commitment to uphold the view that so-and-so's opinion (perhaps when expressed in a certain context) is to count as the opinion of the group as a whole. Here 'the opinion of the group as whole' is itself understood in terms of joint acceptance of the opinion in question. The deferential spouse understands that once the dominant spouse has spoken, he has whatever obligations would flow from their joint acceptance of the relevant view.

I have now distinguished two senses for group belief sentences, a 'deferred' authority use and a (more basic) 'diffuse' authority use, as we might call it. The existence of these two uses alone indicates the complexity of the phenomena that exist 'on the ground', so to speak.

It is not necessary to try to legislate that group belief sentences must always be used in either the joint acceptance sense or some derived sense. Obviously people can use sentences of the form 'Group G believes that p' in whatever sense they please. Theorists may stipulate that they are interpreting such sentences in terms of the simple summative account I have discussed, or in terms of some other summative account. There may be uses not touched on here that are current in both the theoretical and practical domains.

In any case there appears to be a central vernacular concept of group belief according to which a group believes that p if and only if its members jointly accept that p. The range of application of this concept is quite wide; it may apply to small groups and to large, to groups where the members are individually known to each other and to groups where they are not.[32]

III. VERNACULAR COLLECTIVITY CONCEPTS AND DURKHEIM'S SOCIAL FACTS

Analysis of everyday concepts of collective belief, shared action, social convention, and the concept of a social group itself, all suggests that there is an important family of vernacular concepts which have the concept of joint commitment at their core. I have elswhere dubbed these the *plural subject concepts*.[33] The phrase 'plural subject' is a technical term: it is intended to convey the underlying perspective of these concepts, the idea that a plurality of persons may by their own actions come to constitute a single subject (or possessor) of belief and other such attributes. They do this by a process of joint commitment to constitute a body with the attribute in question.

Our speaking of 'beliefs', 'attitudes', and 'feelings' in the group case has its own warrant. We use the concept of belief, as applied to individuals, in our constitution of group beliefs: we constitute ourselves as members of a body precisely with a certain belief. Our joint commitment is to act appropriately, as far as that can be done: we will together make ourselves a 'believing body', a single 'person' made up of many individuals, but 'of one mind'.[34]

Wherever concepts such as that of belief come from, we have a recipe for creating the corresponding group properties in general: jointly commit to being members of a body with that property. Join forces in creating a body with that property. We know what the property is. We apply that knowledge in creating new group psychological properties.

Though the term 'social group' is sometimes used very loosely, I conjecture that the 'intuitive principle' lying behind the standard lists of social groups that sociologists and others give is the concept of a plural subject. Thus *those who constitute a plural subject of any kind thereby constitute a group*. If I bump into someone on the street, turn to them, and say, 'Gosh, I'm sorry!' and get their 'Oh, don't worry about it!' in return, though we were not a group before we become one by virtue of our brief interaction. I am supposing that this can be analysed as a shared action, perhaps characterizable as 'getting over the embarrassment of this disorder'. At this point we may stop and talk, and perhaps endow our little group with some beliefs and attitudes.[35] If social groups are plural subjects, they are indeed a *sui generis* form of human association.

If I am right about them, our everyday collectivity concepts are almost perfectly reflected in Durkheim's conception of a social fact as I described that earlier. Group beliefs, for example, are not group beliefs by virtue of being general. They can be fully in place even if group members do not personally share the belief of the group. They require for their existence a social group, which is a special, *sui generis* type of human association. They possess coercive power: their existence has normative implications for the group members. Not only does each member have and recognize a set of performance obligations, but each has and recognizes a set of rights to criticize and condemn, and a responsibility to accept criticism. If there are indeed group beliefs, as these are tacitly conceived of in everyday thought and talk, then there are social facts as characterized in Durkheim's central statements in the *Rules*.

Analysis of our vernacular concepts shows how Durkheim's rather schematic descriptions can be filled out. Thus sense can be made of the claim that group beliefs 'inhere in' a social group which itself is a '*sui generis* synthesis' of human individuals by reference to the idea that an underlying joint commitment is involved in group formation, something from which obligations are understood to flow. Whether or not Durkheim himself would have accepted this amplification of his claims, it is clear that such amplification is available: it is part of our everyday understanding of how things are.

In sum: according to Durkheim, entering a group involves a radical transformation of the individual. The individual is indeed no longer free to act as he or she wishes. Our vernacular understanding accords perfectly with this picture. There is a 'we' now, as well as a 'me'.[36] This is a more consequential thought than is dreamt of in many philosophies.

NOTES

1 The original version of this chapter was a paper given at St Antony's College, Oxford, Hilary Term 1990. Another version was presented to the Departments of Philosophy and Sociology at Reading University. I am grateful for comments received on those occasions,

and to Frank Stewart and Charles Kamen for comments on written material. I should also like to thank Rodney Needham and Steven Lukes for encouraging my emerging interest in Durkheim on social facts in the early 1970s. Responsibility for the views expressed here is mine alone.

2 Except where otherwise noted, all references to the *Rules* are to the Halls translation (Durkheim t.1982a).

3 See Durkheim (1895a/t.1982a pp. 50–1).

4 Ibid.: 59.

5 See Durkheim (1895a/1901c: 39).

6 Compare Mill (1970: 573).

7 Compare Weber (1964: 101–2).

8 See section II, below.

9 See Gilbert 1989 (*On Social Facts*). See also Gilbert 1987, 1990a, and elsewhere.

10 The discussion in this section is based on that in Gilbert 1989, see ch. 5, section 2. See also ch. 1, section 3, and ch. 2, section 4. Some things are dealt with slightly differently here; the overall interpretation is the same.

11 Terms used by Durkheim in the second edition preface to denote this relationship include *résider dans, être situé dans, s'incarner dans, être dans, avoir pour siège*.

12 Gane 1988 and elsewhere.

13 My emphasis.

14 Compare Durkheim (1895a/t.1982a: 128–9), where this idea is quite clearly expressed.

15 See ibid.: 56: '. . . it is collective (that is, more or less obligatory)'. See also p. 50, where he refers to 'obligations which are defined in law and custom and which are external to myself and my actions'.

16 At one point Durkheim writes '. . . *ils sont doués d'une puissance impérative et coercitive en vertu de laquelle ils s'imposent à lui, qu'il le veuille ou non*' (Durkheim 1895a: 6). W. D. Halls translates this as 'they are endowed with a compelling and coercive power by virtue of which . . . they impose themselves upon him' (Durkheim 1895a/ t.1982a: 54). Halls's term 'compelling' sounds very close to 'coercive' so that the phrase 'compelling and coercive' could be read as a conjunction of synonyms, as essentially repetitive. However, it is possible that '*impérative*' could be intended to have a sense closer to 'obligatory' ('*obligatoire*') so that a possible translation would be 'normative' or 'prescriptive' and the sequence of terms could carry the tacit implication 'coercive *because* prescriptive'. Clearly, 'obligatoriness' is in a sense a type of 'coerciveness' or 'constraint' in itself, but I take it that to say that a form of behaviour is obligatory (*obligatoire*) in some context is not simply to say that one is constrained in some way to follow it. Obligations proper will have specific types of basis (see Gilbert 1993).

17 See Durkheim (1895a/t.1982a: 72ff).

18 Durkheim suggests that a restrictive definition will be most useful theoretically in *Rules*, chapter 1: 'Thus they constitute a new species

and to them must be exclusively assigned the term *social* . . . .' and the rest of the paragraph (1895a/t.1982: 52). On the utility of limiting the scope of the 'social' in theoretical discussion see Gilbert 1989: 441–2 . See also Gilbert 1991.

19 I take the term 'summative' from Quinton 1975–6 who uses it in a slightly different sense, p. 9.

20 The discussion in this section draws on that in Gilbert 1987 and 1989.

21 This account has also been proposed in the philosophical literature, see for instance Quinton 1975–6.

22 Compare Durkheim and Mauss 1903a(i): 44. My imaginary statement is not intended to reproduce their exact words.

23 See Lewis 1969, Schiffer 1972, Heal 1978, Gilbert 1989 for a variety of attempts to describe the essentials of common knowledge.

24 See also the discussion in Gilbert 1989: 268 ff.

25 See Gilbert 1987: 191–2; 1989: 290.

26 For further discussion, see Gilbert 1987: 192–4, and 1989: 291–2.

27 For a fuller treatment of conversations, see Gilbert 1989: 294–8; for the discussion group case, see Gilbert 1987 and 1989.

28 The reader is referred to Gilbert 1989, especially chs 4, 5 and 7, and related papers, for further argumentation in favour of the type of account given here.

29 See ibid.: 198, 205, and elsewhere.

30 See Gilbert 1990a, 1990b, 1993. An interesting parallel to these remarks is to be found in something Durkheim wrote about the 'consensual contract': 'Here, however, there are only volitions, or states of will in question, and yet this state of wills may be enough to bring about obligations and therefore rights. It is for the bonds that have this origin that the term "contractual" has to be reserved' (Durkheim 1950a/t.1957a: 177).

31 On shared action see Gilbert 1989, ch. 4, and 1990a. On social convention see Gilbert 1989, ch. 6. On group languages see ibid., ch. 3, section 6.

32 In many cases group belief ascriptions will doubtless be made rather loosely, with the intention of indicating that 'something like' joint acceptance of the view that p is present in a given group. Thus the joint acceptance model of group belief that has been sketched here may be regarded as something of an 'ideal type' in Weber's sense. This may be true of many such models: they represent paradigmatic or prototypical cases falling under a given concept.

33 See Gilbert 1989, 1990a.

34 Why speak, then, of 'jointly accepting that p', as I have done, rather than of 'jointly believing that p'? I inadvertently fell into the former phraseology some while ago. On reflection I find that the phrase 'jointly believe' has an odd ring, whereas 'jointly accept' does not. This could have to do simply with the aesthetics of these phrases. Or it could be because the general concept of belief in particular requires (for some reason) a single or unitary subject. Then 'believe

as a body' would be less rebarbative than 'jointly believe', as I find to be so.

Some philosophers (including Robert Stalnaker and Bas Van Fraassen) have argued for significant distinctions between belief and 'acceptance'. Insofar as these distinctions are valid, one would want to give different analyses for group belief and group acceptance, and it might be clearest not to use the phrase 'joint acceptance' in an account of group belief. The following would presumably suffice: a group believes that p if and only if the members of the group jointly commit to believing that p as a body (this is what I have here referred to as 'jointly accepting that p'); a group 'accepts' that p if and only if the members of the group jointly commit to 'accepting' that p as a body. The main thing is to understand the general structure of plural subject concepts. See the next paragraph in the text.

35 For further discussion of the idea that social groups are plural subjects see Gilbert 1989, 1990a.

36 I argue at length in Gilbert 1989, ch. 4, that there is a central sense of the first person plural ('we') such that 'we' is only properly used to refer to a plural subject. See also Gilbert 1990a.

Chapter 5

Durkheim: the modern era and evolutionary ethics

W. Watts Miller

In the preface to the first, 1893 edition of *The Division of Labour*, Durkheim sets out the basis of his lifelong project for a science of morals which is also the key to ethics. As a science, it observes, describes, classifies and seeks to explain the 'facts of moral life'. As the key to ethics, it helps us to address practical problems, propose reforms, and clarify, correct, decide on ideals. In both roles it very much involves a comparative approach to social and moral life. In the original introduction to *The Division of Labour* – unfortunately omitted in standard modern editions – Durkheim insists on the need to identify societies according to their type and stage of development.[1] Practices and institutions can qualify as 'normal' if they are general throughout societies of the same type and at the same stage of development of this type. Hence a whole society can be in some way deviant compared with others of its type and stage of development. We might think of slavery in nineteenth-century America, or apartheid in modern South Africa, as well as Durkheim's own example of the tolerance in Italy of acts of brigandage (1893b: 34/t.1933b: 432). But the point of importance here is Durkheim's concern with the dynamics of change and development *within* a social type.

Discussion of evolutionary ethics is often preoccupied with how morality changes in the course of the world's history, or at least with how it changes in the transition from one basic type of society to another. Durkheim's interest in such issues is considerable. So, however, is his interest in moral change and development within the same social type, not least within our own, 'modern' society. It is on this which I wish to focus.

It involves an idea of an underlying and unfolding dynamic at work in modern society. This dynamic, it will be argued, does not and cannot just consist of the division of labour. It consists of two interdependent elements, the division of labour and the basic ideals of individualism–humanism. The argument is necessary since in *The Division of Labour* Durkheim himself can seem to cast their relationship as one in which the division of labour is the fundamental, unidirectional cause, and individualist–humanist ideals are its mere product and effect.

I. THE DYNAMIC OF MODERN SOCIETY

Durkheim is interested in the development of a modern ethic in which the individual has value because of the humanity that we all share, and not just because of particular qualities that might very much vary between us. He discusses this as an ethic of 'the individual in general', or of 'the individual in the abstract', or of 'the human person', and sometimes simply as 'individualism', sometimes simply as an ethic of 'humanity'. He does not himself refer to it as 'individualism–humanism', or even as an ethic of 'the individual as man'. But these terms are of help in making clear the kind of individualism which he has in mind.

In *The Division of Labour*, Durkheim locates individualism–humanism at the core of the modern *conscience collective*, and sees it as a 'sort of religion' (1893b/1902b: 147/t.1933b: 172). It is true that he worries, at this point, that it does not really constitute a social link (ibid.). But he ends with an enthusiastic endorsement in his conclusion, insisting that 'if we hold on to humanity, and must hold on to it, it is because it is a society in process of realizing itself', and that 'the ideal of human fraternity can be achieved only in proportion as the division of labour progresses' (ibid.: 402/t.: 496). He also insists, in a later article, that the cult of the individual as man is the only system of beliefs nowadays capable of ensuring moral unity (in 1970a: 270). As always, he still sees the division of labour as underlying the development of individualist–humanist ideals (ibid.: 271). The problem, however, is that it is difficult to see how the division of labour can develop and 'progress' as Durkheim envisages unless it is in turn directed by these ideals. They attack, *inter alia*, barriers of class, caste, race, gender. They attack inherited position and wealth, unequal opportunity, unmerited advantage, the social squandering and suppression of individual talents. They attack, in a word, the injustices in terms of which

Durkheim describes the 'constrained', 'abnormal' division of labour (1893b: Bk3, chapter 2).

It is often asked how Durkheim can consistently complain about the 'constrained' division of labour, when it seems so general and persistent in modern society. Asking this might overlook how long, complex and difficult processes of reform can be. It certainly overlooks the role in such processes of individualist–humanist ideals. These constitute the 'normal' morality of our era, drawn on by Durkheim – but also by his radical critics – to define and complain about injustices in modern society in the first place.

Durkheim himself sees a 'spontaneous' development of the division of labour as the route out of the injustices of its constrained form. But it is again difficult to see what he can mean, without bringing in individualist–humanist ideals to guide the division of labour in a 'spontaneous', 'normal' direction. Indeed, this is precisely what happens in the 1902 preface to *The Division of Labour*.

Durkheim argues for a revival of occupational corporations to promote solidarity, and to overcome a general demoralization of our social and economic life. But what sort of solidarity has he in mind? What is the demoralization which worries him? It is unenlightening just to identify this as 'anomie', and list the detailed economic and other functions assigned to the corporation to tackle it. 'Anomie' is dealt with and the functions are assigned in terms of specific moral ideals. Running through Durkheim's discussion there is a sense of the need for a more civilized, harmonious way of settling wages, conditions of work and disputes over them. This requires mutual regard plus the appropriate organizational machinery. But it also requires something else, and Durkheim repeatedly appeals to the ideal of justice. The corporation is a moral power, which in promoting solidarity prevents 'the law of the strongest from applying so brutally in industrial and commercial relations' (1893b/1902b: xii/ t.1933b: 10). To end the crisis from which we are suffering, it is not enough to establish some sort of regulation where necessary; 'it must also be what it ought to be, that is to say, just' (ibid.: xxxiv/ 29). Durkheim immediately spells this out as involving just contracts and a just distribution of wealth, and for further discussion refers us – where else? – to his chapter on the constrained division of labour.

There are also implications for another ideal, freedom. Society alone can prevent the abuses of power in which some people take advantage of their economic superiority to deprive others of their rightful freedom, and 'it is now known what complicated regulation is necessary to secure individuals the economic independence without which their freedom is only nominal' (ibid.: iv/3). It is taken for granted that the occupational groups involved in this regulation will run their affairs democratically through elected assemblies (ibid.: xxviii n.2/25 n.34). Moreover, their involvement in regulation is not just because of a specialized competence which central government lacks. They constitute autonomous, intermediate groups which are vital to escape the oppression of atomized individuals by an overmighty, hypertrophied state (ibid.: xxxii/28).

Indeed, this is the argument picked out by Durkheim in discussing the need for corporatist reform in his first publication, a review in 1885 of the German sociologist, Albert Schaeffle. The revival of corporations is essential if modern society is to steer a course between two great evils. On the one hand, the individualism of an economic war of all against all means that the strong oppress and overwhelm the weak. On the other hand, a state which concentrates and centralizes power to defend people's interests for them results in their subjection under a 'despotic socialism' (in 1975b,1:370–1). It is also significant that in the same review Durkheim discusses Schaeffle's belief in the need to tackle the massive inequalities of wealth in modern society by generalizing property and bringing it under collective ownership and control (ibid.:360–1). Durkheim does not distance himself from such a view. His sympathies are explicit in a lecture of 1892 on the family. He argues for a generalization of property through its collective ownership and control by occupational groups, in arguing for an end to the inequalities of undeserved, inherited wealth – an 'injustice which seems more and more intolerable to us', and 'more and more irreconcilable with the conditions of existence of our societies' (in 1975b, 3: 44–7). Like the appeal to freedom, this appeal to justice reappears as a central argument for corporatist reform in the 1902 preface, and is evidence of the basic continuity of Durkheim's views.

These invoke liberty, the equality of justice, human fraternity – Durkheim's trilogy of the ideals of the Revolution and of the modern era. Is fraternity the most important? Yes, since solidary feelings and attachments are the very source of moral life.[2] They power moral motivation and concern. Reason is inert without them, unable to stir us up. No, since they must be attachments to something, to a society and to its ideals. In modern society, they must be attachments to freedom, justice, reason itself, everyone's status and dignity as a person. Durkheim's case for a socially meaningful solidarity, through the intermediate groups of corporatist reform, depends on an appeal to these ideals, the ideals of the religion of humanity. It deepens attachment to them and to one another, by locking us into particular connections that lock us into the world.

Hence, there are at least two ways in which the division of labour and individualism–humanism emerge, in Durkheim's theory, as interdependent elements of his modern social dynamic. Ideals cannot constitute moral life by themselves. It is vital to have the solidariness of real, concrete, particular relationships and connections. But it is just as vital to have connections which express, foster and sustain the only system of beliefs nowadays capable of achieving moral unity. Ideals cannot arise *ex nihilo*. The division of labour underlies the development of individualist–humanist aspirations. But its own development must in turn be guided by them.

This still leaves the division of labour as the general, very basic source of individualist–humanist ideals. Yet although they cannot arise *ex nihilo*, cannot they have at least some origin that is relatively independent and autonomous?

II. 1789

The question takes us to Durkheim's idea of times of collective, creative ferment. The idea has had its critics, and has been discussed and analysed in detail by W. S. F. Pickering, especially with reference to Durkheim's sociology of religion (Pickering 1984: chs 21 and 22). Here its interest is as an idea of historically decisive periods which usher in the ideals of a new era – as, above all, in the case of the ideals ushered in by the French Revolution.

Durkheim's first mention of times of creative ferment occurs in his first discussion of the Revolution. This is in his review of Ferneuil's *The Principles of 1789 and Social Science*, a book published during the 1889 centenary. Durkheim insists that the famous principles must be studied, not as scientific theorems, but as social facts. He emphasizes that the men of the Revolution were 'men of action who believed themselves called on to reconstruct society on new foundations'. Their efforts, 'at once destructive and reparative', answered to needs and aspirations of all kinds at work in French society. Their ideas were 'articles of faith', which 'arose from the very activity of life'. Indeed, 'they were a religion, which had its martyrs and apostles, which deeply moved the masses, and which, in the end, achieved great things' (in 1970a: 216). Durkheim sees the formulae of the Revolution as expressions, however inadequate, of an 'underlying reality' (ibid.: 218). They are inadequate because bound up with the needs of action, and also because of their absolute character. Why expect otherwise? It is in criticizing Ferneuil's view of such absoluteness as exceptional that Durkheim remarks: 'But this taste for the absolute is not specific to the Revolution; it is found in all creative epochs, in all periods of a new and audacious faith' (ibid.: 224). He immediately comments on the Revolution's particular, substantive ideals:

> They have survived over time and spread well beyond the country of their birth. A large part of Europe believed in them and believes in them still. They therefore depend, not on accidental and local circumstances, but on some general change which has taken place in the structure of European societies.
>
> (ibid.)

So we have an emphasis, in the same passage, both on the Revolution's creation of new ideals and on their rootedness in general, long-term social processes. Is there any inconsistency in this?

The new 'religion' of humanity reappears in *The Division of Labour*. So does the notion of ferment, when Durkheim describes how assemblies can create collective sentiments and beliefs of a tremendous intensity (1893b/1902b: 67/t.1933b: 99). So does the insistence that individualism does not suddenly show up in 1789, but, like the division of labour itself, involves a long development (ibid.: 146/171). Durkheim continued to work with and combine these ideas throughout his career.

One of his most interesting and sustained treatments of them is in the lectures on the evolution of educational thought, first given in 1904–5. Both the Reformation and the Revolution emerge in these as important moments in the long march of individualism. In the case of the Revolution, Durkheim emphasizes its generation of ideas when he underlines the task of practical realization of these that lay ahead:

> the achievement of the Revolution in the realm of education was more or less what it was in the social and political realms. Revolutionary effervescence was immensely productive of brand-new ideas; but the Revolution did not know how to create organs which could give these ideas life, institutions in which they could be embodied.
>
> (1938a, 2: 169/t.1977a: 305)

But there is also his discussion of the Revolution in the lectures on socialism, given in 1895–6 (1928a).

Durkheim sees the Revolution as involving 'two fundamental principles', issuing from 'a double movement' of individualism and statism. In one of these movements, a new concept of justice rejects traditional inequalities to demand that the place of the individual in the body politic must be decided by personal worth. In the other movement, the state has the power and is the way to realize this demand.

Moreover, they are closely bound up in the sense that the stronger the State is constituted and the higher it is raised above all individuals of every class and origin, the more, therefore, they are seen as all equal in relationship to it (1928a/1971d: 93–4/t.1957a: 102).

Durkheim immediately emphasizes the centrality of such ideas, so that economic reforms which they inspired in the eighteenth century 'always present themselves as appendages of political theories' (ibid.: 94/ 103). He emphasizes this, because he wants to explain why socialism, as a movement, did not really develop until the nineteenth century. Yet the fundamental principles combined in individualism and statism already contained it as a possibility. So did the economic situation – 'riots and strikes were extremely frequent', and 'the lot of workers was much the same as it became later' (ibid.: 95/104). Durkheim's explanation is that it was the Revolution, as a political event, that mobilized such possibilities and ushered in socialism as a movement for far-reaching reform:

What was necessary for these factors to be able to produce their social or socialist consequences was that they first had to produce their political consequences. In other words, may it not be the political transformations of the revolutionary epoch which caused the extension to the economic order of the ideas and tendencies from which they themselves resulted? May it not be the changes introduced in the organization of society which, once realized, demanded others that also derived in part from the same causes which had given rise to them? May it not be that socialism, from this double point of view, issued directly from the Revolution?

(ibid.: 96/105)

It is clear that Durkheim's modern dynamic is a complex of interdependent elements in which a vital role is played by ideas, but also, in the development of our society, by formative moments such as the Revolution. This is consistent from a 'double point of view'. It is a picture of things which Durkheim consistently works with throughout his career. It is also a picture of things which, if it involves all kinds of tensions, does so in grappling with tensions and complexities in the world itself. It is inconsistent only with the 'consistency' of rigid, one-dimensional theoretical schemes, whether these see ideas as all-important or reduce them to mere epiphenomena, or lack a sense of the different rhythms of social life and its *durée*.

Durkheim's own sense of such rhythms, at their most intense and explosive, is evident in a note in *Suicide*:

It is likely that the suicides so common amongst the men of the Revolution were due, at least in part, to an altruistic state of mind. In these times of internal struggles, of collective enthusiasm, the individual had lost value. The interests of country or of party came before everything. The great number of executions resulted, no doubt, from the same cause. One killed others as readily as one killed oneself.

(1897a: 247, n.1/ t.1951a: 228, n.34)

Similarly, he writes in *The Elementary Forms of Religious Life*:

This explains . . . the many scenes, sublime or savage, of the French Revolution. Under the influence of the general

exaltation, the most mediocre or the most inoffensive bourgeois can be seen transformed, whether into hero or butcher.
(1912a: 301/t.1915d: 241–2)

We might also note the remark, in a lecture course of 1907 on religion, that 'the French Revolution felt the need for a new cult, to replace the old one which it wanted to destroy' (in 1975b, 2: 122). This contrasts with the point, in the 1898 article on the definition of religious phenomena, that 'our country, the French Revolution, Joan of Arc, etc. are sacred things for us, which we are not permitted to tamper with' (in 1969c: 157). But it also contrasts with Durkheim's usual emphasis on the positive and creative rather than destructive aspects of collective ferment. For example, in a lecture course of 1909, again about religion, it is in order to explain the creation of new moral ideals that he mentions, in the case of the Revolution, 'the effervescence of assemblies through which the individual is transformed . . . swept away by the collective élan' (in 1975b, 2: 14). In the 1911 article on judgements of value and of reality, the Revolution is once more listed as one of the great moments of creative, collective ferment (in 1924a: 134). In *The Elementary Forms of Religious Life*, published a year later, there is the remark about the bourgeois turned butcher. But the overwhelming emphasis, as far as the Revolution is concerned, is on the establishment of a new religion with 'its own dogma, symbols, altars and feasts' (1912a: 306/t.1915d: 245), and on 'those hours of creative effervescence, in the course of which new ideas arise and new formulas are found which serve for a while as a guide for humanity' (ibid.: 611/475). Nor is this so different from the message, twenty years earlier, in the 1890 review of Ferneuil.

Collective, creative ferment is thus a consistent part of Durkheim's theory. It gives ideas another origin besides underlying, long-term social processes. Hence it gives modern ideals a life of their own because of such an origin, and not only because, once generated by the division of labour, they help to direct it. But creative ferment also has a significance that goes beyond this.

III. RELIGION AND ENLIGHTENMENT

It is noticeable how Durkheim identifies periods of such ferment with the ushering in of the ideals, not just of a new era, but of a new 'faith' and 'religion'. This is partly because of his view, as in *The Division of Labour*, that a morality and *conscience collective* must consist of a core of beliefs held as intense, religious-like convictions (1893b/1902b:143/t.1933b: 169). However, much more is involved. Durkheim insists, in the 1913–14 lectures on pragmatism and sociology, that there is and always will be a place in social life for religious-like 'mythological truths' (1955a: 184/t.1983a: 91). These are collective beliefs which have the character both of not-to-be-questioned dogmas and self-evident, taken-for-granted axioms. But they are also beliefs which are both socially created *and* socially creative. They are socially created, since ideals must have a basis in reality. They are socially creative, in that they are beliefs which help to constitute a society, to give it a consciousness of itself, to define, identify, make up what it is. There then seems a clear implication of the need for 'mythological truths', as socially creative dogmas and axioms. It is that there is and always will be an epistemological gap in social life between our beliefs and a rational power to explain, justify and establish them.

But we do not have to wait for this implication until the 1913–14 lectures. It is already contained in a review, in 1887, of J.-M. Guyau's *Non-Religion of the Future* (1887b). In a review of Herbert Spencer in the previous year, Durkheim had argued that 'religion begins with faith, that is, with every belief accepted or submitted to without discussion' (in 1970a: 195), that a society without such beliefs 'would be a monstrosity incapable of living', and that 'as long as men live together, there will be a faith held by them in common' (ibid.: 197). But his appeal to the inevitability of faith boils down to an appeal to the inevitability of habit. In the review of Guyau, Durkheim's argument for the continuing importance of religion is more challenging. It runs as follows. There are limits to science and to its ability to demonstrate truth. We can and should learn, as a society, to accept these limits. We therefore can and should give up a mystical, metaphysical urge to reason our way to answers to everything. We still have to act in the world, but must do so on the basis of beliefs we just assume and accept as true (in 1975b, 2: 164–5).

In this and subsequent work, Durkheim never really addresses, in a sustained and explicit way, the tension which he thus sets up between his insistence on the need for religious-like, dogmatic beliefs and his hopes for an ethic which the science of morals can explain, justify and establish on a rational foundation. Given the tension, his vision is still one of enlightenment. But it is not the enlightenment of an illusory, mystical rationalism that, in questioning everything, seeks to answer everything too. It is the enlightenment of scientific rationality, always trying to push further, yet recognizing its own limits, and recognizing belief that must take us beyond them. Commitment to such enlightenment fits in with Durkheim's insistence on the continuing need in modern, secular society, not only for a 'religion', but for the symbolism and ritual that are part of it. Symbolism and ritual shore up mythological truths, in helping to fill the gap between knowledge and belief, and to inculcate an authority which reason by itself cannot provide. But it has to be appropriate symbolism, in keeping with the mythological truths of our times. Although, once again, Durkheim never really comes out and tells us what this might be, all his concern with a new secular cult of the human person points to an obvious suggestion. It is that individuals themselves are the central symbols of 'man', the central mythological truth constitutive of modern society and of our identity as members of it. 'Man' could not be a mythological truth without a real basis in things, above all in the development of the division of labour and of some sort of worldwide human society. But it also has a real basis in our history, in a past which is a 'social fact' of the present, and constitutive of our identity. Above all, it has this basis in certain formative, decisive moments, in ideals which emerge from them as the ideals of the modern era, and which Durkheim associates with the ideals of the Revolution. Studying these as 'social facts' implies that continuing, fundamental attack on them is futile – as is a continuing, fundamental, rationalist defence. They are just the central moral data of our time, just to be accepted as such. The only meaningful question is how they might unfold and develop.

IV. IS THE REVOLUTION OVER?

But let us stay with the Revolution a little longer. As already noted, Durkheim acknowledges its destructive aspects on a number of occasions. His overriding concern is with its creativity. This is to identify collective ferment as a way in which new ideals can enter decisively into the world, and inspire and take hold of consciences. Even so, the concern might have another, more political reason.

In 1904, the up-and-coming historian, Albert Mathiez, published *The Origins of the Revolutionary Cults, 1789–1792*. In arguing that there was a revolutionary religion, he drew on Durkheim's article on the definition of religious phenomena. He was promptly criticized by Durkheim's nephew and disciple, Marcel Mauss, for misunderstanding the master, and has been criticized on similar lines since.[3] Whether or not the criticism is justified, the point of interest here is how, in one of his arguments, Mathiez compares the revolutionary movement with other religions and identifies it as itself a religion. He emphasizes its intolerance, not just of people with different beliefs, but in its 'destructive rage against the symbols of other cults' (Mathiez 1904: 12). He gives a long list of examples of this iconoclastic 'fanaticism', and cuts the list short by remarking that the examples are so numerous that they could fill a vast volume (ibid.: 38). When, in *The Elementary Forms of Religious Life*, Durkheim discusses the establishment of a revolutionary religion with 'its own dogma, symbols, altars and feasts', he in turn draws on Mathiez, to cite his study in support (1912a: 306, n.1–5/t.1915d: 245, n. 15–19). It is noticeable that Durkheim does not draw on Mathiez to emphasize the new religion's iconoclasm. Wisely, perhaps.

Mathiez was not a conservative, implacably opposed to the Revolution. He was a radical, very much in sympathy with it, and went on to found the Society for Robespierrist Studies. But he was venturing, somewhat simplistically, into a political minefield. He was seen as compromising the Revolution in the way in which he identified it as a religion, and as playing into the hands of the right in the way in which he stirred up the whole issue of the Revolution's 'fanatical' destruction of paintings, statues, libraries, churches, monuments, tombs and even the corpses of the royal dead.

The issue did not just become a political minefield in the Third Republic. It was already this in the Revolution. The revolutionaries themselves invented the term 'vandalism'. They did so in a campaign to preserve something else they invented, 'cultural heritage', while waging war on something else they invented too, the 'old regime'.[4] Yet how was it possible to attack the symbols that represented and sustained the hated 'old regime' without attacking objects that constituted a 'cultural heritage'? Paintings, statues, libraries, churches, monuments, tombs and even the corpses of the royal dead can constitute, at one and the same time, a 'cultural heritage' and political symbols continuing to secrete the ideology of the past.

In his article on judgements of value and of reality, Durkheim himself touches on the problem when he observes how symbols can consist of 'figurative designs, emblems of all sorts, written or spoken formulas, animate beings, objects' (in 1924a: 138). It is important to notice his inclusion of 'animate beings'. Debates on revolutionary iconoclasm rarely if ever include the most spectacular case of all – the killing of persons as symbols, or, in a word, iconocide.

Thus, was the king tried and executed because of his 'treason'? Or, was he killed as a symbol of the old regime, and to kill off kingship itself? Yet how can killing someone as a symbol have anything remotely to do with a new era of justice and enlightenment? How could a show trial, in which only one verdict was politically thinkable, mark the beginning of this era of justice and serve as a symbol of its ideals? Indeed, what does capital punishment have to do with humanity and enlightenment? Is it not, like torture, a hallmark of barbarism? Was it necessary, even so, to kill Louis to demystify kingship and save the republic? Again, the revolutionaries wrestled with the issue in terms not only of the ideals but of the symbolism at stake, as did the great historian, Jules Michelet, in the nineteenth century, and as do some philosophers and historians today.[5] But although iconocide involves very specific problems of its own – above all in an era which sacralizes the human person – it should not be kept completely separate from the general issue of iconoclasm. In turn, this issue should not be debated as just concerning the destruction of objects which, although political symbols, are at the same time works of art. As well as iconocide of the living, there is also the case already mentioned of iconoclastic attack on the corpses of the dead. There is also such attack on flags, insignia and other 'emblems of all sorts'. There is also such attack on sacred formulas – whether of the Bible, or of the American Constitution, or of the Revolution itself. There is also such attack on the very memory of saints and heroes, for example, Joan of Arc. But the case of works of art remains, of course, important, and a number of points can now be made.

The very ideals of the modern era work against a total break with the past. They require an accommodation with it, to respect its achievements, to continue to enjoy its works of art, to foster a civilized, enlightened regard for all that forms our 'cultural heritage'. But the result is that even in the palace turned 'museum' of Versailles the old symbols can continue to work some of their old ideological magic. It is understandable, in a way, that there was a proposal in the Revolution to flatten the place completely (Hermant 1978: 712). It has been suggested that the Revolution's creation of 'the museum' solved its icono-clastic problem, by conserving objects as works of art – whether in the museum or as a museum – while destroying and depoliti-cizing them as symbols (Idzerda 1954). Although there is much in the suggestion, by itself it is too simple. It overlooks the influence and importance of literature, music, opera, drama. It also overlooks the destruction of works of art when they are destroyed as an ensemble, removed from the context for which they were created, and installed piecemeal in some or other museum. Indeed, this was a persistent criticism, at the time and subsequently, of Alexandre Lenoir's revolutionary Museum of French Monuments (Poulot 1986). It is doubtful if it was a purely aesthetic criticism. Preserving 'works of art' as an en-semble and in their original setting – whether Notre Dame or Versailles – helps to preserve their power as living, ideological symbols. But it is anyway extremely difficult, as already remarked, to suppress their old magic completely, and enlightenment cannot contemplate their wholesale physical annihilation. Mona Ozouf describes, in a brilliant article, how the revolutionaries oscillated between belief in an almost instan-taneous emancipation and awareness of the long struggle that lay ahead against the vast system of symbols that sustained the old regime and penetrated consciences at the deepest levels (Ozouf 1988a).

It is not surprising, therefore, that like Durkheim the revol-utionaries themselves looked to the emancipatory power of 'effervescent assemblies', of a vast new system of 'symbols, altars and festivals', of 'a new cult, to replace the old one which they wanted to destroy'. But this inevitably set off a continuing battle

of symbols – the 'palace' versus the 'museum' of Versailles, the
Festival of St Joan versus Bastille Day, Mary versus Marianne,
pacific versus militant versions of the latter's personification of
the Republic, the tricolour versus the red flag, the Place de la
Concorde versus the Place de la Révolution.[6] Maurice Agulhon
echoes Durkheim when he writes, in *Marianne au combat*:

> The theoretical ideal of republicans was certainly rationalist
> ('philosophical' as it was said at the time). Emancipated minds
> do not need cults. But could an elitist ideal of philosophers
> have won the battle? It is only too true that enemies are never
> fought without resembling them a little . . . To change the
> form of the State and its principle is to abolish its symbols and
> to have to invent others as a result.
>
> (Agulhon 1979: 232, 236)

If the idea of a symbol-free society is an illusion, it is as much as
anything because of the symbolism needed to combat the past,
even in the name of humanity, enlightenment and reason.

Moreover, although some sort of consensus around symbols
might emerge, it cannot escape compromise, eclecticism or
banality. A good example of compromise is Bastille Day itself, as
the Third Republic's choice of a national festival. 21 January,
the day of the king's execution, was never even suggested. 10
August, the day of the monarchy's overthrow by an insurgent
'people', was much canvassed by radicals, who wanted to emphasize liberty's dependence on armed struggle, while drawing a
veil over the Terror. It did not appeal to moderate and conservative republicans, just because of this militancy, association
with the Terror, and opening of old wounds. They were far
more attracted by the pacific, constitutionalist symbolism of days
such as 26 August, when the National Assembly adopted the
Declaration of the Rights of Man and the Citizen. In the end, 14
July was endorsed with an overwhelming majority, since it belonged to this liberal, constitutionalist phase of the Revolution,
attacked the Bastille rather than, say, Notre Dame, did not
involve too much violence, and yet still involved, to placate the
radicals, the insurgent 'people' (cf. Sanson 1976: ch. 2).

One of the best examples of eclecticism, in Durkheim's own
time, is a provincial church's stained-glass window featuring
Joan of Arc in red, white and blue, and a crowned medieval
France bearing the tricolour (Girardet 1984: 5–8). It exactly

captures Durkheim's remark, some years before its installation, that 'our country, the Revolution, Joan of Arc, etc. are sacred things for us'. But a problem with the symbolism of compromise, pluralism and eclecticism is if it replaces 'sacredness' with banality. Louis XVI was guillotined in the Place de la Révolution, now renamed the Place de la Concorde. It has a small plaque recording the event, on a large monument to someone else, surrounded by several lanes of heavy and constant traffic. It has nothing 'sacred' about it. It is a site of meaninglessness and amnesia. Perhaps the *places de la révolution* which survive elsewhere, the *rues Jeanne d'Arc*, the *boulevards Victor Hugo* and so on have been similarly emptied of significance (cf. Milo 1986). Perhaps, along with Versailles, Notre Dame, etc., they have become like the plastic 'cultural heritage' in EuroDisneyland, which now has a whole Michelin guide devoted to it. On the other hand, as Rosemonde Sanson argues in the case of 14 July, symbols which seem to have exhausted their meaning can still come to life when the occasion requires. This still need not entail a bright future, in our secular society, for a secular 'religion'.

In invoking Durkheim to identify a revolutionary 'religion', the young Mathiez challenged an older man's views. This was the professor of modern French history from whom he eventually took over in the republican apostolic succession, Auguste Aulard (cf. Sironneau 1990). Many have entered the lists in the debate thus set off, including another in the same succession, Albert Soboul, and, nowadays, Mona Ozouf (Soboul 1957; Ozouf 1988c). But Durkheim's own emphasis on 'religion' might be misleading. He could just have talked of 'faith', or, better still, 'belief'. The real issue in Durkheimian theory concerns the inevitability of 'mythological truths' and of the epistemological gap which they involve. If enlightenment is about trying to close the gap, it is also about recognizing that it cannot close it completely, and accepting the mythological element in modern belief in the individual as man.

IV. FACTIONALISM

This enlightenment still means that, in the words of Celestin Bouglé, a close member of his circle, Durkheim seeks our acceptance of individualism–humanism as the only 'sociologically justified' morality today (Bouglé 1924: 139). But he never sees the science of morals as simply rubber-stamping the status quo. On the contrary, he sees it as the only possible route to informed, critical reflection, proposals for reform, and clarification, correction, endorsement of basic ideals. Such reflection and argument might in itself guarantee continuing conflicts of interpretation of these ideals. But conflict is guaranteed by Durkheim's own dynamic account of things. As his thesis on Montesquieu explains, 'the nature of societies contains opposites, which struggle against each other, just because it frees itself from an earlier form only little by little and moves little by little towards one which is born out of this' (1892a: 68–9/ t.1960b: 59). Moreover, *The Division of Labour* explicitly rejects an enlightened Chinese stationariness; 'there is and there always will be . . . a free field open to our efforts' (1893b/1902b: 336/ t.1933b: 344). The result is that Durkheim's science of morals might eliminate some points of view as hopelessly reactionary or as hopelessly utopian. It cannot decide between points of view which remain. It cannot answer the individual's question of which of rival versions of our basic ethic to adopt – the more 'conservative' and, for the time being, established, or the more 'radical', looking firmly to the future, or the more 'moderate', somewhere in between. They are all part of the same social and moral dynamic.

The problem is built into other evolutionist accounts, such as Leslie Stephen's *The Science of Ethics*. Stephen, who was admired by Guyau, also gets an honorary mention from Durkheim (in 1975b, 1: 335). He is as concerned as they are with social *life*, or, as he puts it, 'social vitality' (Stephen 1882: 120), and talks of a moral code 'which is fixed and elastic in the right place' (ibid.: 367). Thus he argues that, although all vice is deviation, not all deviation is vice. It can be part and parcel of 'vitality'. It is true that 'every reformer who breaks with the world, though for the world's good, must expect much pain' (ibid.: 418). Yet he 'would not teach if he were not in advance of his fellows, nor find a hearing unless he were giving articulate shape to thoughts obscurely present to countless multitudes' (ibid.: 152). In *The Ethics of Naturalism*, first published in 1885, W. R. Sorley seizes on such ambivalence within an evolutionary account of the good to question the possibility of 'our getting from it any clear and consistent notion of the ethical end to which it leads' (Sorley 1904: 306). The difficulty is hidden in *The Division of Labour*. It is

very apparent in a book published in the same year, by James
Bonar:

> The Hegelian idea of development might be taken up (as it
> was by the Right), with an emphasis on its conservation of the
> past and its relative justification of the present; – or it might
> be taken up (as by the Left) with an emphasis on the ceaseless-
> ness of change, and the inevitableness of revolution; – or
> finally, by moderate men (of the Centre) the balancing of the
> two might be kept in the forefront, as it was by Hegel himself.
> (Bonar 1893: 391)

Of course, Durkheim was also greatly concerned with the
recognition and balancing of opposing tendencies in society.
This is not at all the same as their uniform expression in individuals, with everyone a dialectical moderate. An 'obvious'
Durkheimian response to the problem is to emphasize the dynamics of opposing tendencies in society, to accept the liberal
moral politics of party and faction, and to see in conflicting
interpretations of basic ideals a kind of division of labour in
which conservatives, radicals and moderates all contribute to
social life as a whole. But it does not seem a view adopted by
Durkheim himself, and certainly not in his vision of corporatist
reform.

Under such a reform, the socio-economic division of labour
itself would mean that we participate in politics, via an occupational franchise, and that the occupational corporation would
be the 'essential organ of public life' (1893b/1902b: xxxii/
t.1933b: 27). There is no recognition, in this scheme of things, of
the liberal politics of parties and factions, and a kind of division
of labour involved in the conflicts between them. The idea of
corporatist politics has made little headway. Indeed, it can be
criticized as misconceived, and in terms of Durkheim's own basic
approach. The liberal politics of party and faction seem normal
in that they are general throughout modern Western society.
More important, they are rooted in its underlying dynamic and
ethic. Corporatist politics are not.

This position is set out elsewhere.[7] But some general obser-
vations might be made. They concern ideal-typical patterns of
diversity in modern society. Durkheim is preoccupied with
'organic' diversity, while many liberal philosophers nowadays
are preoccupied with pluralism. At its most abstract, organic

diversity is the solidariness of complementary, interlocking and interdependent differentiation. As such, it is not equated by Durkheim with the socio-economic division of labour, although he is very much concerned with it as this. At its most abstract, pluralism is our freedom as individuals to have our own ideas of the good and, whenever they diverge or indeed conflict, to be able to act on them by going our separate, undisturbed and unobstructed ways. The only solidariness or collective decision involved is that there should be this freedom, in pursuing our ideas of the good, to go our separate ways. But the preoccupations with organic diversity and with pluralism both ignore a pattern of diversity that is central to liberal democratic society and culture. This is factiousness. At its most abstract, factiousness unites us in conflicts over which collective policy to adopt, but that when adopted, and although still opposed by some as wrong, is accepted by all as legitimate. Factiousness depends on a consensus. But it is first and foremost a consensus around procedural norms, about how to conduct our disputes and arrive at collective policies which, because of the way of arriving at them, can take on legitimacy. Hence they are norms of due process, of freedom of speech and association, of civility, and, not least, of concession and compromise. If a group refuses to compromise and exploits formal mechanisms of due process to force through one controversial policy after another, this threatens the very legitimacy of these mechanisms in threatening to alienate other groups from them. Similarly, an important kind of collective decision remains a decision, on this or that issue, to adopt a pluralism which lets people go their separate ways.

But a general procedural consensus cannot flourish on its own. It needs to be fostered by and rooted in the kind of solidariness of concern to Durkheim, which is the solidariness both of organic diversity and of attachment to basic, substantive ideals, such as of justice. Indeed, like a substantive justice, the tolerance which underlies the procedural norms of liberal democratic factiousness is itself part and parcel of individualism–humanism and regard for one another as persons.

It remains the case that it is impossible, given the Durkheimian dynamic of modern society, to have an extensive, detailed consensus on the content of the good. Factiousness has the role, in this situation, of civilizing our disputes, not just over particular policies, but over the interpretation of fundamental ideals. Symbolism again comes into the picture, for example, as an essential part of norms of civility. So does the division of labour, in that the conflicts of parties and factions might constitute and might be understood as constituting the mutually complementary differences of a kind of division of labour. This in turn re-involves the Durkheimian view of a dynamic development of modern society's ideals. Instead of the same, unending disputes, and instead of a miraculous jump from one consensus to another, it is through the very process of continuing, factious conflict over justice and other ideals that there can be movement in the terms of their debate and change to the assumptions, arguments and agenda of a new centre of gravity.

Durkheim's interest in such change and development spans a wide range of issues – contract, property, occupational life, women's emancipation, the family, divorce, education, punishment. But let us stay with politics and consider a question which is one of the most important of all. What is the city of citizenship?

V. URBI ET ORBI

Durkheim developed two rather different views of how, on this question, modern society might evolve. They can be discussed as ideas of 'macrocosm' and 'microcosm', although these are not his own terms. The idea of macrocosm envisages the emergence not only of a European but of a global political society. The idea of microcosm stays with a system of sovereign nation-states, but envisages each of them as an embodiment of humanity and its ideals. It is another way of locking us into particular connections that lock us into the world.

It is the development of existing states as 'microcosms' of humanity which is pictured in the lectures of the 1890s on civic ethics (1950a), and again in the lectures of the 1900s on moral education (1925a). A narrow, aggressive chauvinism will be replaced by a cosmopolitan nationalism, in which people's peaceful concerns are with their own country's realization of individualist–humanist ideals. A picture like this is endorsed by Durkheim in his first publication, the 1885 review of Schaeffle (in 1975b, 1: 362–3). There is also a hint of it in the beginning of *The Division of Labour*'s conclusion. But a switch takes place, and the final, macrocosmic vision is of the evolution of a larger, European political community and even of a worldwide human society; 'if we hold on to humanity and must hold on to it, it is because it is a society in process of realizing itself'. Durkheim qualifies and hedges on this in his notes, but does not at all rule it out (1893b/1902b: n. 2 and 3/t.1933b: n. 6 and 7). In a debate of 1907, Durkheim again envisages the emergence of both a European and a human *patrie* (in 1970a: 293–300). In lectures of 1909, he continues to see the emergence of ever larger political societies, but retreats from the idea of one which will be world-wide (in 1975b, 3: 222–4).

It is impossible to assign the ideas of microcosm and macro-cosm to different periods of Durkheim's thought. They occur throughout his work, and even, as with *The Division of Labour*, in the same text. They are united in a continuing concern with the city of modern citizenship, and in a continuing vision of it as the city of man.

It is of considerable interest, for an understanding of Durkheim's ideas, to turn to a debate of 1905. He distinguishes '*patrie*' both from 'nationality' and 'nation', but also from the 'state' (in 1975b, 3: 178–86; and see Chapter 6 here). In his own time, the Poles and Finns constituted 'nationalities'. Very roughly, nationalities are peoples who have a cultural identity and sense of their own history, but who lack their own state, and lack feelings of attachment to that of which they are subjects. 'Nations' are one-nationality states. 'States' themselves are simply legal-political organizations, such as the Austro-Hungarian and Russian empires. They do not necessarily arouse in their many and various subjects great loyalty or affection. In contrast, a '*patrie*' does involve attachment to it. But this is not necessarily the attachment, as in a nation, of a shared nationality. It is a shared sense of *civisme*. Examples readily come to mind. A *patrie* could be former city-states such as Geneva and Venice. It could be modern Luxembourg. It could be an emerging Europe of different peoples and nationalities. It could be a human *patrie*. After all, this does not have to mean a world government which is remotely like the old nation-state. It can be a polity of different and indeed changing identities, of new Europeans, resurgent Scots, or, quite possibly, non-disinvented Britons. In the lectures on civic ethics, Durkheim himself includes entities as loose as the 'confederation' amongst the legal-political entities which he sees as states. Moreover, there is already a considerable development, not just of international law, but of a whole range of governmental and also non-governmental worldwide institutions. If this helps to foster, it might also stem from the development of, a human *civisme*.

Durkheim's ideas on the city of modern citizenship continue to be of relevance, and indeed seem challenging and exciting. He is much misrepresented when portrayed as a conservative stalwart of the nation-state, as, for example, by Lewis Coser (1960). We get a more accurate as well as sympathetic picture from Jean-Claude Filloux (1977: 353–63). But let us finish with a general issue at stake in Durkheim's commitment, whether in ideas of microcosm or macrocosm, to the city of man.

The issue concerns the form of ethical relativism in which Durkheim endorses the morality appropriate in each type of society, and rejects a universal morality, supposedly valid for every place and time. But in endorsing individualism–humanism as the locally valid and appropriate ethic of modern times, Durkheim's relativism endorses a 'local' ethic which seems thoroughly universalistic. It is not an ethic of morals = *mœurs* = *Sitten*. It is an ethic of morality = *la morale* = *Moralität*. It is the ethic, as he himself says, of Rousseau, Kant, the Declaration of the Rights of Man, and, some would add, of Hegel. Indeed, a standard translation of Hegelian usage of the term, *Sittlichkeit*, is 'ethical life'. Similarly, Durkheim's repeated talk of '*la vie morale*' can straddle the localism implicit in *mœurs* and the universalism implicit in *la morale*.

This universalism has generated all kinds of philosophical searches – for example, by Wilhelm Wundt for an immanent, world-historical idea of man, something explicitly rejected by Durkheim (1893b/1902b: xxxviii; and in 1975b, 1: 331); by Dominique Parodi for an immanent, world-historical reason, something also explicitly rejected by Durkheim (in 1975b, 2: 373); in our own day by Alan Gewirth for an atemporal reason that would again have been rejected by Durkheim, and that is rejected by Alasdair MacIntyre in *After Virtue* (1981: 64–5). MacIntyre might be correct to insist that rights are socio-historical conventions. But in his nostalgia for community he continually sneers at liberal individualism and its Rights of Man. In a Durkheimian view, in contrast, liberal universalistic discourse has a real socio-historical basis in the development of international law and institutions, of a sense of a human *patrie*, and of the division of labour itself. It might also help to invent 'man' as a socially creative myth and identity. But that this is both socially creative and based in social realities is precisely the point of a Durkheimian ethical relativism which offers a powerful, coherent and 'communitarian' legitimation of universal human rights in the modern world, and of the ethic of which they are part.

Again, Durkheim is much misrepresented if viewed as unable to condemn the atrocities of, say, Nazi Germany – a view that seems urged on us by Zygmunt Bauman (1989: 170–5). Durkheim both explains and justifies our condemnation of such things, as citizens of the universalist world of modernity, committed to everyone's status and dignity as a human person. In a study of the emergence of new and appalling forms of man's inhumanity to man, the historian, Edward Peters, concludes:

> It may be possible to make torture disappear by making it effectively illegal and dangerous to those who practise it, but it seems necessary also to preserve the reason for making it illegal and dangerous – to preserve a notion of human dignity that, although not always meticulously observed, is generally assumed in the public language, if not the the unpublic actions, of most modern societies, and assumed, moreover, in a generally universal and democratic sense.
>
> (Peters 1985: 186)

He appeals to Kantian anthropology as an essential basis for such a public culture. Durkheimian anthropology incorporates this, but with a sense of 'man' as more than a philosophical postulate, and, instead, as a living, sacred, religious-like truth, which we tamper with at our peril.

In sum, Durkheim's ethical relativism can and does endorse universality in that, amongst other things, it can and does condemn man's inhumanity to man whenever or wherever this occurs in the modern world. But Durkheim does not condemn 'man's inhumanity to man' in, say, ancient Babylonia. That is, he rejects retrospective moral legislation. He refuses to endorse the universality either of a timeless Good or of an immanent, world-historical Spirit. His critics do not always make clear if they really want to defend such notions. If they do, their problems might be rather greater than any we encounter in Durkheim.

NOTES

1 Most but not all of the sections of the 1893 introduction deleted or altered in the 1902 edition are reprinted, giving original page numbers, in 1975b, 2: 257–88, and are translated in 1933b: 411–35.

2 Cf., 'non seulement la solidarité n'est pas un devoir moins obligatoire que les autres, mais elle est peut-être bien la source de la moralité' (1893b: 10/t.1933b: 415).

3 The argument is that the cults do not constitute a real religion, although they might fit Durkheim's definition of religious *phenomena*; cf. Mauss 1905, and Philippe Sand, 'La question de la religion révolutionnaire dans l'œuvre de jeunesse d'Albert Mathiez', unpublished paper, reported by J. Godechot in *Annales Historiques de la Révolution Française*, vol. 54 (1982), 314–15.

4 On 'vandalism' see, e.g., Idzerda 1954, Cornu 1956, Hermant 1978, Sprigath 1980, Baczko 1989: ch. 4. On 'cultural legacy' see Chastel 1986, Poulot 1986, Pommier, 1988. On the 'old regime' see Venturino 1988.

5 Michelet 1847: vol.9; and Walzer 1977 and 1988, Fehér 1987: ch. 5, Ozouf 1988b; Watts Miller 1993.

6 On the 'museum' of Versailles see Gaehtgens 1986. On festivals generally see Weber 1977: ch. 21; on Bastille Day see Sanson 1976 and on May Day see Dommanget 1953. On Marianne see Agulhon 1979 and 1989. On flags see, on the tricolour and the royalist white flag, Girardet 1984, and, on the red flag, Dommanget 1966. On street names see Milo 1986.

7 W. Watts Miller, 'Les deux préfaces: science morale et réforme morale', in *Division du travail et lien social: La thèse de Durkheim un siècle après*, P. Besnard, M. Borlandi, W. Paul Vogt, eds., Paris: PUF, 1993. For a general discussion of liberal moral politics see Watts Miller 1992.

Chapter 6

Durkheim and the national question

Josep R. Llobera

INTRODUCTION

This chapter brings to the fore some of the lesser-known contributions of Durkheim to the study of nationalism. To that end it shall concentrate on material (mostly public discussions) hitherto ignored or little commented upon. These texts, which could be called occasional contributions to the study of the national question, correspond to the period between 1905 and 1909, although consideration will also be given to Durkheim's wartime writings, particularly his *Allemagne au-dessus de tout* (1915c). Perhaps there is no explicit Durkheimian theory of nationalism, but it is my conviction that many of Durkheim's works can be read profitably in the light of a nationalist *problèmatique*.

Before embarking on the subject I would like to describe briefly the state of the art, within the social sciences community, concerning Durkheim's contribution to the study of nationalism. For that purpose I will rely on a relatively recent article by Anthony D. Smith (1983). In addition, there is the need to clear the path of some accusations, mostly from the 1930s, which make of Durkheim a precursor of fascism. Many misunderstandings concerning Durkheim's ideas about, and attitudes towards, nationalism, even in those authors who might otherwise be reasonably familiar with his work, stem from a lack of understanding of the intellectual and political milieu of the Third Republic. Some attention will be dedicated to this issue as well.

DURKHEIM AND THE SOCIOLOGY OF THE NATION

In an article published a decade ago, Anthony D. Smith could write: 'If we look at the writings of classical sociologists from about 1800 to 1920 (and even of many sociologists thereafter), we find little explicit attention paid to problems of nationality and nationalism, as if the subject did not merit special, or separate, investigation' (1983: 19). Following Steven Lukes (1973), Smith admits that although 'Durkheim wrote little directly about nationalism or nationality problems, he became increasingly interested in the subject, and not only with the drift towards world war' (1983: 29).

As is well known, the formative period of Durkheim's life culminated in *The Division of Labour in Society* (1893b), in which he made use of concepts such as 'mechanical solidarity' and *conscience collective*. According to Smith, there are two major areas of concern in Durkheim which have implications for the study of nationalism. First, the emphasis he put on what in modern terminology is called ethnic solidarity. In describing the early societal types, Durkheim insisted that 'cohesion is due essentially to a community of beliefs and sentiments' (1893b/ t.1984a: 219). The causes that draw human beings together are mechanical, but instinctive forces (*forces impulsives*), such as common descent, ancestor cult, common habits, attachment to the same soil, etc. are also important in keeping society together. The mature Durkheim also pointed out that, although the process of modernization may dissolve some ethnic ties, the sentiment that every society is a moral society and that individuals have a strong attachment to it because they are not self-sufficient, is still paramount or perhaps even more pronounced in modern industrial societies than in 'primitive' ones.

The second area of interest was what Smith called in-depth analysis of the 'roots of community and identity' (1983: 30). Here the main source of material is, of course, *The Elementary Forms of Religious Life* (1912a), published some twenty years after *The Division of Labour in Society* (1893b). However, Durkheim's interest in religious issues dates approximately from 1895. Until then his main scientific project, Filloux argues, had been the constitution of a social science which would bring to modern societies a rational consciousness of themselves so that they could take charge of their social change (Filloux 1970: 68). Sociology was, in Raymond Aron's words, the scientific counterpart of socialism. It is at this stage, as Bernard Lacroix (1981) and W. Paul Vogt (1976) have remarked, that Durkheim also became progressively interested in so-called 'primitive societies' and proceeded to a *refoulement* of the political sphere. This double shift was far from total (and this will be made clearer in the course of this chapter), but it is fair to say that the inventory of concepts that Durkheim had developed in his formative period – and in particular the ideas of *organisme social, conscience collective* or *commune, représentation collective, solidarité*, etc. were mostly applied to 'primitive' societies.

In his early writings (particularly in the 1880s), Durkheim drew from a variety of authors (Fouillée, Schäffle, Tönnies, Gumplowitz, etc.) who had made contributions on how national consciousness was formed and maintained. We can gather from Durkheim's course on *Professional Ethics and Civic Morals* (1950a) (first taught in Bordeaux in 1889–90 and then repeated in Paris in 1904 and 1912), how his conceptual framework could have been applied to the study of national consciousness in contemporary societies. But it is perhaps in his educational works – *Moral Education* (1925a) and *The Evolution of Educational Thought* (1938a) (based on lectures delivered in 1902–3 and 1904–5 respectively) that the potential for this type of application can be best judged.

Anthony Smith has reminded us that what Durkheim may say about 'primitive societies' à propos of what constitutes the religious sphere, that is, 'systems of beliefs and practices related to sacred things' (1983: 30), has not been eroded in modern societies. Religion, in the wider sense of the term, is still crucial for the survival of society. Religion converts societies into moral communities. As Durkheim put it: 'Religious forces are human forces, moral forces' (1912a/t.1915d: 419). The main aspects of collective life were initially aspects of religious life. In the final resort religious life is the pre-eminent form and the concentrated expression of the whole collective life.

In a nutshell, 'if religion has given birth to all that is essential in society, it is because the idea of society is the soul of religion' (ibid.). It is in this sense that Durkheim can say that 'there is something eternal in religion' (ibid.:427). Modern as well as ancient societies have to restate and defend or sustain with regularity 'the collective sentiments and collective ideas which make its unity and its personality' (ibid.). The way to do this is by inducing individuals to gather together and participate in rituals and ceremonies. It is by being together that individuals reaffirm their common sentiments.

Now, Durkheim maintained that it was of no consequence whether what was celebrated was the life of Christ or the life of the nation. The best example that he provided of a society setting itself up as a god or creating new god(s) was his own country in the three years immediately after 1789. What occurred at that time was the sacralization of the secular (and particularly of the idea of the nation). He quoted approvingly Albert Mathiez's (1904) classic study of the origins of the revolutionary cults, and shows how the new religion (with its saints, dogmas, symbols, rituals, altars, etc.) appeared. It could perhaps be said that Durkheim transferred the features of the modern nation to the 'most primitive and simple' (1912a/t.1915d: 1) society and tried to throw light on how the society is re-created through its rituals. Furthermore, the emphasis on symbols as things which have no value in themselves but bring to mind the reality that they represent, is aptly used by Durkheim in the analogy between the flag of the nation and the totem of the clan. For Durkheim the totem is the flag of the clan (ibid.: 206). However, the power of symbols is so great that individuals may become totally absorbed in them, and even forget what they stand for and be prepared to sacrifice their lives for them.

Smith concludes that

> lacking an adequate sociology of specific cultures and of politics, however, Durkheim stopped short of applying his ideas directly to modern nations and their secular faiths. Nor was he able to give an account of the genesis of nations and nationalism; his wholly 'internal' analysis addresses itself to the functions of collective symbolism, ritual and ideals.
>
> (1983: 31)

Gellner's theory of nationalism would incorporate some of Durkheim's elements (role of anomie and role of the withering away of tradition), insists Smith. And one should add as perhaps a more direct Durkheimian influence, Bellah's theory of civil religion (with specific reference to America) (1970).

DURKHEIM AS A PROTO-FASCIST

To the best of my knowledge there are only two major articles dedicated to defending the proposition that Durkheim's conception of the nation made him a fascist precursor. These were both published in the 1930s: one by M. Marion Mitchell (1931) and the other by Svend Ranulf (1939).

Mitchell's was the first article ever to be published on Durkheim's ideas on nationalism (and to date perhaps the only one exclusively focussed on the subject). We can quickly establish Mitchell's position, which is made obvious in the second page of the paper. In characterizing Durkheim, Mitchell says that

> out of the gospel of social determinism which exalted the group or society, and minimized the importance of the individual, there evolved a conception of the nation which foreshadowed some of the principal doctrines of the militant Action Française, of the Italian fascists, of the Russian Bolshevists, and of 'one-hundred-per-cent Americans'.
>
> (1931: 88)

In the end, Durkheim's thought is envisaged as the transition from nineteenth-century humanitarianism to twentieth-century jingoistic nationalism. Durkheim is seen as having paved the way for the 'integral nationalism' of Charles Maurras (ibid.: 106). These are serious accusations which require careful consideration. Mitchell's article was published in a respectable American journal and it is basically a scholarly article, that is, it makes use of a wide range of primary sources (some in the original), as well as some of the then standard secondary sources on Durkheim.

Mitchell focuses initially on *The Elementary Forms of Religious Life*, which he labels a 'sociological interpretation of religion [which] is strikingly original' (ibid.: 91). The idea that God and society are a single reality, that societies are simply worshipping themselves and that sacred things 'are those whose *représentations* society itself has fashioned, (. . .) all sorts of collective states, common traditions and emotions', called for nationalist implications. So far as the ills of modern society (anomie, egotism, lack of moral fibre, etc.) are concerned, Durkheim developed a plan of political reconstruction to solve them.

The moral regeneration required to create a healthy society

could not be provided by the traditional institutions (family, regional units, religion, etc.). As to the educational system, it was not sufficient in itself to effect the changes. Given the complexity of social labour in modern society, the only institution which could be re-created was the occupational group, working under the supervision of the state, but having an active part in regulating the functioning of the professions and its internal conflicts. These new groups would become intermediate associations which would fill the social emptiness that existed between the individual and the state in modern industrial society. Again, Mitchell sees in Durkheim's applied sociology, aimed at creating solidarity by reinforcing the professional groups, 'the subjection of both individual and economic interests to the discipline of the state' (ibid.: 95).

It is not the intention here to enter into a detailed presentation and critical analysis of Mitchell's evidence concerning Durkheim's so-called nationalist philosophy. Mitchell managed to bring a lot of written material to bear on the issue at stake: only a few relevant, short Durkheimian texts escaped attention. The problem is elsewhere: in the interpretation given to the material and in the conclusions extracted from it. The crux of Mitchell's position concerning Durkheim can best be illustrated by reference to the following passage of the article. Because Durkheim treated social facts as things, it followed that he 'exalted the group as a personality infinitely superior to the individual [and] came to regard the nation as the supreme reality of his time' (ibid.: 96). Part of the problem stems from the inability of Anglo-Saxon critics of Durkheim in the inter-war period to handle collective concepts without seeing in them unacceptable metaphysical constructs, collective ghosts or Leviathan reincarnated. This led them to ignore the overwhelming evidence of the centrality that human values had for Durkheim in modern society. Furthermore, Mitchell's case is pinned on Durkheim's reluctance to brand all patriotism as national egotism, as jingoism or chauvinism. Even when Durkheim defined the *patrie* as a partial incarnation of the idea of humanity, he was still found wanting. One aspect which Mitchell refuses to consider is that even if it could be shown that Durkheim was a narrow-minded French nationalist (which was certainly not the case), it could still be possible to show that his ideas about how national solidarity works or the importance of the beliefs, symbols and rituals of nationalism, are relevant to understanding the modern nation.

Ranulf's article is predicated on the assumption that there is a line of sociological thinkers (Comte, Tönnies, Durkheim) who, by emphasizing the idea that modern industrial society is poorly integrated and too individualistic, have, perhaps unwittingly, helped the emergence of fascism. In particular, the idea that there is something superior in the idea of community (*Gemeinschaft*) over that of society (*Gesellschaft*), is for Ranulf tantamount to 'fascist propaganda' (1950: 34). It is interesting to note that some aspects of this thesis were repackaged and sold by Robert Nisbet (1952) in his thesis about the conservative origins of Durkheimian sociology. In Nisbet's case the genealogy extended as far back as the reactionaries against the French Revolution, such as de Bonald and de Maistre. Recently, Isaiah Berlin (1990) has published a book in which he depicts Joseph de Maistre as a forerunner of fascism, although I am not suggesting that in his book Durkheim is considered a precursor of fascism. Ranulf's demonstration is rather thin on the ground, creates superficial analogies between authors and misunderstands Durkheim's position concerning individualism. In no way does he show any connection between Durkheim's ideas and fascism, except those already present in his mind. Perhaps a greater familiarity with Durkheim's public life would have helped him to dispel his outrageous suggestions.

There is something interesting in Ranulf's article, however, and that is a long quote from a letter by Marcel Mauss, in which Durkheim's nephew states that neither he nor Durkheim had foreseen that modern societies could have been so easily open to suggestion through gatherings, processions, rituals, etc. as traditional ones (Australian aborigines). Mauss describes the events that were taking place, presumably in Italy and Germany, as a 'return to the primitive', made possible by the existence of the modern media. However, Mauss also seems to be saying that these events are proof, no matter how tragic, of the importance of collective representations. And yet he still concludes by saying that it is only in the collective spirit (*esprit collectif*) that the individual can find ground and sustenance for his/her freedom, independence, personality and self-improvement (ibid.: 32).

Mitchell and Ranulf are not the only authors to put the blame on Durkheim for the excesses brought about by nationalism. A well-known specialist on nationalism, Carlton Hayes, could write in 1941:

> It must not be imagined that the sowers of totalitarian nationalism were all anti-semites. Some Jews were effective planters – for example, Emile Durkheim, who started out to be a rabbi and ended up as a world famous sociologist. He taught that the national state, the *patrie*, is a 'psychic being', that of all 'societies' – family, class, church, etc. – it is the most basic and by right the most powerful, and that, as its function is the supreme one of directing and giving harmony to the ideal 'corporative society', so its members owe it supreme allegiance and the highest public worship.
>
> (Hayes 1941: 247)

The fact that in *The Division of Labour in Society* Durkheim insisted that intermediate associations ought to play an important role in modern industrial societies, surely left him open to the charge of corporative bias and, in the ideologically polarized atmosphere of the 1930s, even of proto-fascist tendencies.

Recent historiography on Durkheim (Wallwork 1972, Bellah 1973, Giddens 1986) depicts him at most as a moderate French patriot, who believed in the progressive emergence of a sort of world patriotism, hardly the chauvinistic, jingoistic, narrow-minded French nationalist portrayed by Mitchell or the proto-fascist described by Ranulf. How is it possible that using roughly the same literary evidence, such diametrically opposed conclusions can be reached? Part of the answer must lie in the different historical periods in which these judgements were produced. The 1930s, obsessed with the rise of fascism, produced numerous knee-jerk reactions, both among liberals and Marxists (think of Lukács a little later), which encouraged dubious intellectual genealogies. More important, though, is the fact that today, particularly after the extensive research of Steven Lukes (1973) and many others, we have a much better knowledge of Durkheim and his milieu than people had in the 1930s. We can map out in reasonable detail Durkheim's intellectual, political and academic developments in the society of the Third Republic, because his writings have to be seen and understood in this very context. Anybody who is familiar with Durkheim's political trajectory would have to be extremely partial or biased to concur with the judgements passed in the 1930s which I have just described. If there is one concept which must be understood as a child of each historical period it is that of nationalism.

DURKHEIM'S FRANCE: THE NATIONALIST BACKGROUND

Trying to account for Durkheim's ideas and sentiments on nationalism independently of the time in which they were written is bound to be at best superficial and at worst grossly misleading.

A proper understanding of Durkheim's position on the national question requires, first of all, a clarification of the idea of nationalism as it developed during the period of the Third Republic. Durkheim's ideas were moulded and developed over a period of time (1870–1914) in which France experienced a number of events which were nothing short of national disasters. I refer, in particular, to France's military defeat by Prussia in 1870 and the subsequent territorial losses of Alsace and Lorraine in 1871, as well as to the Paris Commune. These events led to a total re-evaluation of the national question in France. At a more general level the period was perceived by quite a few intellectuals as one of decadence (Swart 1964). There developed the belief that France was lagging behind both the United Kingdom (economically) and Germany (educationally and militarily), and that a solution to these ills had to be found. This was a propitious cauldron in which to brew anti-democratic and anti-liberal solutions to problems both real and imaginary.

So far as the national question is concerned, 1871 was a dividing line for intellectuals and politicians alike. Before 1871 French thought had embraced the idea of national self-emancipation for oppressed nationalities; even Napoleon III had sympathized with Italian and German nationalism, as had many of the leading intellectuals of the period. In the aftermath of the defeat, two important and closely related attitudes appeared: an anti-German, revanchist state of mind and an outright rejection of the ethnic principle in the making of the state. During the nineteenth century Germany had been admired by many as a philosophical, scientific and political beacon. Soon after the 1870 defeat the voices of Michelet, Fustel de Coulanges, Taine, Renan and many others expressed sentiments of shock and disbelief, of hatred and humiliation at the

Prussian affront. Germany was no longer a romantic, liberal, creative country, but a state under the Prussian boot geared towards absolute power and with no respect for the will of the people; the annexing of Alsace-Lorraine was an obvious example (Digeon 1959).

There follows a retrenchment from the universalist pretensions of the French idea of nation to a process of inward-looking which tended to concentrate the mind on the history of France, on how France came to be what it was. The historical criterion of nationality triumphed, while language, culture, race, etc. were rejected as criteria of nationhood. These ideas concerning the nation crystallized in Renan's famous lecture 'Qu'est-ce qu'une nation?', delivered in the Sorbonne in 1882 (Renan 1947). Renan's nation is anchored in the strong moral sentiment of togetherness. The nation is an historical precipitate, not of race, language, religion, geography or economic interest, but of the will of the people to live together. The material is not sufficient to constitute a nation, because the latter is a spiritual principle which is the result of the desire to preserve historical memories and common traditions. A nation is a solidarity of past and future sacrifices. Renan is emphatic about the element of consciousness and will, to the point of requiring for the existence of the nation the clearly expressed desire of the people to live in common, hence his metaphor of the nation as a 'daily plebiscite'.

The Third Republic emerged, then, in the context of a military defeat and a loss of national territory. Michelet's idea of France as a 'vessel of humanity', with a mission to free the oppressed peoples of the world, no longer made sense in a humiliated country, obsessed with revenge and with military values. The Third Republic was poised to create a progressive, secular, liberal and democratic country; in other words, a truly modern France; a country free from political and religious tyranny, able to take the lead in world affairs. But the republican regime was far from being free from tensions and contradictions; and the integration of the different layers of the French population into a modern society was slow, uneven and problematic. The period between 1870 and 1914 was characterized by violent class struggles, controversial imperialist adventures abroad, popular movements like Boulangisme, acute social divisions like the Dreyfus Affair, and so on. From the 1890s onwards an open nationalist movement made its appearance. It was, as Raul Girardet has remarked, 'a right-wing, conservative nationalism, which essentially presents itself as a meditation on decadence' (1983: 17). This was the nationalism of the Ligue des Patriotes of Paul Déroulède and Maurice Barrès, of Edouard Drumont's *La France juive*, of La Ligue de la Patrie Française, of Action Française led by Charles Maurras, of the writings of the Catholic convert Charles Péguy. For the nationalists, France was in extreme danger of falling into oblivion, undermined by external and internal factors. The main enemy abroad was, of course, Germany: an ever-aggressive and expansionist Germany which threatened the survival of the French nation. At home, the anti-patriots were at work; cosmopolitans, Jews, socialists and Masons constituted the forces that had progressively weakened the defences of France.

For the period preceding the First World War, it is not easy to establish the relative strength of the nationalism of the 'nationalists' (as defined in the previous paragraph). As we shall see, neither Durkheim nor the overall majority of the intellectual class, for that matter, shared this kind of nationalism. For one thing, the nationalists were mostly anti-republican, as Claude Nicolet emphasizes (1982: 18), while Durkheim was fervently in favour of the ideal of the Third Republic. This was particularly the case after the Dreyfus Affair which, in the words of Eugen Weber, gave rise to a 'rebellious nationalism, antirepublican, whose assertive traditionalism rejected a whole century of French tradition, revolutionary because royalist, and chauvinistic by reaction against the foreign elements that it felt were swamping French life and culture' (1977: 195). Much has been made of the influence that the disciplines of history and geography had on the development of French nationalism. But even if this is true for the period immediately after 1870, by the beginning of the century the new geography of Vidal de la Blache was a far cry from any nationalist leanings; the same can be said about the new academic history. The academics of the Third Republic no doubt contributed to the consolidation of patriotism, but it was a conception of the historical *patrie* tempered by a commitment to republican values.

As has been said, nationalism was a right-wing, traditionalist ideology; it was mostly an urban phenomenon, particularly strong in Paris, which affected mainly the petty and middle bourgeois, but had little impact on the upper echelons of the bourgeoisie. It found obvious allies in the Church and in the Army. The new brand of Catholicism typical of this period preached the iron union between God and the Fatherland (*patrie*), and abhorred the evils of pacifism and internationalism. As for the Army, most officers were nationalists, though perhaps in the old-fashioned way. What is important, however, is that the Army was the object of nationalist solicitations and worship; it appeared as the saviour of the fatherland, which would deliver the beloved provinces of Alsace and Lorraine from the hated Germans. Part of the youth was also in favour of a bellicose nationalism. In a survey published in 1913, *Les jeunes gens d'aujourd'hui* by Henri Massis and Alexis de Tarde, Parisian students and *lycéens* showed themselves strongly against the intellectualism of the previous generation and expressed a desire for action; the elite among the young were in favour of extreme patriotism, Catholicism, heroism, tradition, etc. They worshipped an aesthetic ideal of martial virtue, which they soon had a chance to put into practice (Becker 1977).

DURKHEIMIAN WRITINGS ON NATIONALISM: A TEXTUAL ANALYSIS

Three pieces written by Durkheim in some way have bearing on the issue of nationalism: three public discussions in which he participated between 1905 and 1907, the summary of a course he taught in 1908–9, and his war writings. These texts spread over a period of ten years of international tension, of inter-imperialist rivalries; a period in which France and Germany clashed a number of times. The main topics of the public discussions in which Durkheim was involved concern patriotism and nationalism, internationalism and pacifism, the state and war.

The first text, chronologically speaking, is also perhaps the most substantial (1905e(2)). It is entitled 'A debate on nationalism and patriotism'. The debate took place in 1905 as part of the *Libres entretiens* of the Union pour la Verité. (They have been reprinted in Durkheim (1975b) *Textes*, vol.III; there is an incomplete translation in Giddens (1986), *Durkheim on Politics and the State*.) This text was a public discussion which brought together, in addition to Durkheim, the leading geographer Vidal de la Blache, the professor of philosophy at the Sorbonne André

Lalande, two philosophers – Paul Desjardins and Frédéric Rauh, specialists in morals and education and teachers at the École Normale Supérieure – and others.

Interestingly enough, the discussion started with a typically Durkheimian ploy: the definition of the basic concepts to be used in the arguments. It will be observed that the need for these definitions, and the major disagreements that followed among the participants concerning Durkheim's definitions, show the confusion that existed at the time concerning the basic terms of reference.

Durkheim was well aware that the problem was both terminological and conceptual, that what was important was 'not to distinguish between words, but to succeed in distinguishing the things covered by the words' (1975b: 179). But now as then common parlance gets in the way and it is not always possible to redefine words or to coin new ones. What is at stake is the ability to separate human groups. Durkheim proposes to differentiate the following groups: political society, state, nationality, nation, *patrie* (fatherland) and *peuple* (people).

Political society and the state are closely related. Political society is the highest and most individualized secondary grouping; although it contains other human groups (family, professional groups, etc.) it is not incorporated into any other grouping (ibid.: 179). A political society which is centralized can be designated by the term state. Here Durkheim is merely pointing out that some political societies, what he would call primitive societies, exist without an organized central power.

If the state is somewhat unproblematic to define, the next concept is extremely difficult to pinpoint. Following established conventions of the time, he introduces the idea of nationality. He defines it as 'human groups which are united by a community of civilization, without being united by a political bond' (ibid.: 179–80). These groups are not political societies, and yet they possess some sort of unity. Durkheim believed that these groups had either been states in the past or were trying to become states. He refers to Poland and Finland (as well as to Germany and Italy prior to unification) as historical realities which should be labelled nationalities. At this stage I would only like to emphasize the ambiguity, and in the final instance, inadequacy of the term community of civilization when used to define the concept of nationality. In a note on the notion of

civilization Durkheim and Mauss (1913a(i)(1)) propose a definition of civilization which is much wider (Christian civilization,
Mediterranean civilization, etc.) than the one used here, and
hence of little use for the purpose of defining nationality.

Wherever the two groups, that is, the state and the nationality,
overlap, merge, or are absorbed into one, we have a nation.
Durkheim uses France as a perfect example of nation. Finally, to
explain the *patrie*, Durkheim introduces the idea of sentiment.
The *patrie* is the political society felt in a certain way; that is,
individuals feel 'themselves attached to it by a bond of sentiment'. We are here in the world of 'subjective impressions'.
Patriotism is then 'a sentiment that attaches the individual to the
political society seen from a certain viewpoint' (ibid.: 180).
Although Durkheim does not define nationalism, it is obvious
that it is perceived as an extreme, morbid form of patriotism.
In an article published in 1899, he had insisted that 'the
tumultuous manifestations of nationalism prevent us from
fostering, as we should, a more serious form of patriotism'
(1899b/t.1986a: 212). Strangely enough, the word *peuple* does
not appear at this stage in the Durkheimian vocabulary: it is only
used in the sense of 'those in a state that have no share in its
government' (1975b: 184).

The first problem encountered in the discusssion is the definition of nationality. Civilization is too vague a word to satisfy
the critics; Vidal de la Blache wanted to see economic facts
included in the definition of civilization, and Durkheim obliged.
But the term civilization still created problems because even
within France we can talk of a civilization of the Midi and of
a civilization of Northern France, as well as accept that there
is a civilization which goes beyond the confines of France. A
speaker suggested that nationality should perhaps be defined as
'a group of people that have common aspirations' (ibid.:181),
but Durkheim did not agree.

By far the most controversial definition proved to be that of
patriotism. Durkheim had initially limited it to the sentiment felt
towards the political society, in other words, the state. However,
in the course of the discussion it became obvious that patriotism
covered three different realities: the sentiment of an individual
towards the state to which he or she belongs, the sentiment that
one has towards the state that one would like to belong to, and

the sentiment that binds an individual to other individuals who belong to the same civilization. So there would not only be a patriotism of the fatherland and of the nationality, but even a patriotism towards the state that may be oppressing one's nationality. Durkheim was only willing to accept the first two.

A more precise definition of modern patriotism as 'an affective and moral bond whereby individuals subject themselves' to the fatherland or to the nationality was given. Durkheim believed that patriotism could be defined by its external characteristics, and that it was a quality that should not be predicated on sentiments which were directed to other human groups. However, there was still the problem of whether we could use terms such as local patriotism or regional patriotism.

The second document to be considered is entitled 'Internationalism and Class Struggle'; the discussion took place in 1906, and it involved a number of philosophers and socialist politicians. The main argument was between Durkheim and Hubert Lagardelle (founder of the journal *Le Mouvement socialiste* and member of the extreme left of the Section française de l'Internationale ouvrière) (Durkheim 1970a).

Lagardelle presented the traditional Marxist doctrine that the workers had no fatherland, that society was antagonistic and that if the bourgeoisie embraced the idea of *patrie* it was because they owned things, while the workers being totally dispossessed could do without the idea. Durkheim criticized the anti-patriotic stand adopted by revolutionary socialists, which he saw as the consequence of the belief that social reconstruction could only take place on the basis of the destruction of present societies.

Durkheim's main objective was to examine Lagardelle's proposition that socialism and destructive revolution go together. He offered three main arguments against it. First, Durkheim challenged the idea that the development of modern industry would lead of necessity to the destruction of the political society as we know it. He envisaged modern industry as part of the normal development of society: in fact, he visualized it as an extension of traditional local industry. There is no reason why the new economic regime should not be compatible with society; after all, there were juridical and moral institutions which were developing alongside the economic ones. Second, it was a weakness of revolutionary syndicalism to believe that the worker was only a producer; the worker also had a moral and intellectual life.

Finally, it was dangerous talk to want to destroy society. Is barbarism desirable? argued Durkheim. It may take centuries to reconstruct society (as happened in the Middle Ages). How can one want to wipe out realities such as Germany or France? When a society disappears, a civilization also disappears.

An additional point referred to the possibility of choosing the *patrie*. Durkheim accepted this choice but insisted that revolutionary socialists were not really in favour of such a choice, since for them all existing societies were capitalists and hence had to be rejected and destroyed. The right of the individual to choose his nationality cannot be denied, once the individual has satisfied the duties towards his native *patrie*. But to want to live without a society is totally impossible, because 'society is the moral atmosphere of human beings, whether they are workers or whatever' (1970a: 287).

The third and final discussion to be considered here is entitled 'Pacifism and Patriotism' and took place in 1907 (1908a(1)/ 1970a). In it a number of leading philosophers and sociologists of the period participated, including Dominique Parodi, Léon Brunschvicg, Ferdinand Buisson, Theodor Ruyssen and Xavier Léon. This is an important discussion, in that it gave Durkheim the opportunity to defend what he called 'open patriotism', and in which he tried, in Filloux's words,

> to reconcile the allegiance to particular nations, with the requisite of universality; pacifism and patriotism are not necessarily contradictory, if in the same way as the cult of the individual means the respect to the human being in general which exists in each individual, the cult of the nation is the love of one's society in abstract.
>
> (Filloux 1970)

The discussion started with a plague on both your houses: on the 'anti-patriot internationalists' and the 'patriot nationalists'. For the first group, international peace follows automatically due to the disappearance of the *patries* as a result of the development of capitalism; for the second, the preaching of pacifism dissolves the instinct of preservation necessary for the survival of society.

With arguments similar to those expressed in his discussion with Lagardelle, Durkheim insisted on the absurdity of the position that we can exist without a *patrie*. The fatherland is simply the highest organized society that we know. But here Durkheim introduces a new angle which is that of which sort of *patrie* we should wish for. Certainly, we all belong to a *patrie* towards which we have certain obligations, but there is another *patrie* which is in the process of being formed, and which encompasses our national *patrie*. Durkheim mentioned the European or even the human *patrie*. The question for Durkheim is whether we should strive to achieve these *patries* in formation, or rather, try to preserve jealously the independence of the *patrie* to which we belong (ibid.: 294).

In trying to provide an answer to this rather complicated question, Durkheim finds inspiration in the evolutionary framework, from the simple to the complex, which he had put forward since writing *Division of Labour in Society* (1893b). By reference to specific historical examples, both from modern times (the formation of the German state) and from the medieval period (the formation of France) he shows how small *patries* have merged into large *patries*, and the latter into still larger ones. There is no reason to believe that a process that has been going on for centuries would now come to a standstill. But in addition to seeing this process of evolution from small *patries* to large *patries*, he is also interested in the normative question of what one should do at present. His answer is to link pacifism with the process of evolution; in other words, to make sure that these changes from the *patries* of today to those of tomorrow proceed along peaceful lines, and no longer through violence and war as happened in the past (ibid.: 297). We should try to realize this new *patrie* of the future, which at present is only an ideal. So pacifism should not hesitate to embrace this ideal of a larger *patrie*, which will make peace possible within the confines of the new organized society. So Durkheim saw the creation of a European order (to which he already referred in *The Division of Labour in Society* (1893b)) as a precondition for peace in the continent; but for him this international society (and not that of the internationalists) once realized would be basically a *patrie*, an organized collectivity.

Another issue that concerned Durkheim is how to justify the love of fatherland when the empirical realities may point at imperfections or failures. And the answer to that was not to celebrate the virtues of one's *patrie*, or to claim superiority over other *patries*. A *patrie* could only be justified in such a way that the explanation provided was applicable to all *patries* without distinction. 'One must show in the *patrie in abstracto* the normal and indispensable milieu of human life', he said (ibid.: 300). Durkheim repeatedly castigated the kind of patriotism that placed France and its culture above everything else and insisted on a love of fatherland with abstraction of the concrete *patries*.

The next document to be examined is a short text entitled 'Civic morals and fatherland', which are the notes taken by a student (Armand Cuvillier) of a course that Durkheim taught in 1908–9 (1975b, III: 220–4).

The course reiterates most of the points made in the previous documents we have examined. However, a number of clarifications and additional points are presented.

First, Durkheim classifies societies into two types:

a) Unorganized and undefined (those which share the same civilization or the same unorganized faith). These societies have no organs or defined duties. As examples Durkheim cites German civilization, Lutheranism, etc.

b) Organized and defined. These can in turn be classified in societies which are part of other groupings (family, etc.) and those which are autonomous (political societies).

As to fatherland (*patrie*), which Durkheim had previously defined as a political society viewed from the perspective of a sentiment, he now sees it as a 'grouping which is able to impose certain defined obligations to its members' (ibid.: 221). A *patrie* only exists when the society is organized and norms are well defined. Its autonomous character is emphasized by the existence of borders. Durkheim envisages the border as the 'limit of the collective personality' (ibid). Borders are recent developments; in the past, there were either no territorial limits or they were only very vague. With the greater individualization of *patries* in modern times, borders become more permanent and fixed.

Following a well-established principle among French commentators, at least since Renan, Durkheim tried to keep *patrie* as separate as possible from community of culture. In fact, he textually says that 'in the idea of *patrie* the notion of community of culture plays no role' (ibid.). He has to admit, though, that 'countries which share the same culture tend to constitute a single *patrie*', although he insisted that 'it is an ideal, not a real *patrie*'. The community of culture is not even a sufficient condition for the *patrie*; it is only an auxiliary condition, and can even be totally absent (as the case of Switzerland proves). If culture is not decisive, what then constitutes the *patrie*? Following Renan, what Durkheim emphasizes is the community of historical memories, which in turn derives from the community of organization.

There is an additional reason to reject the community of culture as the essential element in the definition of *patrie*: in this way we avoid the chauvinism and the nationalist pride which considers one's own *patrie* as having the best civilization. This attitude, which is the result of ignoring other civilizations, leads to an aggressive nationalism and constitutes a danger to international peace. National exclusivism has to be excised from patriotism.

Finally, Durkheim sees perhaps a limit to the growth in the size of *patries*. He cannot quite envisage the existence of single world *patrie*. The idea of a single organized society is rather unthinkable because human affairs oscillate between diversity and unity (ibid.: 224).

The final document that I propose to consider at some length is *L'Allemagne au-dessus de tout*, published in 1915 (1915c). Durkheim's small book purports to be an analysis of a morbid form of patriotism – namely, nationalism understood as an exclusive and blind preference for one's own nation-state cum empire. Durkheim's objective was to depict the morbid character of the German spirit, of the German *mentalité*, which the First World War had made only too obvious. The major negative features of the German national character, such as aggression, inhumanity and contempt for international law, should not be envisaged as a result of war circumstances, but were implict in this mentality. Durkheim was eager to show that in modern times the Germans never belonged to the moral community of the civilized world. The exemplification of this mentality he found in Heinrich Treitschke's *Politik* (Durkheim used the second edition of the book, that of 1899). He considered Treitschke to be a typical representative of German collective ideas and sentiments. He was the author who had best expressed the mentality of his milieu: the Germany of the late nineteenth century. His ideas were extremely popular and were presented in an open and naked way; later, they were implemented insidiously by the German army and diplomacy during the war.

The crucial issue for Durkheim was the German conception of the nature and functions of the state as presented by Treitschke. Three points are worth emphasizing here. First, the state is above international law, that is, it is not bound by international treatises. War is inevitable and acceptable as the consequence of inter-state rivalries. If a state is not powerful, it will inevitably either be absorbed or become a satellite. Second, the state is above morality; the Machiavellian doctrine that the end justifies the means is the rule. Third, the state is above civil society and assumes that the duty of the citizen is to obey. I will examine these three points in succession and in some detail.

1 The state is above international law

Durkheim maintained that the German conception of the state was an extreme interpretation of the idea of sovereignty. Traditionally, the state was seen as sovereign in the 'sense that it is the source of all legal power to which citizens are subject to, and that it recognizes no other authority as superior' (ibid.: 7). Durkheim emphasized, however, that this sovereignty is relative because it depends on a variety of moral forces which, independently of their status, have a tangible effect on reality. Among those we can mention: treatises agreed upon, voluntary engagements, moral principles, public opinion, international opinion, etc.

In the German conception the state is totally self-sufficient and accepts no other authority above itself, except God or a mightier sword. The state has a highly developed sense of honour; any challenge against its domination or even any offence against its symbols (flag, etc.) has to be punished either by obtaining apologies from the offender, or if these are not forthcoming, by going to war. On the other hand, the state has no sense of long-term commitments to other states, except when it finds it convenient. In this conception of the state there is no sense of morality binding the parts that have signed a treaty. No international tribunal can be accepted, because this would be to limit the boundless sovereignty of the state. It follows, then, that war is the only available procedure to solve disputes among states (ibid.: 11). In fact, Treitschcke maintained that while states are sovereign, war is inevitable. 'Without war the state is not conceivable' (ibid.); the right to declare war is what distinguishes the state from other human groupings. War is moral and sacred; it is moral because it is the source of the highest moral virtues (heroism, sacrifice, etc.); it is sacred because it is the necessary condition for the existence of the state. War is the situation where individuals share with their compatriots a common feeling of self-sacrifice for something bigger that transcends them.

If the state, in Treitschke's words, is *Macht*, it follows that small and weak states will tend to be dominated by large and strong ones. Now what makes a state powerful is its army, and Treitschke considered it the 'cornerstone of society, the incarnation of the state' (ibid.: 14). The existence of small states which cannot defend themselves militarily is a remnant of the past; in fact, they do not deserve to be called states, and although tolerated today they have no reason for surviving in the future.

2 The state above morality

Durkheim maintained that morality is 'generally accepted as superior to the state' (ibid.: 18). Morality may consist only of ideas, but these ideas are forces (here there is a shadow of Fouillée's conception of *idées-forces*) which move and dominate men. For Treitschke the state is not subject to morality, and hence it is not human in Durkheim's terms. Treitschke emphasized that Christian morality had no 'fixed code made of inflexible precepts' (ibid.: 21). Christian standards cannot be generalized; the same act act done by two different persons is not the same in both cases. This way of interpreting Christian morality surprised Durkheim because it conveyed the wrong idea that there are 'no actions which are objectively good or evil' (ibid.: 22).

In addition, Treitschke maintained that humanity had no meaning, because no duties were derived from this concept; there was nothing outside the state. The *Deutschland über alles* meant that there was nothing above the German state: no ideal, no morality. Durkheim saw this attitude as a return to a form of tribal morality. Instead, he defended the morality of civilized nations which was based on Christianity and which had as its primary objective the realization of humanity (the increase of love and fraternity among humans).

To conclude this section, the state, according to Treitschke, has no other objective than the aggrandisement of its power and any means are acceptable to accomplish it. He was particularly brutal in justifying the oppression of colonial peoples with the argument that mentally inferior people have to be tackled with an iron fist; in his own words: 'he who knows not how to terrorize is lost' (ibid.: 25).

3 The state above civil society

In this section the state is opposed to the people (*peuple*) or to civil society (*die bürgerliche Gessellschaft*). What is at stake here are the relations of the state to its citizens, with the mass of the nation, with the people. For Durkheim, in a 'democratic society people and state are two aspects of the same reality' (ibid.: 27). The state is the people taking consciousness of itself, of its needs and aspirations. The state is a more clear and complete consciousness. For the Germans, on the other hand, state and people are clearly distinguished, and are even antagonistic.

Here Durkheim introduced the concept of civil society, which according to him is used by German authors (Treitschke included) to mean the opposite of the state. Civil society comprises the family, trade and industry, non-state religion, science and the arts. What characterizes all these different institutions is that they are voluntary associations which follow the natural inclinations of human beings. Now for Treitschke civil society is a mosaic of individuals and groups which pursue divergent aims, and the whole of these relations lack unity; the relations that arise out of these groups and individuals do not constitute an organism, a personality. So, for Treitschke, while the 'state is a unity, the civil society has no unity of will' (ibid.: 28).

It was in this context that Durkheim contrasted Treitschke's conception of civil society with the ideas of Niebuhr, Savigny, Latzarus and Steinthal – German scholars who in previous generations had attributed to the nation (conceived independently of the state) a sort of soul or spirit (*Volkseele*, *Volksgeist*), and consequently a personality. These authors had maintained that

a people, from the mere fact that it is a people, will have an intellectual and moral temperament, a character which will assert itself in every detail of its thoughts and acts, but in the formation of which the state will bear no part. This soul or spirit of the people will find expression in literary monuments, epics, myths, legends, etc. which without being created by any particular author, will have a kind of internal unity like the work of individuals. It is from the same source which derive those bodies of juridical customs, the first forms of law, which the state may codify later on, but does not create.

(ibid.: 28–9)

It is important to see in this long quotation from Durkheim's text a change of heart concerning his previous concept of the nation. He acknowledged that the German scholars of the past, by pointing out that these 'impersonal, anonymous and obscure forces' are important factors in history, rendered a scientific service to the understanding of the national question. Treitschke, however, rejects the conception of the *Volksgeist* as an 'abstract construction', and as a passing fad.

Treitschke's civil society is plagued with conflict at all levels; if it were left to itself it would result in the Hobbesian war of all against all. The state is the very opposite; it means unity, order and organization; and it is conceived as a person, with a self which is constant over time and a will. The state is essentially power; its natural tendency is to expand and dominate. To this conception, Durkheim opposed the idea that the state was, in fact, 'one of the most superficial aspects of social life' (ibid.: 31), much less important than economic life, the arts, technology, etc. He maintained that greatness did not follow from the might of the state, but from how civilized a society was.

The final point made in the book concerns the right of nationalities. It is interesting to note that here Durkheim offered a definition of nationality which, by emphasizing the ethnic element, was much more comprehensive than the one to which he had adhered before. He defined a nationality as a

human group whose members, either for ethnic or simply historical reasons, want to live under the same laws and constitute the same state (no matter whether big or small). And it is today a principle among civilized nations, that this common will, if expressed with perseverance, should be respected, but even that it is the only solid foundation of the states.

(ibid.: 40)

Now the German mentality is impervious to this idea of nationality, and it denies the rights of the small nationalities. In fact,
argued Durkheim, Germany never recognized the rights of nations
to dispose of themselves, and the goal of the German state has been
universal hegemony. With *L'Allemagne au-dessus de tout* we have
come full circle: the Germans, who appeared in the aftermath of
1871 as the heralds of ethnic nationalism, are shown in fact to have
adhered all the time to the doctrine of state imperialism.

CONCLUSIONS

In the light of the analysis of Durkheim's texts on the national
question, the following provisional conclusions can be
enunciated:

1 There is obviously no explicit Durkheimian theory of
  nationalism, but certain parts of Durkheim's corpus can
  be read as offering an implicit theory of some key issues of
  national identity.
2 Durkheim was a nation-builder. As one of the leading intellectuals of the Third Republic, he made a vibrant contribution to
  the shaping of the modern French nation. He can be seen, as
  Bellah put it, as 'a theologian of the French civil religion'
  (1973: xvii).
3 There is an undeveloped theory of the evolution of the *patrie*
  from the simple to the complex, from the Greek city-state to
  the modern nation-state.
4 Durkheim may have been a French patriot, but he was not a
  narrow nationalist (in the pejorative sense of the term as used
  in his time). However, his wartime writing (and particularly
  L'Allemagne au-dessus de tout) constituted an attempt to analyse
  morbid forms of patriotism, exemplified by a case study of
  the German mentality which conceives the state above international law, above morality and above the people.
5 In Durkheim's work there is a progressive recognition of the
  role played by cultural and ethnic factors in the shaping of
  nationalities. This is particularly obvious in his wartime
  writings where the theories of the *Volksgeist* are given
  prominence.
6 In the context of the European Community it is interesting
  to see Durkheim favouring a European *patrie*, and consider

that it is essential to build it if we want to achieve peace in Europe. The only way in which the humanitarian ideals could be realized in the context of Europe would be to channel patriotism towards achieving a higher morality at all levels, towards the improvement of society in general and towards fostering the development of artistic and scientific talents.

Chapter 7

A Durkheimian approach to the study of fashion
The sociology of Christian or first names[1]

Philippe Besnard
(Translated by H. L. Sutcliffe)

It is quite clear that Durkheim never referred to the choice of Christian names as a subject for sociology, even though he may have alluded to the problem of the transmission of 'names' in primitive societies.

Durkheim himself had two first names, David and Emile. David was the sign of his Jewishness (a characteristic which this name was to lose in France in the 1970s); moreover, it was the second of the first names of his paternal grandfather (the first was Israël). Emile, a Christian name, became Durkheim's habitual first name. It had been coming into fashion since the 1830s and 1840s, but did not reach its peak until the end of the nineteenth century when Durkheim, born in 1858, started to become well known as an academic.

This duality of first names seems, with hindsight, like an expression of Durkheim's intermediary position in his family lineage. Above him, there are nothing but typically Jewish names as far as the men are concerned, for example, his father's name was Moïse, and those of his grandfathers, Israël, David and Joseph Marx. Durkheim, who distanced himself from Judaism, was to call his daughter, born in 1888, Marie, a very conformist choice. It had been the most popular female Christian name in France for centuries and was given at the time to one infant girl in seven (not counting all the Marie-Louises, Marie-Annes, etc.). For his son, born in 1892, Durkheim chose André, a Christian name then fast becoming popular – a popularity which peaked in the 1920s, though it had been among the top first names from 1900 onwards. It was not even of Hebrew origin.[2]

THE CHOICE OF FIRST NAME AS A DURKHEIMIAN SOCIAL FACT

How can there be a place for the topic of first names in a book on Durkheim? But the topic does indeed belong here – at least, my aim is to show this. First names constitute very rich material which can be exploited, and which moreover benefits from being exploited, from a general Durkheimian, even a rigorously Durkheimian, methodological standpoint. Indeed, when dealing with this type of material, there is no need to introduce subtle nuances or slight adjustments into Durkheim's clearest formulations – those he has been most reproached for, those which have always been disputed, those which now seem outdated to many people, namely, 'Social facts must be treated as things' (1895a/t.1982a: 35). 'Social phenomena must therefore be considered in themselves, detached from the conscious beings who form their own representations of them. They must be studied from the outside' (ibid.: 70). We must not 'accept as such the causes that are pointed out to us by the agents themselves' (ibid.: 228). The sociologist has to break with the common-sense knowledge of the social world.

Statistical objectivization is one of the procedures that makes this break possible. It is particularly appropriate in the case of first names for various reasons, and the chief one is this. A phenomenological or ethnomethodological approach would miss the essential point of the most interesting social phenomenon, namely, the fashion which has governed the choice of first names in France for almost a century. How would one see this by limiting oneself to the reproduction of reasons, given by the actors themselves in deciding on first names for their children? One never encounters parents who announce that they have chosen a first name because it is currently fashionable. They will produce all kinds of other reasons, such as – often – long-established personal preferences, which they have had to accept in the face of the reticence displayed by the family circle; or attachment to a family, a religious or regional tradition. The sociologist may be interested in the reconstitution of the motives; but if he goes no further, he will have no idea of the social mechanisms underlying the giving of first names. This alone provides some indication of how Durkheim would have revelled in the topic.

The giving of first names possesses all the characteristics of a social fact as Durkheim thought or dreamed of it. This act is obligatory, but above all, its legal constraint is accompanied by less visible social constraints, of which the actors are only vaguely aware. To be sure, most parents have a spontaneous idea of the first names currently in use; moreover, it is this spontaneous idea which supplies the spring driving the rotation of preferences, and hence, the merry-go-round of first names. But this idea is false, vague and varies according to a number of social determinants.

DURKHEIM ON FASHION AND DIFFUSION

Fashion is one of the first illustrations Durkheim gives, in the early pages of the *Règles de la méthode sociologique*, of the 'coercive power' of the collective types of behaviour and thinking (1895a: 51). Thus, the sociological question of fashion and diffusion is not absent from Durkheim's work; it merely occupies a secondary place. Why is there this relative lack of interest? The reason is that Tarde's theory of imitation occupied the centre ground and Durkheim was to encounter the problem in the context of his polemic with Tarde. This is why he was to minimize its sociological importance.

The first chapter of the *Rules* on the definition of the social fact bears the hallmark of an obsessive reference to Tarde, even though Tarde's name only appears in a footnote. Durkheim proposes two definitions of the social fact. The first and best-known emphasizes 'the power of external coercion' which it exerts upon an individual and the sanction to which the individual exposes himself by not conforming to this constraint. The second definition is based on the notion of 'diffusion'; the word 'diffuse' is understood to be more or less the equivalent of 'general' or tending to become general or widespread.[3]

Let us quote the relevant text, originally stated in the earlier articles (1894a) but reworded for the 1895 edition of the *Rules*:

> However, it can also be defined by ascertaining how widespread it is within the group, provided that . . . one is careful to add a second essential characteristic; this is, that it exists

independently of the particular forms that it may assume in the process of spreading itself within the group.

(1895a/t.1982a: 57)

The original wording in 1894 was: 'It can also be defined as follows: a way of thinking or acting which is general within the group, but which exists independently of its individual expressions' (1894a: 474).

The new formulation is more abrupt than the original one. The 'individual expressions' clearly look as though they are derived from the social fact. The use of the word 'diffusion' perhaps stems from the position that this definition could appear to contradict what was said earlier, namely, 'It is not the fact that they are general which can serve to characterize socio-logical phenomena' (1895a/t.1982a: 54). However, Durkheim returns to the word 'general' when he summarizes the two definitions at the end of the chapter.

When he wishes to illustrate the usefulness of this dual defi-nition, Durkheim quotes fashion not as an example of diffusion but as an example of constraint, together with law, morality, beliefs and customs. The second definition may be useful when constraint is less 'clearly discernible'. However, Durkheim adds that these two definitions are one and the same: 'this second definition is simply another formulation of the first one: if a mode of behaviour existing outside the consciousnesses of indi-viduals becomes general, it can only do so by exerting pressure upon them' (ibid.: 57).

This dual definition enables Durkheim to take a stand against 'the ingenious system of Tarde' in the footnote attached to the sentence we have just quoted, namely:

> Doubtless every social fact is imitated and has. . . . a tendency to become generalized, but this is because it is social, i.e. obligatory . . . One may speculate whether the term 'imi-tation' is indeed appropriate to designate a proliferation which occurs through some coercive influence. In such a single term very different phenomena, which need to be distinguished, are confused.
>
> (ibid.: 59)

What are these different phenomena? Durkheim answers this question in *Suicide* (1897a). An entire chapter is devoted to the task of rejecting, in an extremely brutal fashion, Tarde's theory of imitation. Here is the climax of the polemic, at least on Durkheim's part.[4]

Durkheim's strategy is clear: to distinguish various different phenomena which are confused, and which Tarde confuses, under the same word, 'imitation', in order to reduce the field of application of the concept to virtually nothing. Durkheim believes he can distinguish three different meanings of the word 'imitation'.

Imitation No. 1 is reciprocal imitation or reciprocal influence as it would be called today. This is the process by which there emerges a sentiment common to persons gathered together both in a crowd – a favourite example of Durkheim in this passage – and in a small group. In this, Durkheim sees 'a highly social phenomenon', even if 'we have only a vague idea of what it is' (1897a/t.1951a: 130; 130n.10).

Imitation No. 2 might be termed imitation-fashion, since the reference to fashion is the first to be used by Durkheim.[5] He immediately adds 'customs' (*usages*) and 'legal and moral practices', since they are 'merely defined and well-established customs (*usages*)' (ibid.: 124–5).

For these first two forms of imitation, Durkheim refers to Tarde, who is explicitly quoted in imitation No. 1 and almost explicitly designated in imitation No. 2, by reference to his celebrated distinction between imitation–fashion and imitation–custom.

Durkheim cannot refer to Tarde in connection with imitation No. 3, which is the only one, he considers, that merits the name imitation. It is automatic reproduction, pure contagion. There is imitation, writes Durkheim, and he emphasized this definition:

> when the immediate antecedent of an act is the representation of a like act, previously performed by someone else, with no explicit or implicit mental operation which bears upon the intrinsic nature of the act reproduced intervening between representation and execution.
>
> (ibid.: 129)

Durkheim has some difficulty in illustrating imitation thus defined. Apart from the literary reference to Panurge's sheep, he provides only two examples: collective laughter, tears or yawning and the more questionable example of 'the thought of homicide', which 'passes from one to another consciousness' (ibid.: 125). Also, Durkheim several times uses the expression 'mimicry' (*singerie*) to characterize imitation No. 3. The term is a poor choice, for to mimic (*singer*) someone is to imitate that person in either a caricatural or clumsy manner: in either case, there is indeed a thought process and a desire to reproduce. It is therefore apparent that Durkheim is hard put to illustrate or describe this pure imitation, this 'contagion', which is supposed to be the only true form of imitation and which 'consists only in more or less repeated repercussions (*ricochets*) of individual phenomena' (ibid.: 132).

To limit imitation, to reduce the sphere of application of this notion to almost nothing, is patently Durkheim's aim. This is why he is so eager to distinguish clearly the three types of imitation and to show that they are three totally different phenomena. It is easy for him to separate type No. 1, reciprocal influence, from the other two types. As for imitation No. 2, it is distinguished from true imitation because it supposes a thought-process, the bringing into play of 'judgments and reasonings, implicit or explicit' (ibid.: 129). In fact, conforming to a fashion or a custom (*coutume*) or to a moral practice, is '*to act through respect or fear of opinion*' (ibid.: 127. Durkheim's emphasis). Like reciprocal imitation, imitation No. 2 is an eminently social phenomenon, 'being due to the obligatory nature and special prestige investing collective beliefs and practices' (ibid.). Only imitation No. 3, true imitation, depends not on social causes but individual conditions.

In this long and slightly repetitive passage, Durkheim is perhaps less sure of himself than he appears to be. He repeats the same arguments in searching for the ideal formulation as though trying to convince himself. A footnote reveals his predicament: 'It may well happen, in individual cases, that a fashion or a tradition is reproduced by pure mimicry; but in that case, it is not reproduction as fashion or tradition' (1897a: 113 n.1. Translation by H.L.S.). In another note, imitation No. 2 is linked to that which stems from 'the moral or intellectual prestige of the original actor, whether individual or collective, that serves as a model'. In his eyes, it is not automatic and 'implies reasoning' (1897a/t.1951a: 129). A little further on, he proposes a distinction between the epidemic viewed as a social phenomenon and contagion viewed as no more than the repetition of individual facts. All these notations help to throw doubt on the contrast Durkheim claims to draw between imitation No. 2 and imitation No. 3, between fashion and contagion.

In reality, this contrast is very difficult to translate into practice. How are the conscious, semi-conscious, unconscious and automatic elements in the adoption of a new item of clothing, or some linguistic mannerism, to be distinguished from one another? Durkheim himself is incapable of maintaining this distinction when he seeks to refute Tarde's thesis empirically, in other words, the theory of imitation reduced to meaning No. 3, by means of a cartographic study of suicide.

The refutation runs as follows: the maps show that suicide 'occurs in great . . . homogeneous masses and with no central nucleus' (ibid.: 137). If the theory of imitation were well-founded, then foci or central nuclei should be found from which the process of contagion would spread. These nuclei should be the capitals, the large cities, because they are visible points, 'cynosures' (ibid.: 134), and also because the great centres are endowed with moral authority. Yet, according to Durkheim, nothing of the kind is found. In Paris, from 1887 to 1891, for example, there were fewer suicides than in the neighbouring *arrondissements*.

Tarde might have retorted that diffusion occurs over time and that a cross-section cannot measure this phenomenon. He might also have observed that, in his argument, Durkheim was confusing imitation Nos. 2 and 3 which he had been at such pains to contrast. More precisely, Durkheim claims a) to refute Tarde by reducing the notion of imitation to something Tarde does not mention, i.e., imitation No. 3, and b) to refute the explanation of suicide by imitation No. 3, using arguments aimed at imitation No. 2.

FIRST NAMES AS STRATEGIC RESEARCH MATERIAL

To deal with the problem of diffusion from a Durkheimian standpoint, one has to be disloyal to this Durkheim who, carried away by his polemic with Tarde, introduces a clear-cut conceptual distinction between two types of imitation, namely, fashion and contagion. This distinction is based on an element from the domain of individual psychology that Durkheimian methodology cannot take as the point of departure for investigation, namely, the individual's awareness of conforming to fashion. In the case of sartorial fashion, one can accept that this awareness exists, however vague. It is much less clear in the case of the adoption of an ephemeral linguistic mannerism. The most interesting phenomena of fashion are those where the individual has no awareness of having the same preferences or of making the same choices as other people; choosing a first name for one's child is one such case.

Since the precursors or founders of sociology – Tarde, Spencer, Simmel – who saw in 'fashion' a central social fact or at least, like Durkheim, the most direct example of the role of the social in individual behaviour, the empirical study of the phenomenon has not progressed. The reason for this is that sociological or para-sociological discussion of the phenomenon has identified it, following popular usage, with sartorial fashion, if not with the clothes themselves. The literature has become entangled in clothes. Yet fashion in clothing or finery is a particularly impure example of the fashion phenomenon understood as the ceaseless, cyclical transformation of the preferences of the members of a given society. First, because the parameters of supply and income are involved in the choice of an item of clothing. But above all because everyone knows (perhaps vaguely) that it conforms, more or less, to the collective trend of the moment. Durkheim drew attention to this in the early pages of the *Règles de la méthode sociologique*. He referred to the sanctions of 'laughter' or 'social distance' which anyone would be likely to incur, if in his mode of dress he was at complete variance with 'what is customary in [his] country and in [his] class' (1895a/t.1982a: 3).

It is quite a different matter where the choice of a first name for one's child is concerned. Here, how far my choice conforms to that of others is not merely unknown; it is even feared. However, individual choices are not merely random. When they are added together, they form the 'collective taste' of the moment – something that Durkheim would not have hesitated to term a 'current of opinion' or some other *sui generis* social reality (as he was fond of putting it).

In order to remain faithful to his methodology, which consists in giving preference to the external, consolidated, objectivizable aspects of the phenomenon being studied, there is no need to venture into this ontological ground, upon which Durkheim sometimes seems to settle. First names, as I shall endeavour to show, are especially well suited to this approach. In my view they are what Merton, in a recent article, calls 'strategic research material'. By this, Merton (1987: 10) means 'the empirical material that exhibits the phenomena to be explained or interpreted to such advantage and in such accessible form that it enables the fruitful investigation of previously stubborn problems and the discovery of new problems for further inquiry' (ibid.: 10). Such a definition may perhaps be deemed a trifle ambitious for first names. But it does not prevent me from laying claim to the epithet 'strategic', though using it in a different sense. This material for research makes it possible to defend and illustrate the necessity for a sociological standpoint, which brings us back to Durkheim's chief preoccupation.

We are perhaps no longer at the stage of the emergence of a discipline. But who can fail to see that the very basis of this discipline is seriously in jeopardy, notably by virtue of the imperialism of economic reasoning?

Let us start with the most apparent traits and advantages of this material.

Choices of first names are objectivized by being recorded in legal or population registers. They are acts, not intentions or replies to questions one does not ask oneself, at least not in these terms.

Since the recording of first names is mandatory, no category of individuals giving first names can elude properly compiled statistics. The ritual criticisms of official statistics, such as the concealment of certain suicides, the social labelling of delinquency, for example, simply do not apply to this material.

Although the first name is a commodity whose consumption is mandatory, it is also gratuitous. It is gratuitous in the two-fold sense that its choice is not determined by objective utility, like that of a medicine, and that it does not cost anything. This latter characteristic is a decisive advantage for sociologists. When they become interested in the social diffusion of an innovation or a new product, sociologists, as they proceed, encounter economists, who show that it is income and not some class culture or other nebulous sociological notion which explains the vertical diffusion of this commodity. And rare indeed are the choices one makes in the course of a lifetime that do not involve a

financial parameter. This material, therefore, makes it possible
to gain access to taste stripped bare of cost and, by so doing, to
put to the test the genuinely sociological model of hierarchical
diffusion, a model commonly accepted by sociologists for a
century, from Simmel (1905) to Bourdieu (1975; 1979), but
whose relevance has scarcely been verified for want of suitable
data. The hypothesis of a temporal hierarchy of the social mar-
kets may find sustenance in common impressions or may even
find verification where the propagation of consumer goods is
concerned, whose acquisition entails a financial cost. Yet the
sociology of tastes postulates this trickling-down of diffusion
without establishing the means to confirm it. In short, first
names are a material particularly well suited to one of
Durkheim's methodological aims: 'to refine out the social fact
from any amalgam and so observe it in its pure state' (1895a/
t.1982a: 55).

The elective affinity of the first name and of fashion also stems
from the dominant motivation – inasmuch as it can be recon-
structed – of the parents giving the first names, at least since the
first name has been chosen rather than handed down. The
choice falls within a spectrum, which varies according to individuals and their social position and ranges from the commonplace to the eccentric. It responds both to the desire to
individualize the child, which leads to the exclusion of over-
popular first names, and to the desire not to choose extravagant
ones, which in turn leads to the exclusion of excessively unusual
first names. The phenomenon of fashion is born precisely from
this tension between originality and conformity. It may be added
that this choice is not an insignificant social act and that it
increasingly forms the stuff of discussions both within the family
and outside it. This perhaps stems from the growing importance
of the first name which, until recently, was not used (certainly in
France) as a term of address except in intimate relationships.
Now it has become a central component of social identity.

One final advantage of first names may be mentioned. They
are well suited to the study of cycles of taste or 'fashion'. Even
though enriched by various novelties or foreign first names, the
stock of possible first names is relatively stable. Hence, the time it
takes for a first name, once having disappeared after a period of
popularity, to re-emerge and become fashionable again can be
measured unequivocally. This task is much more difficult, not

to say impossible, where dress or decoration is concerned. By reconstituting the career of a first name over a long period, one can follow the progression from the eccentric to the distinguished, then to the commonplace, then to the vulgar, then to the old-fashioned, then to the antiquated. After it has spent a long period in purgatory the adventurous pioneer, sensitive to its period charm, will unearth it. The duration of the period depends on its former success.

THE LIFE-CYCLE OF FIRST NAMES

And so to the results actually achieved by the statistical study of first names. The first investigation of first names used in France since 1890 was based on large representative samples produced by a number of surveys conducted by the Institut National de la Statistique et des Études Économiques (on mortality, families and employment), supplemented by samples of birth certificates in the register of births, marriages and deaths. First or Christian names of 2.5 million people were used. This survey resulted in a book (Besnard and Desplanques 1986) and made it possible to reconstitute the career of every first name in use since 1930. It therefore became possible to break down the trajectory of every first name into sections, determined by how far ahead or behind fashion the choice was, in other words, the first name's diffusion in time. The procedure makes it possible to substitute the unit represented by the first name for the unit represented by the position of the choice in relation to fashion. Thus, it was possible to ask: Was the choice far ahead of its time? Innovative? Conformist? Outdated? And so on. One can therefore work on a smaller scale and with more manageable samples, like certain ongoing studies, which should substantially refine results already obtained. We will confine ourselves here to mentioning some of the general results which seem to us to merit most the attention of sociologists.

All the first names which have enjoyed a degree of success since 1930 are first names of the 'fashion' type: they follow a curve of diffusion in time, which is normal or virtually normal, and are in general distinguished by a certain asymmetry on the right-hand side. This indicates that the period of decline of a first name is, in general, longer than its period of ascent.[6]

The frequency attained by these first names of the fashion type when at their peak is rather variable, ranging from 1 per cent (in other words, the first name is given, at its peak, to one boy out of 100 born in France or to one girl out of 100), to over 7 per cent, examples being Michel in the 1940s or Nathalie at the end of the 1960s.

There are virtually no truly 'classical' first names, in other words, names whose frequency is stable in time over a long period. In the twentieth century, François and Hélène are those which most closely approximate to the classical type; but their success is quite modest. In France there are no very popular first names which are classical. However, there is a not inconsiderable number of first names whose career is intermediate between the fashion trajectory and the classical trajectory. These classical-tending first names do not generally exceed the level of 1 per cent.

The life-time of fashionable first names is becoming shorter and shorter. The period involved, however, varies considerably. Nicolas 'emerges' eight years after Sébastien, yet reaches its peak four years later and succeeds it as the most popular first name. Isabelle enjoys less startling success than its contemporary Nathalie, but its career lasts longer. Traditional first names stand up to use better, even when captured by fashion, than new or nearly new first names.

After their 'death', first names of the fashion type go through a period of purgatory, varying according to the success they have had, at the end of which they can be reborn. Cycles can thus be observed lasting 150 years for the most popular first names, but perhaps appreciably less for names which have only enjoyed modest popularity. The great traditional first names take even less time to come back into vogue.

It is also easier to account for our dislikes than our likes. A first name will thus necessarily be abandoned, because it is considered unaesthetic, if it meets three conditions, namely, 1) its career has been brilliant in that it has achieved a high frequency; 2) it has been concentrated in time around a peak; and 3) this peak is situated between ninety and forty years prior to the time of the observer.

VERTICAL FLOW AND HORIZONTAL FLOW

The statistical study of first names corroborates the classical model of vertical social diffusion. First names spread from the top of the social scale downwards. 'Senior executives and professionals' are the quickest off the mark in the pursuit of fashion, followed, in this order, by the 'intermediate professions', 'craftsmen and shopkeepers', 'salaried employees', 'blue collar workers' and last of all 'farmers'. Since what we are dealing with here is a gratuitous commodity, this corroboration is an important one. It shows that, in the hierarchical diffusion of commodities, there is a genuinely social element, which cannot be reduced simply to income.

However, together with this vertical flow in the diffusion of fashion, allowance also has to be made for a horizontal flux stemming from the frequency of contacts with other people. This is no doubt the origin of the special place occupied by 'media, arts, cinema and theatre people', who have a clear lead over other professional people. The same can be said of the lead of shopkeepers over craftsmen or social workers over technicians. Where social position is comparable, the degree of sociability produces a sizeable difference.

Since the 1970s, this social trajectory of first names has tended to alter and diversify. Farmers have almost made up the gap. And many new first names are seen to spread simultaneously, or virtually so, in all social groups. Many of these find their most fertile ground among the working classes. As a rule, such names are Anglo-American imports (Anthony, Christopher, Kevin, Cindy, for example). Conversely, certain first names which come back into fashion (always taken from the traditional French repertoire), tend to remain confined to the upper classes and do not gain an absolutely secure foothold amongst the population at large. The horizontal flows, which are internal to each social category, are increasingly gaining ground at the expense of the vertical flows. Hitherto, social divisions were essentially expressed in the form of a time-lag in the adoption of the same first names; now they tend to be revealed by different choices of first name. If this trend towards increasing social diversification in the choice of names persists, it would call into question the customary diagnoses of the homogenization or standardization of the social palette of tastes and colours, whose distinctions mass society is supposed to level out.

Moreover, a study of the diffusion of first names puts paid to all spontaneous or commonplace interpretations of the fashion phenomenon. An explanation based on the influence of famous personalities, real or imaginary, does not stand up to serious examination. To confine oneself to just one example already mentioned, Brigitte Bardot has had nothing to do with the success of the name Brigitte. On the contrary, her fame hastened its decline, for it had become too visible and was therefore perceived as too commonplace.

Even television does not have the impact commonly attributed to it. The recent vogue for Anglo-American first names probably stems from the massive diffusion of American soap operas, which retain the characters' original first names, pronounced more or less as in English. But it should be emphasized that this influence is diffuse and not direct. It operates through impregnation, which accustoms the ear to the exotic sound of the English or American first names and not through mechanical transmission of the first names of the characters or actors in the best-known soaps. Evidence of this is the recent success of the name Audrey or the current triumph of the name Kevin, which first appeared in France in 1979 and which, since 1989, has been the most popular first name for French infants.

In general, the effect of the media is, above all, one of amplification, and it is very hard to find unequivocal examples of their role in the launching of a first name, particularly as the choices of the authors of films, songs and novels also conform to the emergent collective taste, though anticipating it to varying degrees.

Everything, therefore, encourages one to see in the merry-go-round of first names, that is, in the cyclical development of preferences, an endogenous – or, as Durkheim would have put it, *sui generis* – process with its own dynamic. This is probably also the case in other registers of taste and it is only second-rate journalists who are capable of seeing everywhere – be it in songs, the colour of walls, the length of skirts, styles of furniture, linguistic mannerisms or ideological trends – diverse expressions of 'the spirit of the times'. The spirit of the times, if such exists at all, is not the generating principle but the result of the cross-fertilization, at a given moment, of these many processes. To postulate the existence of a Supreme Clockmaker, linking together or synchronizing these processes, would be to lapse into a species of sociological hyper-realism which Durkheim himself would surely not have endorsed.

NOTES

1 Certain parts of this text have already been published in French in *Recherches sociologiques*, 22 (3), 1991.
2 The first names of Durkheim's nephews and nieces were Marcel and Henri (Mauss), Henri (Durkheim), Albert, Paul and Juliette (Cahen).
3 As we know, Durkheim also uses the word 'diffuse' (*diffus*) through-out his works in a quite different sense, by contrast with 'differen-tiated' (*différencié*) and 'organized'(*organisé*).
4 Yet Tarde had greatly facilitated Durkheim's task. As head of the legal statistics department, he had sent Durkheim the individual files of people who had committed suicide in France in 1889 and 1891. It should be noted that the excellent presentation by Stephen Lukes (1973) of the Durkheim–Tarde debate curiously contains only one brief reference to *Suicide*.
5 The English translation of *Suicide* systematically renders *mode(s)* by 'manner(s)'. This is particularly unfortunate when Tarde's distinction between fashion (*mode*) and 'custom' (*coutume*) is concerned.
6 Moreover, this tendency towards the asymmetry of the curve is difficult to fathom. It is not observed in all cases. The asymmetry is most marked for first names whose life-span is short. It is more frequent for female first names which, moreover, do not, by and large, last as long as male first names. In certain cases, the asymmetry is inverted: the period of ascent is longer than that of decline. Yet these anomalies are understandable. A first name with a specific regional origin takes time to spread throughout the country and its national decline is rapid once it has travelled round the whole of France. What is more interesting is a case where the success of a first name (i.e., when it is at its peak) coincides with the success of a character bearing this name. A good example is that of Brigitte and Brigitte Bardot. In this case, the first name's visibility was so great that parents quickly turned their backs on it.

Appendix

Items by Durkheim relating to anti-semitism

Introductions by W. S. F. Pickering

(*Translations by H. L. Sutcliffe*)

1 DURKHEIM AND DAGAN'S INQUIRY INTO ANTI-SEMITISM

Introduction

During the height of the Dreyfus Affair in 1899, Henri Dagan published a small book of just under 100 pages, *Enquête sur l'antisémitisme*. Its purpose was to help diffuse the then high wave of anti-semitism raging throughout France, and more precisely 'to inform the public of the intellectual attitudes of cultured people in connection with one aspect of the social conflict' (1899: vii). So it was that, encouraged by Dagan, twenty-one intellectuals expressed their views on anti-semitism: they were writers, politicians, and academics of various disciplines. Among the better known names were Emile Zola, Albert Réville, Lombroso, Charles Gide, Garofalo and Durkheim.

Dagan, a Jew, and by profession a sociologist, had published two not very well-known books, *Les sociologues contemporaines* and *Essais sur les questions sociales*. Sociologist or not, his selection of informants for the inquiry was obviously subjective. Each person selected was either interviewed or else asked to submit a written reply. There were no German-speaking respondents: Germans and Austrians were perhaps not invited to submit their views, or they did not reply. Anti-semitism was at that time much more virulent in Germany than in France. The only English contribution was from Sir John Lubbock, writing from the House of Commons. He, together with the Italian contributors, held that in their countries there was no anti-semitism as there was in France. Surprisingly, in the conclusion, Dagan stated that the replies he had received showed that French anti-semitism was not due to religious, ethnic or political causes. By contrast, he emphasized economic ones. Conflicts in France which involved Jews were, he argued, due to capitalism (ibid.: 84ff.). No one could deny the fact of capitalism but it existed, according to him, without reference to any doctrines, to ethnic characteristics or political forms. That Jews did well within the capitalist system merely showed they had an aptitiude for making money, not for being originators of the system. Anti-semitism is therefore no panacea for the evils of capitalism which engenders revolutions and other forms of conflict. To be rid of Jews will not drive away such problems. Quite clearly Dagan offers little more than a scapegoat theory for anti-semitism based on capitalist evils.

How did Durkheim's response fit in with the general trend of the contributors and with Dagan's conclusion? First, along with other writers, especially Jewish, he distinguished French anti-semitism from that of other countries, notably of Germany and Russia, where the phenomenon is seen to be traditional and lingering (*chronique*) (and see Marrus 1971: 99). France had led the way in emancipating Jews and was seen as a Jewish haven. This was not the case in Germany and Russia. In France, therefore, in Durkheim's eyes, the contemporary situation was unique in that anti-semitism had emerged from an acute internal crisis which was directly due to the Dreyfus Affair. He agreed that such anti-semitism was due to the need for a scapegoat, not, as with Dagan, to placate a public incensed against the injustices in capitalism but to assuage more general feelings of failure and dissension in the country itself. In 1870 the Jews, especially in Alsace, were blamed for the French defeat at the hands of the Germans; and Durkheim, as a Jew, could testify to it by what he had seen while he was living in Épinal. Further, Jews were said to be behind the 1848 Revolution. The position in France for them in the 1890s was indeed acute. Behind these events, Durkheim argued, was a social malaise, and for this, blame once again fell on the Jews. Some would argue by implication that the simple and complete cure would be to eliminate the Jews. For Durkheim, there was also a panacea: it was the reverse –

eliminate the social malaise and anti-semitism will wither away. But he added that the solution will not come about in a day. In the meantime simple practical measures had to be undertaken.

Durkheim looked for an optimistic solution – a truly liberal position – in believing that Jews will be happily assimilated into French culture (see Chapter 1). Assimilation was relatively easy, according to Durkheim, since the ethnic qualities of Jews disappeared extremely quickly, even within two generations. Such optimism was not shared by Theodor Herzl and his followers in the Zionist movement who held that the very social structure of Europe contained an eternal vein of anti-semitism. That structure, it might be added, was based largely on Christianity. What happened in later decades, and especially in Vichy France, shows how naive Durkheim was. But he was not alone in his optimistic attitude. According to Marrus there was a general tendency, say in the middle of the nineteenth century, to assert that anti-semitism was an anomaly in France and 'did not fit into the life of the nation' (1971: 99). What France had done at the time of the French Revolution, in creating Jewish emancipation, made most people believe that the issue was now closed. But then the Dreyfus Affair broke out. There had been plenty of warning in the writing of Edouard Drumont (*La France juive* (1886)) and others, and in the growth of anti-Jewish journals and societies. (Incidentally, in the appendix of Dagan's book there are interesting comments on anti-Jewish journals of the time.)

Durkheim was not original in separating French anti-semitism from that in Germany and Russia. Others, such as the anti-semitic writers Maurras and Drumont, had made the same point. But, soaked in a fervent nationalism, some saw the German empire, and particularly Bismarck, as being the root of French anti-semitism. It was a German import – 'the anti-semitic virus' (ibid.: 99; see Chapter 6). To assume that anti-semitism was a German product was one way for French Jews to demonstrate their loyalty to, or identification with, La Nation. Durkheim's originality was to suggest that the 'cause' lay not in the economic state of France and its capitalist mode of production, nor in the religion and ethnic qualities of Jews, but in an internal moral malaise. He does not use the word anomie as he did in other contexts but the word might be loosely applied. The crux of the argument is to know how far French people at the time, including political leaders, were also aware of a prevailing condition of social malaise and whether this could be established as a social fact. And if so, whether it was in fact the major cause of French anti-semitism. It is a subject which needs careful documentation.

Dagan's survey, limited though it was, is of considerable value, not only in showing various views of intellectuals about anti-semitism in France, but in pointing to debatable and so far unresolved issues. Durkheim's contribution is particularly valuable in revealing attitudes he held but did not commonly express.

A contribution to Dagan's survey on anti-semitism (1899d)

(First published in French in H. Dagan, *Enquête sur l'antisémitisme*, Paris: Stock, 1899, pp. 59–63)

To discuss anti-semitism properly, replies M. Émile Durkheim, would require a certain amount of research, which I have not done. So I can only give you an impression.

To begin with, I think a distinction needs to be drawn between French anti-semitism and anti-semitism in other countries – two phenomena which strike me as meaning very different things. The proof of this is that the countries in which anti-semitism is the most deep-seated have completely failed to grasp the significance of recent events in France. In my view Germany did so grudgingly; yet Russia, which is above suspicion, nevertheless manifested the same disapproving surprise.

If it was so surprised and shocked, the reason is that, in the passions then stirred up in France, it could find nothing in common with its own feelings.

What to me seems to differentiate these two attitudes is the fact that German or Russian anti-semitism is chronic, traditional, whereas ours is an acute crisis brought about by chance circumstances. The former is aristocratic in character, composed as it is of haughty disdain. Ours draws inspiration from violent, destructive passions, which seek any and every means to gain a foothold. Moreover, it is not the first time the phenomenon has surfaced in this form.

It was already observed in eastern France during the war of 1870. As I am of Jewish origin myself, I was able to observe it on that occasion at close quarters. It was the Jews who were blamed for the defeats. And in 1848, an explosion of the same type, albeit much more violent, had occurred in Alsace.

These parallels substantiate the conclusion that our present anti-semitism is the consequence and the superficial symptom of a state of social malaise. This was the case in 1870 as it was in 1848 (in 1847 there had been a very grave economic crisis).

When society is ailing, it feels the need to find someone to blame for this ill, someone on whom it can take out its disappointments; and those who are already out of favour with public opinion are tailor-made for the role. It is pariahs who serve as expiatory victims. What bears out this interpretation is the nature of the reception reserved for the outcome of the Dreyfus trial in 1894. There was an outburst of joy in the streets. What should have been an occasion for public mourning was celebrated as a success. So now at last everybody knew whom to blame for the economic crisis and the moral anguish from which they were suffering! It was the Jews who were the source of the ill. This fact was now officially recognized. By dint of this alone, everything suddenly seemed better and people felt somehow reassured.

Secondary factors may well also have played a role. The vaguely religious aspirations which have just surfaced may have benefited from this development; certain defects of the Jewish race have been invoked to justify it. But these are secondary causes. The shortcomings of the Jew are offset by undeniable qualities and, though better races there may be, there are some which are worse. Moreover, Jews lose their ethnic characteristics extremely fast. Two more generations, and the process is complete.

As to religious causes, suffice it to note that faith was no less strong twenty or thirty years ago; yet anti-semitism was not then what it is now.

So above all, anti-semitism is one of the many clues which reveal the serious moral disorder from which we are suffering. The true way of curbing it would therefore be to put an end to this state of disorder, though this is not achieved in the space of a day. However, there is something which can be done immediately and which is urgently needed.

If the ill cannot be struck at its source, then at least this special manifestation which exacerbates it can be controlled. Precisely because we need all our strength to recuperate, it is vital not to waste it in futile battles.

One does not allow a patient to take revenge upon himself for his sufferings and to tear himself apart with his own hands.

To bring about this result, all incitement to hatred by one citizen against another should first be severely curbed. Repressive measures alone would doubtless not be enough to change attitudes; however, they would remind the public conscience, which is beginning to forget, how odious such a crime is. Then, while theoretically censuring anti-semitism, steps would have to be taken to ensure it was not granted any of the real satisfactions which encourage it; and the Government would have to undertake to enlighten the masses as to the error in which they are being encouraged and would have to do so in such a way that it could not even be suspected of seeking allies on the side of intolerance.

'Lastly, instead of resting content with platonic censure, all men of good sense' should 'have the courage to express their feelings out loud, and join forces to ensure victory over public madness'.[1]

As we see, M. Durkheim's impressions are bound to arouse the keenest interest. The author of the *Division of Labour* and the *Rules of Soociological Method* here treats us to a lesson in social psychology which even a M. Tarde would probably not disown . . .

Note

1 It is difficult to know why this paragraph appears within inverted commas. Is it a literal quotation from Durkheim's reply? If so, what has gone before must be a résumé by Dagan of what Durkheim wrote. Or, is it what Durkheim said in an interview? Or, is it a quotation, pertinent to what Durkheim wrote or said, and given without a source?

2 DURKHEIM AND THE COMMITTEE FOR RUSSIAN REFUGEES

Introduction

'I am also concerned about the Jewish question in Russia, which I am studying for the first time.' So Durkheim wrote in a letter to

Xavier Léon in 1916 from a hotel in Biarritz (20 April 1916; in
Lukes 1973: 557). He had gone there to try to recover from a
bout of overwork in Paris but, above all, from the news confirm-
ing the death of his beloved and only son, André, killed in the
war at Davidovo in Bulgaria, on 5 December 1915. But why was
he studying the Jewish question in Russia? One may now hazard
a guess that it was the result of being the vice-president of the
Committee – Durkheim was in fact the senior person in later
meetings – whose report is translated below. The first meeting under the president, Brelet, conseiller d'État, was at the
Préfeture de Police. That no one has considered that the reference in the letter was related to the report of the Committee on
Russians living in the Département of the Seine has been due to
the fact that it has only recently come to light. After being
hidden in the archives of the Préfeture de Police in Paris for
many years, it appears, it was eventually published in 1990
(see 1990a). Without doubt Durkheim was prominent in draft-
ing the report, which was not signed by any one person. The
Committee, consisting of four members, came into being as the
result of a government order dated 26 December 1915, and
the ensuing report was submitted in the remarkably short time
of perhaps less then two months, in February 1916. The issue
at stake was whether the Russian population of Paris, put at
30–40,000, could be said to be loyal to the cause of the Allies,
expressed not least in volunteering for the Army. As many as 95
per cent of the Russians in the Département were Jews. The
Committee had as its obvious concern issues relating to anti-
semitism. English readers might wonder why the Russian
emigrants should have to volunteer for service in the French
Army and were not conscripted. Conscription in France dates
from the time of Napoleon: the law has never been rescinded. It
applies to French citizens only and not to immigrants who have
not become citizens. The latter can, however, volunteer. When a
war progresses badly, as was the case in 1915, the greater
is the pressure on friendly aliens to volunteer. The Committee
had to answer the allegations that the Russian refugees were
not supporting the country in which they were living: in short,
they were not suffering as much as the French and their allies.
The Committee brought to light cases of Russian volunteers
being maltreated, especially those drafted into the Foreign
Legion. There were doubtless several reasons for this. The

Foreign Legion had always recruited a good number of
Russians, and presumably non-Jews. Jews at that time were
reckoned to be poor fighters and it was probably on account of
their Jewishness that the volunteers in this case were given such
a bad time at the hands of gentile officers. But one must not
forget the fact that there were a good number of Jewish officers
in the national army – something which became generally
known at the time of the Dreyfus Affair. Around 1915 and 1916
a wave of anti-semitism broke out in France and doubtless one of
the reasons for calling the Committee was the hope that it would
show that France could still be seen to be a safe place for Jews to
live in and to be accepted as good citizens (see Chapter 1). The
ideals of freedom and equality which inspired the 1789
Revolution could thus be seen to be still being put into practice.
Strangely enough, while Durkheim was working with the
Committee, he was himself the subject of attack by anti-semitists
(Lukes 1973: 557, and also for some of the details which follow).
In a show of hostility in *Libre Parole* on 19 January 1916
Durkheim was accused of being a German agent. It was a very
cruel blow because just a few days before, on 10 January, he had
received the terrible news that André had been officially
declared missing. That Durkheim and his wife had an inklng
that such news was on its way did nothing to soften the blow.
Again, just after the Committee had finished its work, another
attack was launched against him in March in the Senate asking
that the Committee concerned with residence permits of foreigners should examine the case of Durkheim to see whether or
not he was a German agent. A Government minister, Painlev,
replied and defended Durkheim by pointing to his great sense
of patriotism, not least in writing a much-admired pamphlet
about the war and about the German responsibilities for it
(1915b or 1915c). Painlev's speech of defence received great
applause in the Senate and the statement of accusation had to be
withdrawn. The publication of the report has cleared up an
obscure reference to Durkheim in the writings of Trotsky mentioned by Lukes and brought to his attention by L. S. Feuer
(1973: 558n.60). Trotsky in *Against Social Patriotism: An Open
Letter to Jules Guesde* stated that Durkheim was president of the
Committee for Russian Refugees and was able to tip off Trotsky
that the Government of the day was preparing to expel him and
his fellow workers from France, and was also likely to suppress

Nashe Slovo. It was obvious that Durkheim was very sympathetic to these groups, as indeed Lukes notes. The identity of this heretofore unknown Committee has now been revealed and Trotsky's statements about Durkheim in these matters seem quite justified. As one might expect, the position over the Russian refugees in the Département of the Seine was much more complicated than anyone might have thought. Some refugees had migrated to various countries, not least the States, where they had been met by German friends, and the word had got around that France was anti-semitic. Meanwhile, Germany was claiming that it offered full rights to Jews. And let it not be forgotten that at this time the United States had not come to the aid of the Allies. The report argued that the Russian refugees were not the only aliens whose patriotism might be challenged. Why, therefore, harass the Russians, that is, Russian Jews? It put forward one practical suggestion – why not employ those who refuse to volunteer in the Army as tailors and artisans? Research on the report still has to be undertaken. One would like to know, for example, how widely, if at all, the report was distributed and what influence it had. And on whom? Nevertheless its coming to light furthers our knowledge of Durkheim's involvement with the state and with Jewish affairs.

Report on the situation of Russians in France in 1916 (1990a)

(First published in French as 'Rapport sur la situation des Russes en France', in 'Émile Durkheim, défenseur des réfugiés russes en France', presented by N. Elkarati, *Genèses*, 2 décembre 1990, pp. 168–77)

February 1916
Chairman of the Aliens Committee
to the Minister of the Interior

Minister,

When, on 8 January last, we came to discuss with you the work of our Committee, we had the honour to put it to you that, before individually summoning Russian subjects resident in the Department of the Seine for interview, it might be useful to undertake an overall examination of the situation. A preliminary survey of this kind seemed essential to us if subsequently we were to discuss matters with those concerned

on a sound basis. You kindly gave us a free hand with regard
to conducting this inquiry. We now beg leave to present you
with the results; for the facts which have thus come to our
knowledge would appear to be of such a kind as to shed new
light on the matter.

The campaign against aliens of Russian nationality, and
more particularly against Russian Jews, who represent some
95 per cent of the colony, actually dates from well before the
war. All kinds of reasons were instanced, varying according to
circumstances, in support of the demand that they should be
removed from the capital. Sometimes it was the singularity of
their customs and language, and sometimes the outbreak of
an epidemic for which they were held responsible; they were
even presented as troublemakers (*Bulletin municipal*, meeting
of 3 January 1911). But the advent of war brought a fresh
accusation against them, one to which public opinion was
naturally to prove highly sensitive. They were accused of
systematically refusing to do their duty with respect to both
their country of origin and their country of residence;
and since it was no doubt felt that this reprehensible absten-
tion was not just a matter of isolated individuals, of the sort
found in all types of groups, but was generalized, collective and wholesale, measures were demanded to put
an end to what was deemed a scandalous state of affairs. It
was under the influence of this feeling that the Municipal
Council of Paris formally recommended the creation of our
Committee.

Our initial task was to investigate how far this complaint
was warranted.

I

As soon as hostilities took a threatening turn, the societies of
Jewish émigrés launched an enthusiastic appeal to fellow
Jews, pointing out all that Judaism owed to France. 'If we are
not yet French by law,' it was stated, 'we are so in heart and
soul and our most sacred duty is to place ourselves forthwith
at the disposal of this great and noble nation in order to play a
part in its defence. Brothers, it is time to pay our debt of
gratitude to the country in which we have found moral emancipation and material well-being. Jewish immigrants, do your
duty. Long live France!'

This appeal was heeded. As soon as the military authority declared itself ready to accept volunteers, large numbers of Russians came forward to enlist. According to a memorandum communicated to us by the Ministry of War, 3,393 Russians had been enrolled in the Foreign Legion by 10 December 1914. This figure, which is already a high one as it stands, is certainly less than the true number of enlistments. To begin with, from August to December 1914, large numbers of people who had enlisted had already been either killed or discharged as sick and wounded. Also, in 1915, people continued to enlist, even though numbers soon started to fall off for reasons given below. If the number of men having enlisted since the start of hostilities is put at 3,500, the actual figure is sure to be substantially greater. It should also be added that many Russians resident in Paris had returned to Russia to do their military service there.

But this only gives us the number actually allowed to enlist. To gauge the size of the subsequent reaction in the Russian colony, those who offered to enlist but were turned down on the basis of the medical examination, must also be taken into consideration. According to a note published in *Le Temps* of 24 August 1914 (page three, column two), the ratio was 57 per cent. It also emerges that over 6,000 Russians (8,139 according to the calculation) came forward to enlist in the French Army. This figure represents over one-fifth of the 30,000 to 40,000-strong Russian population of Paris.

Hence, on the outbreak of war, there was an impressive wave of enthusiasm among Russians in Paris. And to get a proper measure of the sacrifice these spontaneous enlistments represented, it should be borne in mind that the bulk of the volunteers, among the Jews especially, were poor workers. In the fourth *arrondissement*, there are now large numbers of families in a state of abject misery because the head of the household is serving in the Army. One person visiting them for charity purposes said it was impossible to understand how these hapless individuals managed to survive. There are 1,750 Jewish soldiers of foreign origin serving on the Front who need the assistance of the aid committees set up for this purpose. There may well be Poles and Romanians among them, but it is the Russians who predominate. Lastly, one organization recently founded, which has assumed responsibility for the upbringing of Jewish war orphans without means of support, has already taken in about a hundred Russian children whose fathers have been killed by the enemy.

Regrettably, a number of deplorable incidents occurred to dampen this enthusiasm. As you are acquainted with these incidents, Minister, there is no need to detail them here. However, we must draw attention to them when appropriate in order to show clearly how one thing led to another.

The volunteers were enrolled in the Foreign Legion. While carefully refraining from any hasty or unwarranted generalization, we know that in certain places the Legionnaires showed themselves to be content with their lot. This was the case, for example, of those who were sent to the Orléans depot, where the benevolent and paternal command of Colonel Adam de Villiers produced excellent results. But this can scarcely have been the rule. Certain officers had absolutely no idea of the very special conditions in which these volunteers found themselves. They were treated as ordinary Legionnaires, or perhaps even more harshly still. They were daily accused of having enlisted solely 'for the grub'. Insults and ill-treatment finally rendered their lives intolerable. 'It's hell,' wrote one of them, a very cultured young man, to his father. In vain did they request the right to transfer to ordinary regiments: their requests were turned down. However, a state of rebellion was brewing which an ugly incident one day brought to a head. Twenty-seven Russian soldiers, all of whom said they were prepared to serve in a French regiment, refused to obey their superiors in order to attract the attention of the High Command. They were court-martialled; seven received the death sentence and were executed. They died courageously, shouting 'Long Live France! Long Live the Army. Down with the Legion!'

Naturally, we are not seeking to pardon a manifestly culpable act. But the fact nevertheless remains that this tragic scene, which might perhaps have been foreseen and avoided, could not but kill off the original enthusiasm. And this should not be forgotten if the current situation in the Russian colony is to be judged fairly. Moreover, the Government acknowledged the error which had been committed since, in the wake of these painful events, it granted the Russian volunteers the right they had been demanding for so long: if they did not prefer to return to Russia, they were allowed to enlist in metropolitan regiments. All but about 400 accepted. Alas, the harm had already been done.

Also, other complaints had meanwhile been added to this central one, thereby only compounding its effect.

1. Some of the Russian volunteers were quickly invalided out. However, it would seem that it was quite exceptional for them to be granted a Class 1 discharge. The Chairman told us that, out of 92 discharged soldiers receiving assistance from a charity, 90 received a Class 2 discharge. Hence only the following were granted a Class 2 discharge:
   GRILICHEN, 42, Boulevard Rochechouart, whose right hand has been paralysed by two bullets which shattered the bones and whose right leg is semi-paralysed;
   NAPTALOVITCH, 25, rue des Rosiers, who has lost an eye, and is also in serious danger of losing the other;
   TINTEROFF, 7 passage Bullourde, who lost his hearing during an exchange of gunfire;
   ELGEL, 88, rue Basfroi, wounded in the chest and suffering from anaemia owing to heavy loss of blood;
   DE MORGUIEVITCH, 24 rue Trousseau, whose left leg was shattered.
   We shall confine ourselves to these few examples, though we have also been told of other similar ones which it would be easy to check. We do not believe that French soldiers as seriously wounded as this would be treated in the same fashion.
2. Only 8 of the 92 families of the persons discharged just referred to receive help from the State in the form of a benefit, and two in the form of unemployment benefit. In most cases, we are told, the families of Russian volunteers only receive assistance thanks to private initiatives.

A number of other instances of unequal treatment have also been reported to us, which we feel it would be pointless to dwell on.

Moreover, we ourselves have not been able to investigate these secondary grievances: our funds would not allow it. But in order to ensure that you have before you all the evidence in the case, we shall confine ourselves to setting it out according to the testimony we have received.

II

One overriding fact is consistent. The Russian population did not display the collective indifference it was accused of and, if the enthusiasm of the early days was not maintained, we ourselves are partly to blame.

But it was not enough to have established that a considerable section of the colony offered to go to the front or actually did so. We also had to find out whether, among those who remained behind, there were many who, in normal circumstances, should have been in the army.

To investigate this, we used the surveys conducted on your instructions by the police last July. In the 10 Paris Districts, just over 4,000 Russian nationals, representing that section of the population between 19 and 43 years of age, were summoned and questioned. However, a substantial number of them did not appear because they had either already returned to Russia, left for the provinces or gone abroad, particularly to America, Spain or Britain. Also, in the ninth district, only a list of names and addresses was compiled; if any people were interviewed, there is no record of it now. Lastly, only 3,108 individuals were actually interviewed. On the basis of their replies[1] they can be divided into three different categories, as follows:

1 Persons complying with military law.
Persons not currently eligible for service in Russia
(liberated, discharged, exempted, not called up,
deferred, etc.) 1,303
Political refugees not entitled to serve 182
Persons enrolled in the French Army, turned down
and deferred at medical review, or discharged as
medically unfit 795
 Total 2,280

2 Persons not complying with military law or refusing
to serve.
Deserters, draft-dodgers 124
Persons rejected from all service 416
 Total 540

3 Miscellaneous cases.

Persons whose intentions are doubtful 147

Persons working in the trenches 41

    Total 188

4 Persons willing to enlist in the French Army
(but not the Foreign Legion) 100

Hence, over two-thirds (71 per cent) of the 3,000 persons questioned were blameless.

In the first place, this includes those whose situation was legal under Russian law, because they had been excused from duty, liberated, or not yet mobilized, etc. There may be some in this category who are young and healthy, which is the case of only sons who are completely excused from duty under Russian law if they are orthodox, in which case, if they are also Jews, they are placed in the second category of the militia (not yet called up). However, there is no question of pressurizing them to do service, since the law of their native country exempts them from it. The conditions imposed upon them in France should not be harsher than those they would be legally entitled to in their own country. Otherwise, the same demands would have to be made on Belgian and British nationals resident in France who, under our recruitment rules, would be liable for mobilization even though exempt from it under their own law.

The same applies to political refugees *who do not even have the right to serve in the Russian army*. As their native country has deprived them of the honour of bearing arms, it is scarcely for us to make it a duty for them. Indeed, some of them who presented themselves in Russia for military service were imprisoned, some even sent to Siberia.

Lastly, 795 individuals were either enrolled in the French army and were thus illegally summoned by the police, or discharged as unfit, rejected or, at the very least, deferred at the medical examination. They cannot be called on either, for they have done their duty.[2]

Finally, representations could only be made to the 418 Russians who, for various reasons (often health grounds or domestic responsibilities), have refused to serve in both Russia and France. To these could be added the 124 draft-dodgers or deserters, despite the fact that many of them must, in all probability, be political refugees. If one also adds the 147 [illegible], whose evasive replies are probably just lame excuses barely concealing their intention to do nothing, this produces a total of 687 individuals, representing the maximum possible number of active soldiers in the Russian colony in Paris.

But this maximum is wholly theoretical. Supposing all of them, convinced by what they were told, presented themselves for service, the number rejected on the basis of the medical examination would be substantial. In August 1914 it was 57 per cent. It is unlikely that it would be less than this, since it was the elite of the population who were the first to enlist. Supposing it were 50 per cent, or even 40 per cent, that would make 343, or at the most 413 new soldiers who, in a few months, would end up serving either on our front or the Russian front.

In reality, there would only be a minute number or perhaps none at all. For if, in July, only 100 declared themselves willing to enlist, not without reservations or reluctance, and notwithstanding the fact that they may sometimes have been threatened, how many would there be today, now that the Russian colony has been reduced by the numerous departures occasioned by all these measures, now that it has lost its best men in those accepted as volunteers, and lastly, now that enthusiasm to enlist has dwindled for reasons we have explained?

III

When you did us the honour of receiving us, Minister, one of us drew your attention to the serious consequences of summoning people to report to the police stations in 1915 and of the inquiry launched by the police. These measures triggered off real panic among the Russian population. Thousands of refugees hastily departed for America or Spain. There, they were taken in by the friends of Germany and everywhere presented as the living testimony to French anti-semitism. 'Exile in France,' wrote the New York newspaper *Die Warhat* (14 July 1915), 'is a new chapter in the tragic history of Jewish emigration. The first living witnesses arrived yesterday on the *Rochambeau*; the 160 Jews who disembarked have all been expelled by the glorious Republic . . . They told us that nearly

10,000 had left Paris for Spain or America . . . The French police are acting at the instigation of the Russian Embassy, giving the Jews an ultimatum – either leave the country or enlist.' We conveyed[3] our concern to you that summoning people to police stations, as the Committee was instructed to do, might have the same effect.

The facts have borne out our apprehensions. Once the creation of the Committee became known, a fresh commotion broke out in Russian circles. The departures resumed. An article appeared in the *Judische ArbeiterKorrespondenz* of The Hague, with the revealing title 'Die New [*sic*.] Anti-semitische Hetze in Paris' (The New Anti-semitic Persecution in Paris, December 1915). Letters arrived from America inviting Parisian Jews to leave in order to escape this new persecution. Not without difficulty, we managed to calm this agitation. We succeeded in getting it across to those concerned that the powers of the Committee set up by you were laid down by the very terms of the reply you sent to Deputy Montet on 1 July 1915. Despite the comments of a press which has set out to maintain a level of disquiet that manifestly runs counter to the country's interests, we eventually managed to gain a little trust. But, abroad, the damage has already been done and it will take more than words to check it.

Yet circumstances could not be more unfavourable. American society is already excited to fever-pitch by anything that touches on the Jewish question. This feeling is due, in part, to the events which took place during the Russian retreat last summer, which it is pointless to go over again here. The recommendation recently addressed by the American Senate to President Wilson, the terms in which this recommendation was formulated, the President's reply, and the institution of a Jewish Day, are further flagrant manifestations of this state of mind. Germany is therefore conducting an ardent, active campaign to win over American sympathies by announcing that she is firmly resolved to defend the rights of the Jews at the peace congresses; she is taking advantage of the attacks in which a section of our press is indulging in order to present France as having been won over to the politics of pogroms.[4] And all this at a time when she is negotiating a loan from the United States and when we, too, are preparing to do the same. Everything which – even apparently – serves to harass the Russian Jews can only make her path smoother and make success for us harder to achieve.

This being so, there is every reason to believe that summoning Russians resident in Paris to appear before our Committee, and bringing any pressure to bear on them, albeit morally justified and paternalistic, would inevitably be interpreted abroad in a way contrary to French interests. There would be no shortage of reasons to justify this interpretation, even speciously. It would be said that France was insidiously violating the right of asylum; that the alternative it seemed to be giving to political refugees and religious refugees was a mere trick. Neither group has any freedom of choice, for if they return to Russia, they are bound to expose themselves to imprisonment or to fresh persecution respectively. The very fact that the measures concerned have been demanded by a notoriously anti-semitic party will be enough to give them an imprint that no subsequent explanation will be able to efface. Lastly, when it becomes known that, out of love for France and out of gratitude for hospitality received, over 8,000 Russians spontaneously volunteered to defend her at the beginning of the war, and that many of them gave their lives for us (it was for us that they volunteered, after all), our country is bound to see itself accused of ingratitude.

Clearly, these very serious drawbacks cannot be offset by the few uncertain benefits possibly ensuing from a handful of new volunteers, which moreover would be problematical and at all events few in number. Hence, looking at the matter from a purely French standpoint, the solution would not seem to call for any hesitation. It is probably natural for the wives and mothers of persons mobilized to exhibit some emotion on seeing young men, belonging to an allied nation, free of all utilitarian obligation. But this is because they are unaware of the numerous exemptions or deferments provided for under Russian law (except for the classes of 1916, 1917 and 1918 mobilized in advance). By virtue of all these various exemptions, many of the young men, although in good health, are fully in compliance with the military authority of their country. Moreover, as we have pointed out, *the Russians are not the only ones in this category; why, then, should they be the only ones to come in for harassment?* Another point is that all the investigations and exhortations in the world could not remedy the situation, unless backed up by coercive sanctions, the idea of which has been dismissed.

To the considerations set out above, whose gravity will not escape you, Minister, allow us, if you will, to add two subsidiary remarks.

To begin with, when we obtained the reports drawn up by the police after the July interviews, we were at a loss to see how the task we had been asked to perform differed from the one performed by the police. They had summoned all the Russians between 19 and 42 years of age, questioned them about their military situation and their readiness to serve in either of the two armies. The replies were entered beside the names of all of those summoned. We are at a loss to see what more we could do and in any case what purpose it could serve were we to begin the work again.

Secondly, we must point out to you that, regardless of how it is carried out, this work could only produce extremely rough and ready results. For many Russians living in Paris are completely unable to establish their military situation on a regular footing for want of the necessary documentation. This is patently the case of the political refugees, for in Russia, anyone who is arrested, subjected to administrative deportation or simply sought by the police, finds himself deprived of all identity papers during the first police raid. They are confiscated. As for the religious refugees, most of them are also without identity papers, since they had to leave Russia in secret or in haste. Apart from this, the Russian Consulate refuses, or at least was refusing until quite recently, to concern itself in any way whatever with Russian subjects whose papers were not in order. Very often, we would be obliged to accept the replies given to us, without it being possible to verify them in any way. This is what the police did and we could but follow their example.

IV

To sum up, contrary to what has been alleged, the Russian colony, taken as a whole, has done its duty. France can be proud of the feelings of gratitude she has inspired in her guests. Of course, in that population of 30,000 to 40,000, there may be and certainly are some mediocre elements on whom noble and generous feelings have no purchase. But we have seen that they are few in number. At all events, their behaviour in this respect is a matter of opinion, of moral conscience, not of action by the authorities. Moreover, we were unable to conceal grave errors that may partly serve to excuse them. By seeking to exert moral pressure on them, regardless of what kind it is, we lay ourselves open to suspicions and accusations which could easily be given some semblance of justification and could only serve the cause of our enemies. We would run the risk of losing sympathies whose value for us is of quite a different order from the small number of new units with which we might enhance our front.

These, Minister, are the very serious facts that we submit for your consideration. We cannot help thinking that, had the representatives of Paris known them in their entirety, their view would have been different. This is why we considered that there were grounds for bringing them to your attention without further delay.

However, far be it from us to maintain that there was nothing useful that could be done.

1 Many Russians who, for family or health reasons (for the state of health of this population leaves something to be desired), are not prepared to do active service, could very usefully be employed as tailors, workers in war factories, etc. We are assured that an appeal to that effect would have every chance of a favourable reception.
2 If the idea is to encourage further people to enlist, the only way would be for the Russian Government to agree to an amnesty for political refugees. Such a measure would have every chance of triggering off an impressive national movement.
3 Moreover, we readily admit that the foregoing considerations do not apply identically to the young men who, born in France of Russian parents, repudiated French nationality on reaching the age of majority. This is a very special situation, but it is not our task to examine the very complex issues it raises and which are not related to the Russians alone. Moreover, we do not know whether, in the Russian population, there are a lot of young men in this category.

We scarcely need to add, Minister, that should the explanations we have given call for further details, we are entirely at your disposal. We could come and provide you with them personally and discuss the matter with you. But if, contrary to our hopes, the facts we have presented to you do not seem convincing, then may we make one last proposal? We feel we have established that there is an international aspect to the question. It is therefore of direct interest to the Foreign Affairs Committee. Might there not be a case for consulting this Committee then?

Yours etc.,

Councillor of State,
Chairman of the Committee

Notes

1 We explain why, in many cases, these replies have to be accepted at face value and cannot be checked. This is a cause of imprecision which, as we shall show, cannot be avoided however this subject is approached.
2 Except perhaps those deferred who might have been able [illegible].
3 [Misprint in French; '*exprimons*' for '*exprimions*'. H. L. S.]
4 [Presumed misprint in French; '*programmes*' for '*pogromes*'. H. L. S.]

3 DURKHEIM'S MEMORANDUM OF 1916 ON RUSSIAN REFUGEES AND CONSCRIPTION IN BRITAIN

Introduction

The following memorandum, written by Durkheim on 14 July 1916, proceeds directly from the Report of the Commission which has just been presented. It furnishes more details about the Paris Commission, such as its members, and the results of its report. It is not clear to whom the memorandum was addressed, but it was clearly intended for Lucien Wolf, who passed it over to Herbert Samuel, the British Home Secretary at the time (Wasserstein 1992: 214–15).

Lucien Wolf (1857–1930) was a political journalist who had some influence over leaders of his day. He was Secretary of the Conjoint Foreign Committee drawn from the Board of Deputies of British Jews (founded in 1878) and from the Anglo-Jewish

Association. Born in England he was the son of a Bohemian Jew, very much an Anglophile, but also greatly concerned with Eastern European and Russian Jews. It is not surprising therefore that Durkheim should have been asked by the Commission to express their fears over Russian refugees in Britain and the problems of anti-semitism to such a person as Wolf.

Herbert Samuel (1879–1963), born into a wealthy Jewish banking family, was a prominent Liberal. He was Home Secretary during the First World War from January to December 1916. His religious convictions, like those of Durkheim, bordered on agnosticism, but unlike Durkheim, he was a strong supporter of Zionism and became the first High Commissioner of British-ruled Palestine.

In the early days of the Great War Britain relied entirely on volunteers for the army and navy. Early in 1916, however, owing to heavy losses on the Western Front and the need for more men, conscription was introduced for those who were single and aged between 18 and 41. Herbert Samuel, who was responsible for the legislation, was opposed to having too wide a loophole for conscientious objectors and saw the need to judge individual cases. He was opposed by many fellow Liberals who felt that conscription was a denial of civil liberties. Durkheim noted that the tardiness of the British to introduce conscription showed it was a controversial subject.

For Russian refugees conscription raised particular problems (ibid.: 213–15). Many of the refugees were socialists, they were nearly all Jews and had fled from Tsarist Russia. The many thousands who had been allowed to settle in Britain had not taken out British citizenship because of the considerable cost. They were theoretically liable for military service in Russia but greatly feared returning to that country because of personal reprisals. Very few volunteered for the British Army, unlike the numbers recruited to the French Army from Russian refugees. In Britain only sons of citizens of the realm could enter the Navy. Initially Russian refugees could not be conscripted and the taunt of the white feather was most applicable to those who had enjoyed the protection of Britain but who did not volunteer for the Army in the hour of crisis, either in Britain or in Russia. Trouble arose in 1916 in the East End of London between Jews and non-Jews and also within the Jewish community. Samuel was forced to intervene and found himself in a difficult position

as a Jew and as the Cabinet member responsible for aliens with
the duty of promoting British interests. In Parliament on 29
June of that year he offered Russian refugees the choice of
conscription in the British Army or returning to Russia for
military service. The speech caused much protest but on 11 July
he reiterated the choice and referred to the existence of tribu-
nals. More protests arose and it was at this time that Durkheim
penned the memorandum. Samuel remained intransigent despite the opposition. Later he slightly relented by pressing for
immediate voluntary service which by October received only a
feeble response. The measure was eventually passed by
Parliament and the result was that a few hundred refugees
returned to Russia and about the same number joined the Royal
Fusiliers (ibid.: 219 n 6). The issue was never pushed to its
logical conclusion. But through it Samuel lost the confidence of
a number of fellow Liberals.

Durkheim's concern for the welfare of Russian Jews in both
France and Britain was that they should be accorded human
rights and also that their presence, their actions, and government legislation would not give rise to anti-semitism or encourage it. Further, any such legislation should not be seen to have
been caused by anti-semitism. In all this Durkheim was acting
both as a Jew concerned for Jews and as a humanist. It appears
that in England, at least, his fears were groundless for as a result
of the legislation introduced by Samuel, no great surge of anti-
semitism emerged (but see ibid.). It merely underlines what
appeared earlier in the Appendix, namely, that anti-semitism
was not as pronounced in Britain as it was in France, nor was the
position of Jews the same in each country.

But Durkheim had another objective. He feared that a harsh
treatment of minorities, especially Jews, would encourage
Germans to maintain that they, the enemies of the *Entente*, were
the true supporters of civil liberties, not their foes, who could be
labelled as anti-semitic. There was also the question of American
hostility towards Britain and France – countries which could be
denigrated as oppressive. America had welcomed 'oppressed'
refugees who felt compelled to leave Paris. Such unfavourable
attitudes were politically undesirable in the face of the French
and British wish that America should join the *Entente* in giving
its full support to the war.

Note

The British Centre for Durkheimian Studies is very grateful to Dr David Feldman of Birkbeck College, London, for bringing to its attention the existence of this memorandum. It is located in the documents of Lucien Wolf in the Daniel Mowshowitch Collection, Yivo Institute for Jewish Research, New York. The Centre also thanks the trustees of the Collection for permission to translate the memorandum. The French text appeared in 1993 in *Durkheim Studies*. This document as it is found in the Wolf Collection is typewritten with hand-inserted accents, which suggests that the original memorandum was hand written by Durkheim – he never used a typewriter – and that he wrote the memorandum from his Paris home. Where it was typed is difficult to say. Durkheim's handwriting was extremely hard to read and one would imagine that Wolf would have had the memorandum typed. Yet the pages are numbered from page 109, suggesting that the typing might have been done especially for the Wolf collection, either in Britain or in the United States.

'Note on the measures aimed at forcing Russian refugees in Britain to enlist in the British Army or rejoin the Russian Army (1993a)

(A translation of 'Note sur les mesures ayant pour objet d'obliger les Russes réfugiés en Angleterre à s'engager dans l'armée anglaise ou à rejoindre l'armée russe', from the David Mowshowitch Collection, New York.)

It should be noted to begin with that in France, similar but much stiffer measures have been demanded by the anti-semitic party. I shall explain below why they have not been implemented. But if they are adopted by the British Government, there is no doubt that the campaign of anti-semitism, which has ceased over the past five months, will in this connection start up again. Indeed, it has already done so since Mr Samuel's speech has become known.

Here are the very serious objections raised by these measures:

I. In July 1915, under pressure from the anti-semitic party, the French Government announced that Russians in Paris eligible for mobilization were going to be summoned to present themselves at police stations. It was immediately stated that no force would be brought to bear on them; the police were only to inquire about their military situation and invite those who would

have had to serve, had they been in Russia, to do their duty. But
again, this invitation was to be no more than an appeal to their
consciences.

Immediately these measures were announced, and despite
their innocuousness, they had the effect on this nervous population of imminent persecutions. Many Russians emigrated to
America and Spain. On disembarking there, they were welcomed by the friends of Germany and presented as the living
testimony to French anti-semitism. (See on this point the New
York Yiddish newspaper *Die Warhat* of 14 July 1915 and the
article entitled 'Die neue anti-semitische Hetze' in Paris in the
Yuedische Arbeiter-Korrespondens of October 1915). Letters arrived
from America urging Parisian Jews to flee this persecution by
leaving France.

It scarcely needs saying how sensitive American society is to all
aspects of the Jewish question, to everything which is or even
smacks of persecution of the Jews. Moreover, it is clear how
vitally important it is for us to humour American opinion,
especially Jewish American opinion. It was to influence this
opinion in the Allies' favour that our Comité d'Action et de
propagande chez les Juifs neutres was set up. These measures
were thus harmful to our cause and ran counter to our
Committee's aim. This is what made us decide to intervene in
the manner described below, to prevent what seemed to us an
enormous blunder.

II. Moreover, it has to be acknowledged that the measures
demanded by the anti-semites which Britain seems about to
adopt, do raise major objections of a general nature.

They are an insidious violation of the right of asylum. In fact,
Russians resident in France, like those resident in England, are
either political refugees or religious refugees. Hence, the
alternative it seemed they were being given was merely a trick;
for they had no freedom of choice. Their return to Russia was
bound to expose them either to imprisonment (in the case of the
political refugees), or to renewed persecution (in the case of the
religious refugees). It is *necessarily unjust* to treat men forced by
religious or political persecution to flee their country as men
who have left it voluntarily. That is a very special situation,
which it is impossible not to take into account.

Political refugees do not have the *right* to do military service in
Russia; so how could we compel them to do so here? As the

victims of pogroms, religious refugees do have the right to serve in Russia. But they would have to return there in order to avail themselves of this right. Experience has proved what awaits them there if they do.

It will be said that the Russians owe something to the country having offered them asylum. This cannot be denied. But it is a debt whose settlement *manu militari* we do not have the right to demand. We do not demand it of Romanian Jewish immigrants. Why should we demand it of Russian Jews who no longer have any vestige of Russianness? Yet refugees offered asylum in a country are not citizens of that country. Nor do they share all its duties, for they do not enjoy all its rights.

Are we to allow the Germans, and the pro-Germans in America, to become the champions of these ideas, champions of the cause of the right of asylum, and present us, France and Britain, to the neutral countries as the persecutors of the Jews? Even if these persecutions were no more than apparent, that alone would be too much.

III. These various reasons seemed telling enough to the French Government for it to rule out coercive measures as a matter of principle, and simply appeal to the conscience of the Russians.

The measures announced by the British Government would be open to still more serious criticism than those which could be levelled at the French Government. It would be said that the British people had shown greater leniency towards themselves than towards the hapless foreigners to whom they had granted hospitality. It took them over a year and a half to make military service compulsory for themselves: their hesitation showed that they regarded it as controversial. And, from one day to the next, only two months after voting in favour of conscription, they would be seeking to impose it on foreigners who are not British citizens.

The contrast would be shocking. The pro-Germans would have a field-day.

It remains for me to explain how the measures demanded in France by the anti-semites came to be deferred *sine die*.

I was saying earlier how, in July 1915, the Russians were summoned to the police stations in Paris. All that this achieved was to ensure the emigration of Russian Jews to America. In November, the anti-semitic party resumed the offensive.

The Paris Municipal Council made a recommendation. The Government then decided to set up a Committee to hear the cases of the Russians. Once again, those liable for mobilization under Russian law were to be admonished. Owing to the standing of the members of the Committee, it was thought that being interviewed by it would be more effective and would not alarm the Russians as much as being interviewed by the police.

The Committee chairman was (and still is) M. Brelet, a senior member of the Council of State; the vice-chairmen are M. Busson-Billaut, former president of the Bar and Professor Durkheim of the Sorbonne. The members of the Committee included two judges, one representative of the Ministry of the Interior, one representative of the Prefecture of Police and one police superintendent.

As just indicated, I had agreed to serve on the Committee, but on condition that, before proceeding with the interviews, the Committee would start by examining, through an inquiry, the situation of the Russians in Paris from the military standpoint, endeavouring to determine how great a part they had played in the war by spontaneously joining up, their record in the Army, etc. This working method was adopted and I was placed in charge of the inquiry.

I was able to establish that, in August 1914, some 9,000 Russians had volunteered for service and that the number of potential conscripts remaining in Paris was small. On the basis of these facts, as well as for the other reasons stated above, the Committee declared that, in its view, it was preferable not to proceed with the planned interviews I have just referred to. When this opinion, which was unanimous, was made known, the Minister postponed the application of the planned measures.

So telling were the reasons put forward by the Committee that the anti-semitic party did not protest against this postponement. Our report was submitted to the Ministry at the end of February. There has been no further mention in the anti-semitic press of the measures previously demanded, except in the last few days, when Mr Samuel's speech became known.

On the other hand, *Die Warheit* recently furnished us with proof that American opinion had been very favourably impressed by the decision I obtained, which we had publicized in America.

Such is the background to the events in France. If I felt compelled to discuss the matter with Mr Lucien Wolf, it was because I was instructed to do so by our Committee, as the common interests of the Allies were at stake.

It is not for me to offer the British Government advice on what to do. However, I wonder if the tribunal responsible for examining individual cases could not be asked to take into account the special situation of political refugees and religious refugees. Coercive measures could be reserved for Russians born in Britain or domiciled there for quite a long time.

However, in this respect and speaking on behalf of our Committee, *I fervently hope* Mr Samuel will publicly declare that the situation of the Russians in Britain is not like that of the Russians in France, for the Russians residing in France enlisted voluntarily in great numbers. Also, that it is thus natural for the French Government not to have taken any measures with respect to them. This would prevent French anti-semitism from using the British Government's example as a pretext. The damage done might thereby be alleviated.

Signed: ÉMILE DURKHEIM
Professor at the Sorbonne

Paris, 4 Avenue d'Orleans
14 July 1916

References

(The dating enumeration for works by Durkheim are those found in Lukes 1992. t. followed by a date refers to the date of an English translation. See References and Notation.)

Agulhon, M. (1979) *Marianne au combat: l'imagerie et la symbolique républicaines de 1789 à 1880*, Paris: Flammarion.

Agulhon, M. (1989) *Marianne au pouvoir: l'imagerie et la symbolique républicaines de 1880 à 1914*, Paris: Flammarion.

Allen, N. J. (1972) 'The Vertical Dimension in Thulung Classification', *Journal of the Anthropological Society of Oxford*, 3: 81–94.

Allen, N. J. (1985) 'The Category of the Person: a Reading of Mauss's Last Essay', in M. Carrithers, S. Collins and S. Lukes (eds) *The Category of the Person: Anthropology, Philosophy, History*, Cambridge: Cambridge University Press.

Allen, N. J. (1987) 'The Ideology of the Indo-Europeans: Dumézil's Theory and the Idea of a Fourth Function', *International Journal for Moral and Social Studies*, 2: 23–39.

Allen, N. J. (1989a) 'Assimilation of Alternate Generations', *Journal of the Anthropological Society of Oxford*, 20: 45–55.

Allen, N. J. (1989b) 'The Evolution of Kinship Terminologies', *Lingua*, 77: 173–85.

Allen, N. J. (1991) 'Some Gods of Pre-Islamic Nuristan', *Revue de l'histoire des religions*, 208: 141–68.

Allen, N. J. (in press) 'The Hero's Five Relationships'.

Anon (1917a) 'Nouvelles diverses', *Archives Israélites*, 78: 188.

Anon (1917b) 'Emile Durkheim', *L'Univers Israélite*, 73: 294–5.

Ardener, E. (1989) *The Voice of Prophecy and Other Essays*, in M. Chapman (ed.), Oxford: Blackwell.

Atran, S. (1990) *Cognitive Foundations of Natural History: Towards an Anthropology of Science*, Cambridge: Cambridge University Press.

Bach, K. and Harnish, R. (1979) *Linguistic Communication and Speech Acts*, Cambridge, Mass.: MIT Press.

Baczko, B. (1989) *Comment sortir de la Terreur: Thermidor et la Révolution*, Paris: Gallimard.

Baudrillard, J. (1993) *Symbolic Exchange and Death*, London: Sage.

Bauman, Z. (1989) *Modernity and the Holocaust*, Cambridge: Polity Press.

Becker, J. J. (1977) *1914. Comment les Français sont entrés dans la guerre*, Paris: Presses de la Fondation Nationale des Sciences Politiques.

Bellah, R. (1970) *Beyond Belief*, New York: Harper and Row.

Bellah, R. (1973) 'Introduction' to *Emile Durkheim on Morality and Society*, Chicago: The University of Chicago Press.

Berlin, I. (1990) *The Crooked Timber of Humanity*, London: Fontana Press.

Berthelot, J.-M. (1988) Introduction à E. Durkheim, *Les Règles de la méthode sociologique*, Paris: Flammarion: 7–67.

Besnard, P. (ed.) (1983) *The Sociological Domain*, Cambridge: Cambridge University Press.

Besnard, P. and Desplanques, G. (1986, 1991) *Un Prénom pour toujours. La Côte des prénoms hier, aujourd'hui et demain*, Paris: Balland.

Bloor, D. (1982) 'Durkheim and Mauss revisited: classification and the theory of knowledge', *Studies in the History and Philosophy of Science*, 13 (4): 267–97.

Bois, H. (1914) 'La Sociologie et l'obligation', *Revue de Théologie de Montauban*, 23: 193–250, 320–79.

Bonar, J. (1893) *Philosophy and Political Economy* (3rd edn., 1922), London: Allen and Unwin.

Bouglé, C. (1924) *Le Solidarisme*, 2nd edn., Paris: Alcan.

Bourdieu, P. (1979) *La Distinction. Critique sociale du jugement*, Paris: Minuit.

Bourdieu, P., Delsault, Y. (1975) 'Le Couturier et sa griffe: contribution à une théorie de la magie', *Actes de la recherche en sciences sociales*, 1: 7–36.

Brown, C. (1984) *Language and Living Things: Uniformities in Folk Classification and Naming*, New Brunswick: Rutgers University Press.

Caron, V. (1988) *Between France and Germany: The Jews of Alsace-Lorraine, 1871–1918*, Stanford, California: Stanford University Press.

Cedronio, M., (1989) *La Societ à organica. Politica e sociologia di Durkheim*, Torino: Bollati Boringhieri.

Chapman, M., McDonald, M. and Tonkin, E. (1989) 'Introduction' to E. Tonkin, M. McDonald and M. Chapman (eds), *History and ethnicity*, London: Routledge.

Chastel, A. (1986) 'La Notion de patrimoine', in P. Nora, (ed.), *Les Lieux de mémoire: La Nation*, vol.2, Paris: Gallimard.

Clifford, J. (1982) *Person and Myth. Leenhardt in the Melanesian World*, Berkeley and London: University of California Press.

Cornu, M. (1956) 'Le Père du vandalisme révolutionnaire', *Europe*, 128–9: 123–9.

Coser, L. A. (1960) 'Durkheim's Conservatism and Its Implications for his Sociological Theory', in K. H. Wolff (ed.), *Essays on Sociology and Philosophy*, New York: Harper and Row.

Cushing, F. (1896) 'Outlines of Zuñi Creation Myths', in Powell (ed.) 1896.

Dagan, H. (1899) *Enquête sur l'antisémitisme*, Paris: Stock.

Davy, G. (1919) 'Emile Durkheim: 1. L'Homme', *Revue de métaphysique et de morale*, 26: 181–98.

Derczansky, A. (1990) 'Note sur la judéité de Durkheim', *Archives de Sciences Sociales des Religions*, 69: 157–60.

di Donato, R. (1983) 'Di *Apollon Sonore* e di alcuni suoi antenati: Georges Dumézil e l'epica greca arcaica', *Opus* 2: 401–12.

Digeon, C. (1959) *La Crise allemande de la pensée française (1870–1914)*, Paris: Presses Universitaires de France.

Dommanget, M. (1953) *Histoire du Premier Mai*, Paris: Société Universitaire d'Éditions et de Librairie.

Dommanget, M. (1966) *Histoire du Drapeau rouge*, Paris: Éditions Librairie de l'Etoile.

Doroszewski, W. (1933) 'Quelques Remarques sur les rapports de la sociologie et de la linguistique: Durkheim et F. de Saussure', *Journal de Psychologie*, 30: 82–91.

Drumont, E. (1886) *La France juive*, Paris: Marpon and Flammarion.

Dubuisson, D. (1991) 'Contribution à une Epistémologie dumézilienne: l'idéologie', *Revue de l'histoire des religions*, 208: 123–40.

Dumézil, G. (1981) *Georges Dumézil* (Cahiers pour un temps), Paris: Centre Georges Pompidou/Pandora.

Dumézil, G. (1987) *Georges Dumézil: Entretiens avec Didier Eribon*, Paris: Gallimard.

Durkheim, E.

(1887b) Review. 'Guyau. L'Irréligion de l'avenir', *Revue philosophique*, XXIII: 299–311.

(1892a) *Quid Secundatus Politicae Scientiae Instituendae Contulerit*, Bordeaux: Gounouilhou.

—— (t.1960b) by R. Mannheim, *Montesquieu and Rousseau: Forerunners of Sociology*, with a foreword by H. Peyre, Ann Arbor, Michigan: University of Michigan Press.

(1893b) *De la Division du travail social: Étude sur l'organisation des sociétés supérieures*, Paris: Alcan.

—— (1902b) 2nd edition by Durkheim.

—— (t.1933b) by G. Simpson with preface, *The Division of Labor in Society*, New York: Macmillan.

—— (t.1984a) by W. D. Halls, *The Division of Labour in Society*, with an introduction by L. Coser, London and Basingstoke: Macmillan.

(1894a) 'Les Règles de la méthode sociologique', *Revue philosophique*, XXXVII: 465–98, 577–607; XXXVIII: 14–39, 168–82.

(1895a) *Les Règles de la méthode sociologique*, Paris: Alcan.

—— (1901c) 2nd edition by Durkheim.

—— (t.1938b) by S. A. Solovay and J. H. Mueller, *The Rules of Sociological Methods*, edited, with an introduction, by G. E. G. Catling, Chicago: University of Chicago Press.

—— (t.1982a) by W. D. Halls, *The Rules of Sociological Method*, London: Macmillan.

(1897a) *Le Suicide: Étude de sociologie*, Paris: Alcan.

—— (t.1951a) by J. A. Spaulding and G. Simpson, *Suicide: A Study in Sociology*, edited, with an introduction, by G. Simpson, Chicago: Free Press, and (1952) London: Routledge & Kegan Paul.

(1898a(ii)) 'La Prohibition de l'inceste et ses origines', *L'Année sociologique*, I: 1–70.

—— (t.1963a) with an introduction, by E. Sagarin, *Incest. The Nature and Origin of the Taboo by Emile Durkheim*, New York: Lyle Stuart.

(1898c) 'L'Individualisme et les intellectuels', *Revue bleue*, 4th series, X: 7–13.

—— (t.1969d) by S. and J. Lukes, with note, *Political Studies* XVII: 14–30.

(1899d) Contribution to H. Dagan, *Enquête sur l'antisémitisme*, Paris: Stock: 59–63.

—— (t.1994a) by H. L. Sutcliffe in Appendix.

(1900b) 'La Sociologie en France au XIXe siècle', *Revue bleue*, 4e série, XII: 609–13, 647–52.

(1901b) 'De la Méthode objective en sociologie', *Revue de synthèse historique*, II: 3–17.

(1903a(i)) (with M. Mauss) 'De quelques Formes primitives de classification. Contribution à l'étude des représentations collectives', *L'Année sociologique*, VI: 1–72.

—— (t.1963b) by R. Needham, *Primitive Classification*, with an introduction by R. Needham, London: Cohen and West.

(1903c) (with P. Fauconnet) 'Sociologie et sciences sociales', *Revue philosophique*, LV: 465–97.

—— (t.1982a) see 1895a.

(1905e(2)) Contribution to discussion of: 'Sur l'Internationisme: définition des termes: internationism économique; Patriotisme national et lutte des classes', *Libre Entretiens*, 2e sèrie, pp. 17ff.

(1908a(1)) Contribution to discussion of: 'Pacifisme et patriotisme, sèance du 30 dècembre 1907', *Bulletin de la Société Française de philosophie*, pp. 44ff.

(1912a) *Les Formes élémentaires de la vie religieuse. Le système totémique en Australie*, Paris: Alcan.

—— (t.1915d) by J. W. Swain, *The Elementary Forms of the Religious Life: A Study in Religious Sociology*, London: Allen & Unwin, New York: Macmillan.

(1913a(i)(1)) Note. 'Sur la Notion de civilisation', *L'Année sociologique*, XII: 46–50.

(1913a(ii)(15)) Review. 'Deploige, Simon, *Le Conflit de la morale et de la sociologie*', *L'Année sociologique*, XII: 326–8.

(1913b) Contribution to discussion of: 'Le Problème religieux et la dualité de la nature humaine', séance de 4 février 1913, in *Bulletin de la Société française de philosophie*, XIII: 63–75, 80–7, 90–100, 108–11.

—— (t.1984b) by R. A. Jones and P. W. Vogt, 'The Problem of Religion and the Duality of Human Nature', *Knowledge and Society*, 5, pp. 1–44.

(1915b) with E. Denis, *Qui a voulu la guerre? Les origines de la guerre d'après les documents diplomatiques*, Paris: Colin.

—— (t.1915e) *Who Wanted War? Origins of the War according to Diplomatic Documents*, Paris: Colin.

(1915c) *L'Allemagne au-dessus de tout: la mentalité allemande et la guerre*, Paris: Alcan.

—— (t.1915f) *Germany Above All: German Mentality and the War*, Paris: Colin.

(1916a) *Lettres à tous les Français*, Paris: Comité de publication.

(1924a) *Sociologie et philosophie*, preface by C. Bouglé, Paris: Alcan.

—— (1951b) new edition.

—— (t.1953b) by D. F. Pocock, *Sociology and Philosophy*, introduction by J. G. Peristiany, London: Cohen and West.

(1925a) *L'Éducation morale*, introduction by Paul Fauconnet, Paris: Alcan.

—— (1963c) new edition.

—— (t.1961a) by E. K. Wilson and H. Schnurer, *Moral Education: A Study in the Theory and Application of the Sociology of Education*, edited, with an introduction, by E. K. Wilson, New York: Free Press.

(1928a) *Le Socialisme*, edited, with an introduction, by M. Mauss, Paris: Alcan.

—— (1971d) new edition.

—— (t.1958b) by C. Sattler, with introduction by A. W. Gouldner, Yellow Springs, Ohio: Antioch Press.

(1938a) *L'Évolution pédagogique en France*, 2 vols, introduction by M. Halbwachs, Paris: Alcan.

—— (t.1977a) by P. Collins, *The Evolution of Educational Thought. Lectures on the Formation and Development of Secondary Education in France*, introduction by M. Halbwachs and a translator's introduction, London and Boston: Routledge & Kegan Paul.

(1950a) *Leçons de sociologie: physique des moeurs et du droit*, foreword by H. N. Kubali, introduction by G. Davy, Istanbul: L'Université d'Istanbul. Paris: Presses Universitaires de France.

—— (1969g) new edition.

—— (t.1957a) by C. Brookfield, *Professional Ethics and Civic Morals*, London: Routledge & Kegan Paul.

(1955a) *Pragmatisme et sociologie. Cours inédit prononcé à la Sorbonne en 1913–1914 et restitué d'après des notes d'étudiants par Armand Cuvillier*, Paris: Vrin.

—— (t.1983a) by J. C. Whitehouse, *Pragmatism and Sociology*, edited, with an introduction, by J. B. Allcock, Cambridge: Cambridge University Press.

(1969c) *Journal sociologique*, with an introduction and notes by J. Duvignaud (selection of Durkheim's articles), Paris: Presses Universitaires de France.

(1970a) *La Science sociale et l'action*, introduction and presentation by J.-C. Filloux, (Collection of articles by Durkheim), Paris: Presses Universitaires de France.

(1975b) *Durkheim, E., Textes*, 3 vols, edited, with an introduction, by V. Karady (Collection of articles, reviews, notes, letters), Paris: Les Éditions de Minuit.

(1990a) (with others) 'Rapport sur la situation des Russes en France'.

In 'Émile Durkheim défenseur des réfugies russes en France', presented by N. Elkarati, *Genèses*, 2: 168–77.
—— (t.1994a) by H. L. Sutcliffe in Appendix.

EJS European Journal of Sociology.

Engler, R. (1967) *Cours de linguistique générale de F. de Saussure, édition critique*. Wiesbaden: Harrassowitz.

Fauconnet, P. and Mauss, M. (1901) 'Sociologie', in Mauss, M., *Œuvres*, 3 vols, Paris: Minuit.

Fehér, F. (1987) *The Frozen Revolution*, Cambridge: Cambridge University Press.

Filloux, J.-C. (1970) Introduction and Notes to Durkheim 1970a.

Filloux, J.-C. (1976) 'Il ne faut pas oublier que je suis fils de rabbin', *Revue française de sociologie*, XVII (2): 259–66.

Filloux, J.-C. (1977) *Durkheim et le socialisme*, Geneva and Paris: Droz.

Freedman, M. (1975) 'Marcel Granet, 1884–1940: Sociologist', Introductory Essay to M. Granet (original 1922), *The Religion of the Chinese People* (translated and edited by M. Freedman), Oxford: Blackwell.

Gaehtgens, T. W. (1986) 'Le musée historique de Versailles', in P. Nora (ed.), *Les Lieux de mémoire: La Nation*, vol.3, Paris: Gallimard.

Gane, M. (1988) *On Durkheim's Rules of Sociological Method*. London and New York: Routledge.

Gane, M. (ed.) (1992) *The Radical Sociology of Durkheim and Mauss*, London: Routledge.

Giddens, A. (1971) 'Durkheim's political sociology', *Sociological Review*, NS, 19: 477–519.

Giddens, A. (ed.) (1986) *Durkheim on Politics and the State*, Oxford: Polity Press.

Gilbert, M. (1987) 'Modelling collective belief', *Synthèse*, 73: 185–204.

Gilbert, M. (1989) *On Social Facts*, London and New York: Routledge, reprinted 1992, Princeton: Princeton University Press.

Gilbert, M. (1990a) 'Walking together: a paradigmatic social phenomenon', *Midwest Studies in Philosophy*, 15, *The Philosophy of the Human Sciences*: 1–14.

Gilbert, M. (1990b) 'Fusion: sketch of a "contractual" model', in *Perspectives on the Family*, Moffat, R., Grcic, J., and Bayles, M. (eds), Mellen Press.

Gilbert, M. (1991), 'More on social facts', *Social Epistemology*, 5: 233–44.

Gilbert, M. (1993) 'Agreements, coercion, and obligation', revised version of paper presented to the political theory conference held at New College, Oxford, February 1990, and at York University, England.

Girardet, R. (1983) *Le nationalisme français*, Paris: Editions du Seuil.

Girardet, R. (1984) 'Les trois couleurs', in P. Nora (ed.), *Les Lieux de mémoire: La République*, Paris: Gallimard.

Gordon, M. M. (1964) *Assimilation in American Life: the Role of Race, Religion, and National Origins*, New York: Oxford University Press.

Granet, M. (1934/1968) *La Pensée Chinoise*, Paris: Albin Michel.

Greenberg, L. M. (1976) 'Bergson and Durkheim as sons and assimilators: the early years', *French Historical Studies*, IX, 4: 619–34.

Halphen, E. (1987) 'Préface affective', in Various 1987: 5–10.

Hayes, C. (1941) *A Generation of Materialism 1870–1900*, New York: Harper.

Heal, J. (1978) 'Common knowledge', *Philosophical Quarterly*, 28: 116–31.

Hermant, D. (1978) 'Destructions et vandalisme pendant la Révolution française', *Annales: Economies Sociétés Civilisations*, vol. 33: 703–19.

Hertzberg, A. (1968) *The French Enlightenment and the Jews*, NY and London: Columbia University Press.

Idzerda, S. J. (1954) 'Iconoclasm during the French Revolution', *American Historical Review*, 60: 13–26.

Jakobson, R. (1971) 'Retrospect' in *Selected Writings*, vol.2: *Word and Language*, The Hague: Mouton.

Kedward, R. (1965) *The Dreyfus Affair*, London: Longmans.

Lacroix, B. (1981) *Durkheim et le politique*, Paris: Presses de la Fondation Nationale des Sciences Politiques.

Lenoir, R. (1930) 'Lettre à R. M.' in 'L'Œuvre sociologique d'Emile Durkheim', *Europe*, 22: 292–6.

Lewis, D. (1969) *Convention*, Cambridge, Mass.: Harvard University Press.

Lukes, S. (1973) *Emile Durkheim. His Life and Work: A Historical and Critical Study*, London: Allen Lane.

Lukes, S. (1982) 'Introduction' to Durkheim 1895a/t.1982a: 1–27.

Lukes, S. (1992), new edition of Lukes 1973, London: Penguin.

MacIntyre, A. (1981) *After Virtue: a Study in Moral Theory*, London: Duckworth.

Marrus, M. R. (1971) *The Politics of Assimilation: A Study of the French Jewish Community at the Time of the Dreyfus Affair*, Oxford: Clarendon Press.

Mathiez, A. (1904) *Les Origines des cultes révolutionnaires 1789–1792* (réimp. 1977), Geneva: Slatkine-Megariotis.

Mauss, M. (1905) Review of Mathiez 1904, *L'Année sociologique*, VIII: 295–8.

Mauss, M. with H. Beuchat (1906) 'Essai sur les variations saisonnières des sociétés eskimos', *L'Année sociologique*, 9: 39–130. (t.1979 by James Fox, London: Routledge.)

Merton, R. K. (1987) 'Three fragments from a sociologist's notebooks', *Annual Review of Sociology*, 13: 1–28.

Meštrović, S. G. (1988) *Emile Durkheim and the Reformation of Sociology*, Totawa, NJ: Rowan and Littlefield.

Michelet, J. (1847) *Histoire de la révolution française*, Paris: Calmann-Lévy.

Mill, J. S. (1970) *A System of Logic*, London: Longman. (First edition, 1843).

Milo, D. (1986) 'Le nom des rues', in P. Nola (ed.), *Les Lieux de mémoire: La Nation*, vol. 3, Paris: Gallimard.

Mitchell, M. M. (1931) 'Emile Durkheim and the Philosophy of nationalism', *Political Science Quarterly*, 46: 87–106.

Needham, R. (1963) 'Introduction' to E. Durkheim and M. Mauss (1903a(i)) (translated and edited by R. Needham), London: Cohen and West.

Needham, R. (1978) Review of A. Giddens, *Durkheim*, *Times Literary Literary Supplement*, 25 August 1978.

Needham, R. (1979) *Symbolic Classification*, Santa Monica: Goodyear.

Nicolet, C. (1982) *L'idée républicaine en France*. Paris: Gallimard.

Nisbet, R. (1952) 'Conservatism and Sociology', *American Journal of Sociology*, 58: 167–75.

Nye, R. A. (1983) 'Heredity, Pathology and Psychoneurosis in Durkheim's early work', *Knowledge and Society*, 4: 103–42.

Ozouf, M. (1988a) 'La Révolution française et l'idée de l'homme nouveau', in C. Lucas (ed.), *The French Revolution and the Creation of Modern Culture*, 2, *The Political Culture of the French Revolution*, Oxford: Pergamon Press.

Ozouf, M. (1988b) 'Procès du roi', in F. Furet and M. Ozouf (eds), *Dictionnaire critique de la Révolution*, Paris: Flammarion.

Ozouf, M. (1988c) 'Religion révolutionnaire' in F. Furet and M. Ozouf (eds), *Dictionnaire critique de la Révolution*, Paris: Flammarion.

Pécaut, F. (1918) 'Emile Durkheim', *Revue pédagogigque*, n.s. 72: 1–20.

Péguy, C. (1910) *Notre Jeunesse*, Paris: Gallimard.

Peters, E. (1985) *Torture*, Oxford: Basil Blackwell.

Pickering, W. S. F. (1984) *Durkheim's Sociology of Religion: Themes and Theories*, London, Boston: Routledge & Kegan Paul.

Pommier, E. (1988) 'Idéologie et Musées à l'époque de la Révolution', in M. Vovelle (ed.), *Les Images de la Révolution française*, Paris: Publications de la Sorbonne.

Poulot, D. (1986) 'Alexandre Lenoir et les museés de Monuments français', in P. Nola (ed.), *Les Lieux de mémoire: La Nation*, vol.2, Paris: Gallimard.

Powell, J. W. (1896) 'Administrative Report', in *idem* (ed.) *Annual Reports of the Bureau of Ethnology*, 13, Washington: Government Printing Office.

Prades, J. A (1987) *Persistance et métamorphose du sacré*, Paris: Presses Universitaires de France.

Quinton, A. (1975–6) 'Social objects', *Proceedings of the Aristotelian Society*, 75: 1–27.

Rabi, W. (1962) *Anatomie du judaïsme français*, Paris: Editions du Minuit.

RFS Revue Française de Sociologie.

Ranulf, S. (1939) 'Scholarly Forerunners of Fascism', *Ethics*, 50: 16–34.

Renan, E. (1947) *Œuvres Complètes*, vol. 1, Paris: Calmann-Lévy.

Sanson, R. (1976) *Le 14 Juillet: fête et conscience nationale, 1789–1975*, Paris: Flammarion.

Sartre, J.-P. (1954) (1st edn. 1946) *Réflexions sur la question juive*, Paris: Gallimard. (t.1948) by Erik de Mauny, *Portrait of the Anti-Semite*, London: Secker and Warburg, Lindsay Drummond.

Saussure, F. de (1985) *Cours de linguistique générale*, edited by T. de Mauro, Paris: Payot (translated and annotated (1983) by R. Harris as

Course in General Linguistics, London: Duckworth).

Scharf, B. R. (1970) 'Durkheim and Freudian Theories of religion: the case for Judaism', *British Journal of Sociology*, XXI, 2: 151–63.

Schiffer, S. (1972) *Meaning*, Oxford: Oxford University Press.

Schoenfeld, E. and Meštrović, S. (1989) 'Durkheim's Concept of Justice and its relationship to Social Reality', *Sociological Analysis*, 50: 111–27.

Sharot, S. (1976) *Judaism: A Sociology*, Newton Abbot: David and Charles.

Simmel, G. (1905) *Philosophie der Mode*, Wiesbaden: Bergmann.

Sironneau, J-P. (1990) 'Les équivoques de la religion révolutionnaire' in Y. Chalas (ed.), *Mythe et Revolutions*, Grenoble: Presses Universitaires de Grenoble.

Smith, A. D. (1983) 'Nationalism and Classical Social Theory', *British Journal of Sociology*, 34: 19–40.

Soboul, A. (1957) 'Sentiments religieux et cultes révolutionnaires pendant la Révolution: Saints patriotes et martyrs de la liberté', *Annales historiques de la Révolution française*, 29: 195–213.

Sorkin, D. (1990) 'Emancipation and Assimilation: Two Concepts and their Application to German Jewish History', London: *Leo Beck Year Book*: 17–33.

Sorley, W. R. (1904) (1st edn 1885) *The Ethics of Naturalism*, Edinburgh: Blackwood.

Sprigath, G. (1980) 'Sur le vandalisme révolutionnaire 1792–1794', *Annales historiques de la Révolution française*, 52: 510–35.

Stephen, L. (1882) *The Science of Ethics*, London: Smith, Elder.

Swart, K. (1964) *The Sense of Decadence in Nineteenth Century France*. The Hague: Martinus Nijhoff.

Tiryakian, E. A. (1978) 'Durkheim and Husserl: A Comparison of the Spirit of Positivism and the Spirit of Phenomenology', in J. Bien, (ed.), *Phenomenology and the Social Sciences: A Dialogue*, The Hague, Boston and London: Martinus Nijhoff.

Tiryakian, E. A. (1979) 'L'École durkheimienne à la recherche de la société perdue: la sociologie naissante et son milieu culturel', *Cahiers internationaux de Sociologie*, LXVI: 97–114.

Turner, S. (1986) *The Search for a Methodology of Social Science*, Dordrecht: Reidel.

Various, (1987) *Durkheim: 100 ans de sociologie à Bordeaux*, Bordeaux: Bibliothèque Muncipale.

Venturino, V. (1988) 'La Naissance de l'"Ancien Régime" ', in C. Lucas ed., *The French Revolution and the Creation of Modern Political Culture*, 2, *The Political Culture of the French Revolution*, Oxford: Pergamon Press.

Vogt, W. P. (1976) 'The Uses of Studying Primitives', *History and Theory*, XV: 33–44.

Wallwork, E. (1972) *Durkheim. Morality and Milieu*, Cambridge, Mass.: Harvard University Press.

Walzer, M. (1977) *Regicide and Revolution*, Cambridge: Cambridge University Press.

Walzer, M. (1988) 'The King's Trial and the Political Culture of the Revolution', in C. Lucas, (ed.) *The French Revolution and the Creation of*

Modern Political Culture, 2, *The Political Culture of the Revolution*, Oxford: Pergamon Press.

Wasserstein, B. (1992) *Herbert Samuel: A Political Life*, Oxford: Clarendon.

Watts Miller, W. (1992) 'Liberal Vegetarianism: Moderation versus Strong Sentiments of Morals', in Milligan, D. and Watts Miller, W. (eds), *Liberalism, Citizenship and Autonomy*, Aldershot, Hants.: Avebury.

Watts Miller, W. (1993) 'Iconocide: the case of the trial and execution of Louis XVI', *Cogito*, 7: 10–8.

Weber, E. (1977) *Peasants into Frenchmen: the Modernization of Rural France 1870–1914*, London: Chatto and Windus.

Weber, M. (1964) (1st edn 1922) *The Theory of Economic and Social Organization*, (translated by Parsons, T., and Henderson, A. M.), Glencoe, Illinois: Free Press.

Wilson, S. (1980) *Ideology and Experience: Antisemitism in France at the time of the Dreyfus Case*, London: Associated University Press.

Index